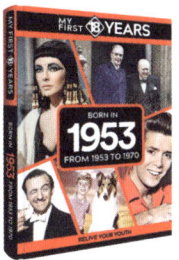
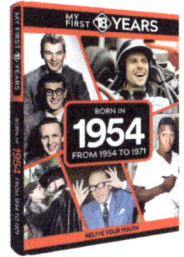

AF128043

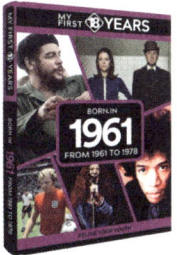
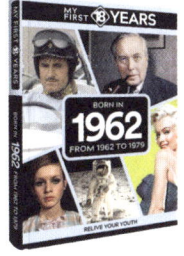
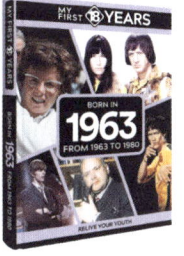
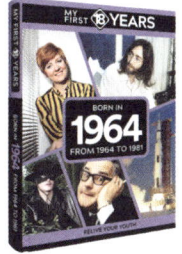

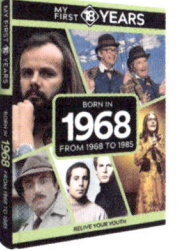

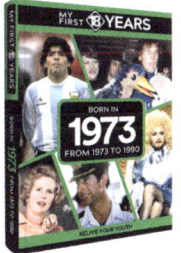
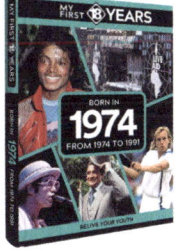
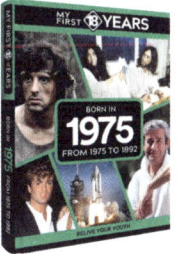

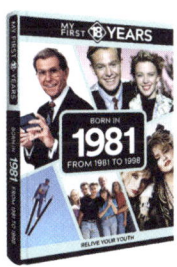

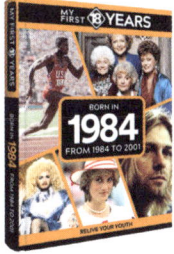

MY FIRST 18 YEARS

BORN IN
1959
FROM 1959 TO 1976

© 2024 TDM Publishing. Rights reserved.

My First 18 Years is a brand of TDM Publishing.
The image, brand and logos are protected and owned by TDM Publishing.

www.mijneerste18jaar.nl
info@mijneerste18jaar.nl

My First 18 Years idea and concept: Thars Duijnstee.
Research and text: Lucinda Gosling, Stephen Barnard, Jeffrey Roozeboom, Katherine Alcock.
Composition and image editing: Jeffrey Roozeboom.
Design: Ferry Geutjes, Boudewijn van der Plas, Jeffrey Roozeboom.
Proofreading: Alison Griffiths.

Every effort has been made to trace the rights holders of all images. If you believe an image has been incorrectly credited, please contact the publisher.

No part of this publication may be reproduced, stored in or introduced to an automated data-file, or made public, in any form or by electronic, digital, mechanical, photocopying, recording or any other means, without the prior written consent of the publisher.

Photos: Sound & Vision, National Archives, Getty images, Mary Evans Picture Library, Shutterstock, BNNVARA, AVROTROS, Veronica, KRO-NCRV, KIPPA, *Mijn eerste 18 jaar* archives.

In writing this series, the authors drew from the following sources: view from 1963-1999, NTS / NOS Annual Review, nueens.nl, vandaagindegeschiedenis.nl, beleven.org, IMDb, Wikipedia, Eye Filmmuseum, Rollingstone.com, image & sound, National Archives, Onthisday.com, Parlement.com. *Complete Book of UK Hit Singles, First Hits 1949-1959* (Boxtree Books), Billboard Books, *Reader's Digest* Music series 1950s-1970s, British Library Newspaper Archive, rogerebert.com

Thanks to: Spotify, Rick Versteeg, Rik Booltink.

The Top 10 list for each year is compiled by Stephen Barnard and is a personal selection of best-selling hits, radio favourites and lesser-known tracks that reflect the popular artists and styles of each year. Some are universally regarded classics, others will be less remembered yet are equally emblematic of the tastes of that year. Each list should provoke many 'Ah yes!' moments, particularly those almost forgotten treasures that are rarely heard even as 'golden oldies' yet tickled the ears in their day.

How to use Spotify playlists:

1. Open Spotify.
2. Click search (the magnifying glass in the image).
3. Click scan (the camera in the picture).
4. Point your camera at the Spotify code in the book.
5. After that, you can play the selected list.

ISBN 978 94 9331 768 0
NUR: 400

1959

MY FIRST 18 YEARS

SPORT

Hawthorn killed
22nd January 1959 Just three months after retiring from motor racing, reigning Formula One world champion Mike Hawthorn dies in a car crash near Guildford.

The Truman show
5th May 1959 Just months after sensationally beating Althea Gibson of the US in the Wightman Cup, eighteen-year-old British tennis star Christine Truman wins her first and only Grand Slam at the French Open. She defeats defending champion Zsuzsa Kormockzy of Hungary in straight sets and achieves the highest ranking of her career as world No. 2. Weeks later she reaches the Wimbledon final but is defeated by Maria Bueno. Admired for her relentless attacking play, Christine remains a top player for the next decade.

The magnificent Beryl
26th July 1959 The greatest female athlete in cycling history, Leeds-born Beryl Burton wins the first of five world championships in the individual pursuit in Liege, Belgium. Having overcome severe paralysis in her early teens, Beryl's story is inspirational, encompassing an eventual 96 national championships in time trialling, track pursuit and road racing, the breaking of both the men's and women's twelve-hour time record, and winning the Britain's Best All-Rounder competition for 25 consecutive years.

Elton at Wembley
2nd May 1959 The FA Cup Final pairs two hard-working but unfashionable clubs making their first appearances at Wembley. Nottingham Forest defeat Luton Town 2-1 despite the scorer of their opening goal, Roy Dwight, breaking a leg. Watching the BBC's coverage at home is Roy's piano-playing cousin Reg, ten years before his name change to Elton John.

Billy Wright retires
25th April 1959 England captain Billy Wright retires from football after guiding Wolverhampton Wanderers to a third league championship in six years. Since debuting for Wolves in 1946, he has made 500 appearances for his club and has amassed a record-breaking 105 England caps.

---

3 JAN 1959
Alaska joins the US as its 49th state.

1 FEB 1959
Swiss men vote against voting rights for women.

2 MAR 1959
A ceremony marks the start of the construction of the Sydney Opera House.

1959

DOMESTIC NEWS

Fog chaos!
29th January 1959 Dense fog causes chaos across the country as roads, train lines and airports are closed. Focused on London, the problem extends across the Midlands, East Anglia, the South of England and parts of Wales, with visibility reduced to only a few metres in places.

CND March!
30th March 1959 The Campaign for Nuclear Disarmament organise their first major march from the Atomic Weapons Establishment in Aldermaston to London. Setting off on the 27th, the march culminates in a rally in Trafalgar Square, and is attended by approximately 60,000 people.

Iceland fires on Brits
30th April 1959 The First Cod War between Britain and Iceland heats up as an Icelandic vessel, *Thor*, fires what appear to be warning shots at a British trawler entering disputed waters. The trawler is pursued by *Thor*, before HMS *Conquest* is deployed to the area and drives the Icelandic vessel off. The disputes will continue well into the 1970s.

Make it Mini
8th May 1959 The very first Mini Cooper rolls off the production line ahead of its official launch in August. The British Motor Corporation's iconic vehicle is ten feet long, with two doors, and a top speed of 70 miles per hour. It is designed to carry a driver and three passengers, although the leg room available is famously extremely limited!

Places get postcodes
28th July 1959 An experiment is launched in the City of Norwich to introduce modern postcodes. In use in some areas, such as London, since the 19th century, the new postcodes stick to a simple formula, and are soon rolled out nationwide.

Auchengeich mining disaster
18th September 1959 47 men are killed at Auchengeich near the village of Moodiesburn when an electrical fault in a colliery fan catches fire. The colliery is flooded with toxic smoke, and later with water to extinguish the fire, leaving only one survivor.

---

2 APR 1959
Seven US astronauts are selected for Mercury space programme.

24 MAY 1959
Death of US Secretary of State John Foster Dulles.

11 JUN 1959
D. H. Lawrence novel *Lady Chatterley's Lover* is banned in US.

1959

ROYALTY & POLITICS

Southend pier fire
7th October 1959 Hundreds of people are trapped as a pavilion on Southend's pier catches fire. The 1.5-mile pier is home to its own railway, which stops due to the blaze, forcing tourists trapped by the fire to climb down into boats which bring them ashore.

A television first
8th September 1959 Prior to visiting France and West Germany, President Eisenhower visits the UK for talks with Harold Macmillan. During the trip, he and Macmillan share a remarkable first when they give a joint live television broadcast in which they exchange pleasantries, reminisce, and discuss the problems currently facing the world.

Airports go duty-free
17th November 1959 Duty-free shopping is introduced for the first time at Prestwick and Renfrew Airports in the UK after the concept was introduced at Shannon Airport in Ireland in 1947 by Brendan O'Regan. Shoppers can now purchase items free of local taxes and duties if they are bringing them home from their travels.

Conservatives retain power
8th October 1959 The Conservatives win the general election for a third successive time and increase their majority to 100 seats. It is a personal triumph for Harold Macmillan and, because of the size of the defeat, an unexpected threat to Hugh Gaitskell's leadership of the Labour Party. Among the new MPs entering the House of Commons are future Prime Minister Margaret Thatcher and future Liberal Party leader Jeremy Thorpe.

Bush TR82 Radio
Bush launch their iconic TR82 Transistor Radio featuring Ogle Design. The portability of these radios, and their edgy design, sees them become enormously popular in the 1960s as the rise of popular music sees more and more time spent huddled around the radio.

8 JUL 1959
First deaths of US military personnel in Vietnam.

7 AUG 1959
The Explorer 6 transmits the first photo of Earth from space.

16 SEP 1959
French President Charles de Gaulle announces proposals for Algerian independence.

1959

The Queen expects
8th August 1959 Buckingham Palace announces that 'the Queen will undertake no further public engagements', which is royal code for saying that she is pregnant with her third child. Royal etiquette dictates that the monarch should not be seen to be carrying a child. The Queen will give birth to Prince Andrew on 19th February 1960.

Revolution in Cuba
1st January 1959 Having defeated the 10,000-strong force of Cuban dictator Fulgencio Batista in May 1958, guerrilla forces under Fidel Castro, Che Guevara and Camilo Cienfuegos head for the capital Havana. Batista flees the country and surrenders. The next day, Guevara and Cienfuegos enter Havana, followed by Fidel Castro six days later. Castro, who becomes President a month later, advocates friendship with the US in his first speeches. Rebuffed by the Eisenhower administration, he will begin transforming Cuba into a communist state.

Princess Margaret is engaged
11th October 1959 Although it will not be announced officially until February, Princess Margaret accepts a proposal of marriage from the society photographer Antony Armstrong-Jones.

Leopoldville riots
4th January 1959 The campaign for independence in the Belgian Congo takes a new turn as riots break out in Leopoldville (latter-day Kinshasa) leaving at least 49 dead. The rioting triggers a rush for independence, which Belgium grants in June 1960.

FOREIGN NEWS

Race for space
The space race between the superpowers is now in full swing. Early in 1959, the Soviets launch Luna 1, the first object to fly past the Moon while the US trains astronauts for its first manned space mission. During May, a US Jupiter rocket launches two primates into space who become the first living creatures to return safely to Earth.

14 OCT 1959 — Death of swashbuckling actor Errol Flynn, aged 50.

2 NOV 1959 — First section of the M1, the first British motorway, is opened to traffic.

1 DEC 1959 — USSR and western nations sign treaty to leave Antarctica as a wilderness.

1959

Barbie's world
9th March 1959 The first Barbie dolls, a blonde and a brunette, are exhibited at the International Toy Fair in New York City. Ruth Handler, co-founder of toy manufacturer Mattel, adapts an existing German design to create an adult dress-up doll inspired by her daughter Barbara's pleasure in dressing up cardboard dolls. Named after her, Barbie is one of the most successful toys of the century. Two years later, a male doll is launched as Barbie's companion and named after Ruth's son Kenneth.

An independent Cyprus
14th December 1959 After Cyprus is granted independence from the UK in August, Greek Cypriot leader Archbishop Makarios is elected President.

Parkas on sale
Originating in Inuit culture, the parka is introduced as part of US Army wear during the Korean war in a version made of nylon with a quilted lining and a fur-trimmed hood. Known as the fishtail parka, it is popularised through sales in army surplus outlets.

Lycra is launched
The enduring search for a replacement for rubber is partly resolved with the invention of spandex by a scientist named Joseph Shivers at US chemical company DuPont. A tough, elastic and heat-resistant synthetic fibre, it is launched as Lycra in Europe in 1959.

ENTERTAINMENT

Ho Chi Minh Trail
26th September 1959 The Viet Cong, as the US calls the National Front for the Liberation of South Vietnam, begins military action as the government of Ho Chi Minh (photo) is building roads through North Vietnam, Laos and Cambodia to South Vietnam - the so-called Ho Chi Minh Trail - to supply the army and the Viet Cong.

Dalai Lama
18th April 1959 The Dalai Lama flees to India when the invading Chinese bomb his palace in Tibet. In India, the refugee Tibetans are allowed to build houses, schools, hospitals and monasteries and so retain Tibetan traditions. From his hiding place the Dalai Lama grows into a spiritual leader of global importance.

Jukebox Jury
Jukebox Jury, hosted by David Jacobs, airs on the BBC on 1st June. Each episode, Jacobs plays a short excerpt from a selection of 7-inch singles to a panel of four celebrities who discuss and ultimately decide if a song is hit or miss. The first show's panel includes DJ Pete Murray and singing star Alma Cogan; later, panellists such as the Beatles and the Rolling Stones help *Jukebox Jury*'s viewing figures hit more than twelve million.

1959

Swashbuckling blunders
ITV's Crusades-era adventure series, *Ivanhoe*, starring Roger Moore with a fabulously bouffant quiff, comes to an end when Moore returns to Hollywood, although ITV continues to repeat the 39 episodes. Moore had insisted on carrying out many of the stunts himself and suffered several injuries during filming; three cracked ribs as a result of a fight scene, and he was knocked out when a battleaxe fell on his head (fortunately he was wearing a helmet at the time).

Avon calling
Pioneering beauty company launch in the UK. Their door-to-door saleswomen are known for visitations where on ringing the doorbell 'Ding-dong' they would call out, 'Avon calling'.

Carry on Teacher
Just six months after *Carry On Nurse* is in cinemas, the Carry On franchise wastes no time in bringing out a third film, *Carry on Teacher*, with Kenneth Connor, Hattie Jacques, Leslie Phillips and Joan Sims among the 'expert gagsters' in what the *Daily Mirror* describes as a 'load of golden, corny laughter'!

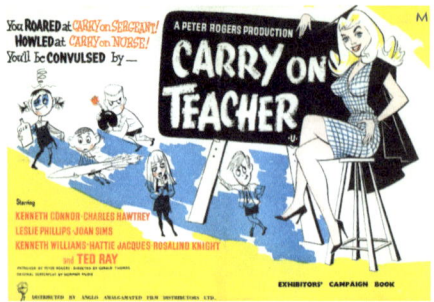

Arctic rollout
Ernest Velden, a Jewish lawyer from Czechoslovakia, sets up the Birds Eye factory in Eastbourne which produces the Arctic roll - a swiss roll-style dessert with an ice cream centre. Capable of producing a staggering 17 million Arctic rolls a year, it is estimated that by the 1980s, twenty-five miles of this nostalgic dessert is being consumed by the British public every month.

Colour *Bonanza*
Bonanza, the TV series about the Cartwright ranching family, and their sprawling Ponderosa ranch in Nevada, airs its first episode on NBC on 12th September, runs for fourteen seasons and is credited with encouraging Americans to invest in colour television sets. The show is first broadcast in Britain on 8th April 1961 and at its peak enjoys a global audience of 400 million. It makes stars of its cast, particularly Michael Landon who plays Joseph 'Little Joe' Cartwright.

Bread ahead
Low-calorie food range Slimcea is introduced by Procea Products with a light-as-air bread as its flagship product. Advertised with the line, 'Show them you're a Slimcea girl' the bread becomes a rival to Hovis's lo-cal loaf Nimble (launched 1955). Nimble uses the metaphorically apt hot-air balloon in its commercials, but both brands do well as women battle to squeeze into the wasp-waisted fashions of the late fifties.

1959

Hot Summer Night
The *Armchair Theatre* play, *Hot Summer Night,* features the first interracial kiss on television, between Andree Melly and Jamaican-born actor Lloyd Reckord. Reckord forms the New Day Theatre Company, which performs at the Royal Court theatre the following year but in one interview insists it must be 'a company for actors of all races.'

Journey to the Centre of the Earth
For true authenticity, the 1959 movie adaptation of Jules Verne's science fiction adventure story is filmed in the stunning Carlsbad Caverns of New Mexico, thought to be the lowest point beneath the surface of the Earth. Working 1,100 feet underground and at night so that the caverns' tourism business would be uninterrupted, James Mason heads the cast as Edinburgh professor, Oliver Lindenbrook, who leads an expedition to the Earth's core via a volcano after finding a message in a piece of volcanic rock. Among the extraordinary wonders Lindenbrook and his party encounter on their adventure are a mushroom forest, the city of Atlantis and gargantuan chameleons with twenty-foot tongues! Pop singer and heartthrob Pat Boone co-stars and is the obvious choice to sing the film's soundtrack.

Sing Something Simple
'Songs simply sung for song-lovers' is how the *Radio Times* describes this half-hour show which is broadcast on the BBC Light Programme for the first time on 3rd July. Listeners can enjoy Cliff Adams and the Adams Singers, accompanied by Jack Emblow on the accordion, with numbers such as *Drifting and Dreaming* and *Sweet Rosie O'Grady*. The show runs for 42 years until 2001, making it the longest-running continuous music programme in the world.

Tiger Bay
Twelve-year-old Hayley Mills makes her screen debut in this beautifully shot thriller set against the decaying industrial backdrop of Cardiff's Tiger Bay. Mills' character, an orphaned young girl, witnesses a murder and befriends the Polish sailor who commits the act; her father, John Mills, plays the police inspector in pursuit. With its glimpses of street culture and multi-racial community in Cardiff, the film paves the way for the social realism adopted by many British film makers in the early 1960s.

Dip pen

1959

Lenny the Lion
Lenny's Den, the latest programme featuring the lion with a lisp, Lenny, worked by ventriloquist Terry Hall, starts on Sunday 18th October. Lenny, whose catchphrase is 'Aw, don't embawass me', is one of the first non-'human' ventriloquists' dummies, and he's fashioned out of fox fur and papier-mâché. Even though Lenny is one of the hardest-working stars in showbusiness, the puppet only has to be remade once.

Ben-Hur
MGM is in serious financial difficulties when it embarks on making the William Wyler-directed Roman epic, *Ben-Hur* and they have to speculate before they can accumulate; the famous chariot race scene alone costs a staggering one million pounds. The gamble pays off and when *Ben-Hur* is released in cinemas, the public flock to see this action-packed, no-expense-spared Roman epic. *Ben-Hur* wins a record-breaking eleven Academy Awards at the Oscars the following year.

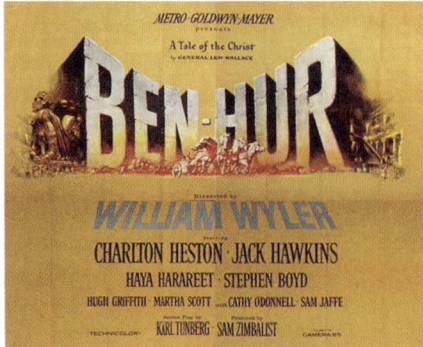

What a drag
Some Like it Hot, Tony Curtis and Jack Lemmon give brilliant turns as jazz musicians on the run from the Mob who drag up to join an all-girl band. But they are just one aspect of Billy Wilder's joyous comedy, which goes on to be voted American Film Institute Best Comedy of All Time. Marilyn Monroe, as singer Sugar Kane, is at her vulnerable, enchanting best.

MUSIC

The day the music died
3rd February 1959 On the day commemorated in Don McLean's *American Pie* as 'the day the music died', tragedy strikes just outside Mason City, Iowa. Buddy Holly, Ritchie Valens and J. P. Richardson (known as the Big Bopper) are killed when their light aircraft crashes after take-off in the middle of a winter tour of America's mid-west states.

1959

Terry in trouble
3rd March 1959 Although one of the better British rock'n'roll singers, Terry Dene has had a troubled time dealing with stardom. Arrests for vandalism and marriage problems have given him a bad-boy image. Called up for National Service in a blaze of publicity, he has now been discharged from the Army as 'mentally unfit', provoking questions in Parliament and an avalanche of hatred from the press. Within a few years Terry disappears completely, his story a salutary lesson in how not to handle fame.

Lady Day departs
17th July 1959 The greatest jazz voice of them all, Billie Holiday, is found dead in New York at the age of 44. She had cirrhosis of the liver complicated by her long-term drug addiction. Nicknamed 'Lady Day', Billie struggled with abuse.

Mourning Mario
7th October 1959 Having entered a Rome clinic for tests just days before, Mario Lanza dies suddenly from a heart attack aged 38. Rumours will persist for years regarding possible Mafia involvement in his death. His grief-stricken wife Betty dies from a drug overdose just five months later.

Kind of Blue
17th August 1959 Jazz takes a giant leap forward with the release of *Kind of Blue* by Miles Davis, which sells over five million albums without making any compromises towards a more commercial sound. Opening with the mesmeric *So What*, it has a tang of sophistication and danger that is the essence of contemporary New York.

A solid second
11th March 1959 The fourth Eurovision Song Contest takes place in Cannes. Having declined to take part in 1958, the BBC is pinning its hopes on *Sing Little Birdie* sung by husband and wife duo Teddy Johnson and Pearl Carr. Their song comes a solid second to the Netherlands' entry *Een beetje*, sung by Teddy Scholten.

1959

Frankie goes to Hollywood

America is the holy grail for UK performers. The latest to try making it there is the high-kicking Frankie Vaughan, whose visit starts well with rave reviews for shows in Las Vegas and New York. He even stars in *Let's Make Love*, a musical with Marilyn Monroe, but the Hollywood experience leaves him rattled and yearning for home. Evading Marilyn's advances and forsaking the American dream, he switches his focus back to the UK.

MY FIRST 18 YEARS TOP 10 1959

1. **A Fool Such as I** *Elvis Presley*
2. **It Doesn't Matter Anymore** *Buddy Holly*
3. **Til I Kissed You** *Everly Brothers*
4. **Only Sixteen** *Sam Cooke*
5. **The Three Bells** *The Browns*
6. **Sea of Love** *Marty Wilde*
7. **Petite Fleur** *Chris Barber Band*
8. **Chantilly Lace** *The Big Bopper*
9. **What'd I say** *Ray Charles*
10. **Mack the Knife** *Bobby Darin*

Tommy and Cliff move on

The first two superstars of British rock'n'roll are starting to leave the rock sound behind. Having played himself in the movie *The Tommy Steele Story*, Tommy Steele is focusing more on family-friendly songs like Lionel Bart's *A Handful of Songs* and *Little White Bull*. Cliff Richard is edging towards a softer, more countrified sound with *Living Doll*, which Bart wrote for *Serious Charge* (Cliff's debut film) but Cliff has now re-recorded in a gentler style. The shift in tone works: the record is his first No. 1, a global million seller and provides the template for such mid-tempo fare as *Travellin' Light* and *Please Don't Tease*.

Sellers takes aim

Offering the last word on popular music in 1959, Peter Sellers makes one of the funniest comedy albums ever. Sellers takes aim at Frank Sinatra, Lonnie Donegan, *My Fair Lady* and much more with brilliant impersonations and merciless parody. Produced by George Martin, *Songs for Swingin' Sellers* also has the most macabre cover of the year - a waist-down view of a body hanging from a tree.

What'd he say?

Blind singer-pianist Ray Charles shows what happens when you mix the sensuality of the blues with the ecstatic energy of gospel music. His freewheeling *What'd I Say* is an epic blend of vocals, piano and big-band blast that takes up two sides of a 45 and sends black music to a whole new level.

PHOTO CREDITS Copyright 2024, TDM Rights BV.
Photos: **A** Klemantaski Collection - Hulton Archive - Getty Images / **B** PA Images - Getty Images / **C** PA Images - Getty Images / **D** Edward Miller - Hulton Archive - Getty Images / **E** Colin Sherborne Collection - Mary Evans Picture Library / **F** Mirrorpix - Getty Images / **G** Evening Standard - Hulton Archive - Getty Images / **H** Keystone - Hulton Royals Collection - Getty Images / **I** Underwood Archives - Archive Photos - Getty Images / **J** Yvonne Hemsey - Hulton Archive - Getty Images / **K** Apic - Hulton Archive - Getty Images / **L** Mirrorpix - Getty Images / **M** Studiocanal Films LTD - Mary Evans / **N** Express - Archive Photos - Getty Images / **O** Kroontjes pen - Algont / **P** AF Archive - Mary Evans / **Q** Fox Photos - Hulton Archive - Getty Images / **R** RB-Staf - Redferns - Getty Images / **S** Keystone - Hulton Archive - Getty Images / **T** Nationaal Archief - Enefo / **U** William P. Gottlieb / **V** Gamma-Rapho - Andre SAS - Getty Images / **W** Gilles Petard - Redferns - Getty Images.

1960

MY FIRST 18 YEARS

SPORT

Burnley are champions
30th April 1960 In one of the tightest finishes to the First Division ever, Burnley snatch the championship from Wolverhampton Wanderers by one point on the last day of the season, so spoiling the latter's dreams of winning the elusive league and FA Cup 'double'.

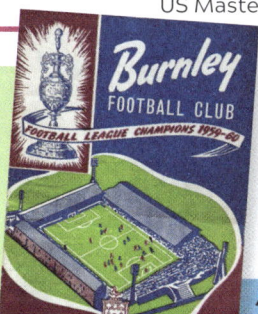

A troubled tour
9th June - 23rd August 1960 South Africa's impending cricket tour of England has been in doubt due to growing feeling against the country's apartheid policy, especially after the Sharpeville massacre in March. Should England be playing against a side that excludes black players? There are demonstrations at the grounds but the tour goes ahead and results in a 3-0 series win for England with two matches drawn.

Arnold at the Open
6th - 9th July 1960 Having won both the US Masters and US Open titles earlier in the year, the charismatic and modest-mannered American golfer Arnold Palmer competes in the British Open for the first time, finishing as runner-up to Australian Kel Nagle by a single shot. He will make a winning return to the Open in 1961 and 1962.

A ten-goal spectacular
18th May 1960 Hampden Park in Glasgow is the venue for one of the most memorable football matches of all time. Real Madrid defeat Eintracht Frankfurt 7-3 in the final of the European Cup in front of a crowd of 127,000.

All roads lead to Rome
25th August - 11th September 1960 In the seventeenth Olympic Games of the modern era, held in Rome, the Great Britain team again achieves only a modest tally of medals - two gold, six silver and twelve bronze. Among the most indelible memories of the Games are Herb Elliott of Australia annihilating the field in the 1500 metres; the young Cassius Clay (later Muhammad Ali) almost dancing to gold for the US in the light heavyweight division of the boxing; and gold medallist Abebe Bikila of Ethiopia running the marathon barefoot and becoming the first black African champion in Olympic history.

29 JAN 1960
French settlers in Algeria begin rebellion against independence.

1 FEB 1960
Civil rights sit-in begins at a lunch counter in Greensboro, North Carolina.

22 MAR 1960
First patent for lasers is granted.

1960

DOMESTIC NEWS

Dr. Martens hit the street
1st April 1960 The iconic Dr. Martens 'AirWair' style 1460 boots are marketed for the first time in the UK. Having bought the patent, the R Griggs Group in Northamptonshire begins producing a smooth cherry-red boot with distinctive yellow stitching. The boots soon become synonymous with counter-culture movements like punk, new wave, and grunge, and remain popular to this day.

European free trade
4th January 1960 The Stockholm Convention is signed to create the European Free Trade Association, with Britain as a founder member. The Association involves seven countries; Austria, Denmark, Norway, Portugal, Sweden, Switzerland, and the UK, all of whom are unable or unwilling to join the European Economic Community, the forerunner of the European Union.

Independence for many
Several countries gain independence from the British in 1960, including British Somaliland on 26th June, Cyprus on 16th August, and Nigeria on 1st October.

Whisky fire kills 19
28th March 1960 A fire breaks out at a warehouse in Glasgow's Cheapside Street. The warehouse holds over a million gallons of whisky and 30,000 gallons of rum, and as brave firemen and salvage corps personnel battle the flames, an explosion destroys the building. The fire claims the lives of 19 men, making this Britain's fire services' worst peacetime disaster.

Miners killed at Six Bells
28th June 1960 An explosion of firedamp at the Six Bells Colliery in Monmouthshire kills 45 of the 48 men on duty. Maintenance work taking place within the colliery meant that less than half of the 125 usual employees were on duty, avoiding a far greater death toll.

Sheerness Dockyard closes
31st March 1960 The closing ceremony at the Sheerness Dockyard takes place, ending almost 300 years of naval history on the Isle of Sheppey and the loss of 2,500 jobs associated with the dockyards.

---

1 APR 1960
World's first weather satellite launched from Cape Canaveral.

7 MAY 1960
Brezhnev replaces Voroshilov as President of USSR.

8 JUN 1960
Argentine government demands that Israel release Adolf Eichmann.

1960

Britain gets binbags
1st November 1960 Black plastic binbags for the disposal of household waste are introduced for the first time in Hitchin, Hertfordshire. This new product, developed by Imperial Chemical Industries, soon becomes a standard household item across the country.

Last man conscripted
31st December 1960 National Service, in place since 1949, finally comes to an end, with the last call ups taking place in November. The last young men to enter National Service will remain in the programme until 1963.

The Lady Chatterley trial
2nd November 1960 Penguin Books is found not guilty under the Obscene Publications Act, after publishing the full, uncensored version of *Lady Chatterley's Lover* by D. H. Lawrence. During the trial, Penguin Books successfully argues that despite the book containing obscene passages, the literary value of the novel is such that censorship is not in the public's best interest.

Traffic wardens deployed
15th September 1960 Two years after getting its first parking meters, the capital welcomes its first traffic wardens. The wardens were the brainchild of Athelstan Popkiss, Chief Constable of Nottingham City Police.

 **ROYALTY & POLITICS**

Goodbye to the farthing
31st December 1960 The farthing, a feature of British purses since 1707 and English purses since the 13th century, finally ceases to be legal tender. Whilst still usable in the Falklands and British Antarctica, this familiar coin leaves British pockets for good from 1961 onwards.

Place your bets
1st September 1960 The Betting and Gaming Act is passed by Parliament, enabling betting shops and bingo venues to operate under licence from local councils. It also aims to stamp out illegal gambling by banning the use of 'runners' by bookmakers to collect money from punters. The measures help change the face of the average British high street and accelerate the conversion of loss-making cinemas into revenue-earning bingo halls.

---

1 JUL 1960
Granting of Belgian Congo independence sparks civil war.

1 AUG 1960
Aretha Franklin's first recording for Columbia Records.

30 SEP 1960
The Flintstones created by Hanna-Barbera premieres in the US.

1960

Wind of change
3rd February 1960 Prime Minister Harold Macmillan makes a speech in the South African parliament calling on the country to recognise what he calls 'a wind of change' sweeping through Africa. Macmillan and his Colonial Secretary Iain Macleod have adopted a policy of preparing British colonies for independence while South Africa has been tightening apartheid and the machinery of white rule. His speech contributes to the South African decision to declare itself a republic and leave the Commonwealth in 1961.

Margaret and Tony wed
6th May 1960 After a six-week official engagement that surprises even the most seasoned royal watchers, Princess Margaret marries Antony Armstrong-Jones at Westminster Abbey.

Prince Andrew is born
19th February 1960 The Queen gives birth to her third child, Andrew Albert Christian Edward, at Buckingham Palace. This is the first time in 103 years that a child has been born to a reigning monarch.

Nye Bevan dies
6th July 1960 Aneurin 'Nye' Bevan dies of stomach cancer at the age of 62. Elected to Parliament for Ebbw Vale in 1928, Bevan was a key player in Clement Attlee's post-war Labour government, where as Minister of Health he oversaw the launch of the National Health Service.

Gaitskell retains leadership
3rd November 1960 After a fractious Labour Party conference, Labour's Hugh Gaitskell sees off a leadership challenge from Harold Wilson. He wins the ballot of Labour MPs by 166 votes to 81.

17 OCT 1960 *News Chronicle* newspaper closes after 30 years.

14 NOV 1960 Belgium threatens to leave the UN due to criticism of its policy in Congo.

31 DEC 1960 Compulsory National Service (conscription) ends in UK.

FOREIGN NEWS

Kenyan emergency ends
12th January 1960 The seven-year state of emergency in Kenya is finally ended as the British colony prepares for independence. Those years have seen vicious fighting between UK forces and the Mau Mau or Kenya Land and Freedom Army, with war crimes committed on both sides.

El Guerrillero Heroico
5th March 1960 At a memorial service for the victims of an explosion on the cargo ship *La Coubre*, Alberto Korda takes the iconic photo of revolutionary leader Che Guevara. *El Guerrillero Heroico* becomes one of the most famous symbols of the 1960s, the portrait appearing on posters and T-shirts across the world.

Under the sea
23rd January 1960 Oceanographers Jacques Piccard and Don Walsh make a deep dive into the Mariana Trench in the Pacific Ocean. After almost five hours, during which a porthole cracks and their bathyscaphe almost collapses under the high pressure, they reach a depth of 10,916 metres, the deepest point ever reached by man.

Sharpeville massacre
21st March 1960 South African police fire indiscriminately into a crowd of unarmed black protesters in the Sharpeville township. Within a week the South African government declares a state of emergency and arrests 18,000 people including the young Nelson Mandela. The scale of the massacre sends shock waves across Africa and moves the anti-apartheid movement in the country towards armed resistance.

Eichmann is captured
11th May 1960 The Israeli secret service Mossad carries out an undercover operation in the Argentine capital Buenos Aires, where they kidnap the high ranking Nazi official Adolf Eichmann and smuggle him to Israel. Eichmann was responsible for the deportation of millions of Jews to concentration camps during the Second World War. A trial for his crimes awaits Eichmann in Israel in 1962.

1960

Congo crisis begins
30th June 1960 The Belgian Congo receives its independence and is from now known as the Republic of the Congo. The country is unprepared for the huge political and social changes and an army mutiny and a bitter, prolonged civil war follow.

Spy plane shot down
1st May 1960 US pilot Gary Powers is flying over the Soviet Union to secretly photograph military installations when his U-2 plane is shot down by a Russian missile. Powers ejects but is captured and given a ten-year sentence for espionage during July.

Kennedy is President
8th November 1960 Democratic presidential candidate John Fitzgerald Kennedy defeats Republican Vice President Richard Nixon by a tiny margin. At 43 years old, Kennedy is the youngest US President in history and the first Roman Catholic.

Three billion people
The world population exceeds three billion, having almost doubled since 1900. In the coming years the population will grow much faster, especially in Asia and Africa.

ENTERTAINMENT

Quick on the Draw
Etch-a-Sketch, a drawing toy which allows children to doodle, erase and doodle again, is launched in the US. Requiring no ink, no mess and no batteries, knobs are used to move a stylus which pushes aluminium powder behind a screen, forming lines to make pictures.

Millions watch Cliff 'Move It'
Hosted by Bruce Forsyth, *Sunday Night at the Palladium* is already essential family viewing each weekend, but in January 1960, when Cliff Richard & the Shadows are on the bill, the programme attracts an incredible twenty million viewers.

1960

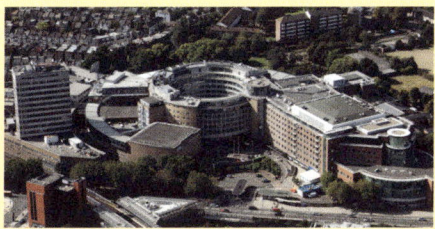

New BBC HQ
The BBC opens its big, shiny, brand new Television Centre at White City in west London on 29th June 1960, the third such purpose-built television headquarters in the world. It was designed by Graham Dawbarn with a distinctive, circular main block (known as the 'doughnut'). For those who spend time watching BBC children's television over the next forty years, the building's postcode - W12 8QT - will become imprinted on their memory.

Nan reads the news
Nan Winton (right), a journalist and continuity announcer, is put in front of the camera and becomes the first female newsreader to present the national news for the BBC. She is not actually the first in television; Barbara Mandall had read the news for ITN in 1955, and unfortunately Winton's new role is short-lived. An audience survey apparently reveals that viewers feel a woman reading the news is 'not acceptable'.

And they're off
Aintree's Grand National is televised for the first time on 26th March and is won by the favourite Merryman II. Sixteen cameras are used and commentators Peter O'Sullevan and Peter Bromley survey the race from a somewhat rickety tower constructed in the middle of the course.

Welcome to Weatherfield
On 9th December, ITV viewers are first introduced to the residents of *Coronation Street*, including barmaid Annie Walker, who works at the Rovers Return, and Elsie Tanner at no. 11, who is dealing with her ne'er do well ex-convict son. And at no. 3, university student Ken Barlow is arguing with his parents who think he's embarrassed about his working-class roots. The creation of Tony Warren, *Coronation Street* initially is commissioned for thirteen pilot episodes, but it will go on to become the longest-running TV soap in the world, airing its 10,000th episode in 2020. The legendary cobbles of 'Corrie' have been the scene of marital strife, neighbourly feuds, murder, betrayal as well as regular doses of inimitable Northern humour. As for aspirational university student Ken Barlow, he never leaves the Street, making William Roache the longest-serving actor ever in a soap.

The Angry Silence
Richard Attenborough co-produces and takes the lead role in this gritty drama about a factory worker whose refusal to take part in an unofficial strike leads to violent repercussions. In the face of criticism that the film was anti-strike and anti-trade union, Attenborough attends several private showings of the film to trade union members and has the opportunity to explain his side.

1960

Psycho Killer
Alfred Hitchcock serves up a frankly petrifying cocktail of sex, madness, and murder in *Psycho*. This classic and hugely influential horror is set in a creepy motel run by the strange but apparently harmless Norman Bates, a character played with pitch perfect awkwardness by Anthony Perkins. As if Janet Leigh's horrifying end in the shower isn't bad enough, audiences are stunned when she's killed off only halfway through the film.

Return of the King
Elvis completes two years of military service and on the flight home from West Germany, his plane stops to refuel at Prestwick in Scotland, the one and only time, the King 'visits' the United Kingdom. Keen to capitalise on the success of his pre-service film career, he makes the very topical *GI Blues* this year, as well as the Western, *Flaming Star*.

I am Spartacus!
Kirk Douglas ripples his oiled muscles as the rebellious slave in Spartacus, in this Roman epic in which 30-year-old director Stanley Kubrick directed a cast of 10,500 and juggled a budget of $12 million prompting the US entertainment magazine *Variety* to suggest, 'he has out-DeMilled the old master in spectacle'. The famous scene in which the army of defeated slaves refuse to identify their leader, bears parallels with the real-life experiences of Howard Fast, author of the original book, who had written it while imprisoned for refusing to name communist sympathisers to investigators from the House for Un-American Activities Committee.

Pig of the Pops
Pinky and Perky's Pop Parade is the latest TV vehicle for the porcine puppet twins, whose high-pitched, sped-up warbling of popular songs has inexplicably turned them into stars. The pair are the creation of Jan and Vlasta Dalibor, refugees from Czechoslovakia where pigs are a symbol of good luck. In order to identify which was which, Perky is given a 'pork pie' hat!

MUSIC

Eddie Cochran killed in crash
17th April 1960 Little more than a year after Buddy Holly's death, another rock'n'roll innovator meets a tragic end - Eddie Cochran, the creator of that great anthem of teenage discontent, *Summertime Blues*. En route for London Airport after completing a UK tour, his taxi hits a tree in Chippenham.

Lonnie's comic cut
31st March 1960 With the skiffle boom in fast decline, Lonnie Donegan is turning away from American folk songs to comedy material. His shift in style is vindicated by *My Old Man's a Dustman*, a relatively clean version of a ditty popular with British soldiers for over half a century. Recorded live during a gig at the Gaumont Cinema in Doncaster, it puts Lonnie back at No. 1 for the first time in three years. Not only that, it sets a new record: it's the first single in UK chart history to hit the top in its first week of sales.

1960

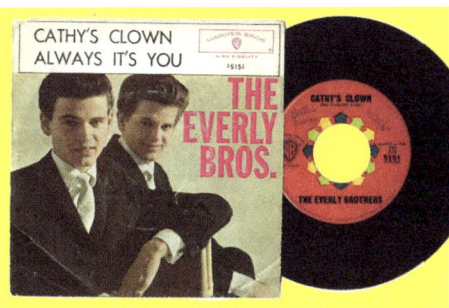

Don and Phil switch labels
17th February 1960 The Everly Brothers leave the small Cadence record label that nurtured them to join Warner Brothers, a new power in the industry. The fee is a record-breaking one million dollars. Their first record for their new home is a 24 carat classic written by Don himself - *Cathy's Clown*.

So long, farewell
23rd August 1960 Oscar Hammerstein, lyricist partner of composer Richard Rodgers, dies at his home in Pennsylvania. He completed work on their final musical, *The Sound of Music*, while fighting cancer. All the lights on Broadway are darkened in tribute.

Beatles in Hamburg
17th August 1960 The Beatles begin six months of performing at nightclubs on the notorious Reeperbahn in Hamburg. When they return to Liverpool they will shock audiences with their vastly improved musicianship and showmanship.

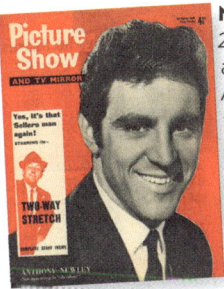

Newley son parade
28th April 1960 A year ago, former child actor Anthony Newley made the film *Idol on Parade*, playing a rock singer conscripted Elvis-style into the Army. By playing a pop idol he has become one, as he now sits proudly at No. 1 with the Lionel Bart song *Do You Mind*. Newley is unusual in that he sings rock'n'roll with an English accent.

The backing steps forward
25th August 1960 Hitherto known as Cliff Richard's backing group, the Shadows launch their own hit-making career with *Apache,* an instrumental spotlighting the crystal-clear lead guitar work of Hank Marvin and the tom-tom drumming of Tony Meehan. Hank's Newcastle pal Bruce Welch on rhythm guitar and charismatic bassist Jet Harris complete the line-up.

New Kidd in town
4th August 1960 In a year of teen idols and Elvis imitators, the chart topping *Shakin' All Over* by Johnny Kidd and the Pirates is a welcome slice of British-made rock'n'roll grit. Johnny's real name is Fred Heath and his band, originally called the Nutters, haven't looked back since changing their name and adopting pirate garb. They wrote and recorded *Shakin' All Over* in less than an hour, intending it as a flipside. Contrary to their publicity, Johnny wears an eye-patch for effect, not because he lost his eye on the Spanish Main.

1960

Chubby does the Twist
19th September 1960 When Hank Ballard fails to turn up to promote a record called *The Twist* on the television show *American Bandstand*, resident dance teacher Chubby Checker improvises some steps on the spot. Twist your body from side to side, he instructs, while stubbing out an imaginary cigarette with your toe. The dance takes off, Chubby makes his own record of *The Twist* and has an unexpected No. 1.

MY FIRST 18 YEARS TOP 10 — 1960

1. **Save the Last Dance for Me** The Drifters
2. **Are You Lonesome Tonight** Elvis Presley
3. **Cathy's Clown** The Everly Brothers
4. **Wonderful World** Sam Cooke
5. **Poor Me** Adam Faith
6. **El Paso** Marty Robbins
7. **Itsy Bitsy Teenie Weenie…** Brian Hyland
8. **Shakin' All Over** Johnny Kidd and the Pirates
9. **Baby Sittin' Boogie** Buzz Clifford
10. **Georgia on My Mind** Ray Charles

DO YOU REMEMBER THIS?
Roller skates

A deathly No. 1
29th September 1960 The controversial fad for 'death discs' in the US spreads to Britain as Welsh singer Ricky Valance's *Tell Laura I Love Her* reaches No. 1. In the same vein as Mark Dinning's *Teen Angel* (girl dies trying to retrieve her boy's high school ring from a car stalled on a level crossing) and Jody Reynolds' *Endless Sleep* (girlfriend attempts suicide), *Laura* is the tale of a boy who dies in a stock car race trying to win enough money for a wedding ring.

Death of Johnny Horton
5th November 1960 Country singer Johnny Horton is killed in a car accident in Texas aged 35. He is best known for story songs with historical flavour, notably the chart-topping *Battle of New Orleans* and the movie theme *North to Alaska*.

Adam keeps Faith
12th November 1960 Adam Faith (left) has come a long way since performing in Soho's coffee bars as plain Terry Nelhams. Now the UK's favourite pop star after Cliff Richard, Adam has a little boy lost image and an ingratiating way of pronouncing 'baby' as 'by-bee' on hits like *Poor Me* and *What Do You Want*.

1961 — MY FIRST 18 YEARS

SPORT

Six goals – and none of them count
26th January 1961 Denis Law scores all six goals for Manchester City in an FA Cup game at Luton. As the game is abandoned twenty minutes from time due to a waterlogged pitch, none of the goals stand. When the game is replayed, Luton win 3-1.

Team tragedy at Brussels
15th February 1961 The entire US team of skaters, officials and chaperones travelling to the World Figure Skating Championships in Prague are among 73 people killed as their plane crashes close to Brussels Airport.

All-British final at Wimbledon
7th July 1961 Wimbledon sees an absorbing all-UK ladies singles final with a ruthless Angela Mortimer beating an injury-hit Christine Truman in three sets to claim her third Grand Slam.

Australia retain the Ashes
1st August 1961 The cricketing summer peaks with a decisive fourth Test between England and Australia at Old Trafford. Richie Benaud's bowling proves crucial on the last day as he takes six wickets for 70 runs. Australia win by 54 runs and so retain the Ashes.

Wage cap abolished
18th January 1961 English professional footballers celebrate the abolition of the maximum wage (currently £20) six decades after the Football Association imposed it. The Professional Footballers Association's campaign for reform has been led by Fulham player Jimmy Hill whose teammate Johnny Haynes is among the first to benefit by becoming English football's first £100-a-week player.

DOMESTIC NEWS

Farewell 'white' fivers
13th March 1961 The old 'white' £5 note, in circulation since 1793, is withdrawn and is no longer legal tender. The note featuring black print on white paper has been slowly replaced since 1957 with the 'Series B' note, a multicoloured version featuring Britannia.

Spurs at the double
6th May 1961 Tottenham Hotspur become the first club this century to secure the elusive league championship and FA Cup 'double'.

---

25 JAN 1961
Military coup in El Salvador.

5 FEB 1961
First edition of *The Sunday Telegraph* goes on sale.

29 MAR 1961
After a 4½ year trial Nelson Mandela is acquitted of treason.

1961

Jaguar E-Type
15th March 1961 The brand-new Jaguar E-Type is launched, capable of reaching speeds of 150 miles per hour and doing 0 to 60mph in under seven seconds. Available in a two-seater coupé or roadster model, the car soon becomes famous for its speed and elegance.

Fire safety
1st May 1961 A fire breaks out at the Top Storey Club in Bolton blocking the venue's exit and 19 people lose their lives. An inquiry shows that an exit that could have saved the victims was prevented from opening by a false dance floor, and public outcry leads to a change in the Licensing Act.

Middlesborough race riots
19th August 1961 Cannon Street in Middlesborough becomes the latest part of the UK to see terrible race riots, which break out following the murder of a young white man, Jeffrey Hunt. The chief suspect in the murder is Asian, and the attack precipitates three nights of violence centred around the Taj Mahal Club.

Mothercare
September High Street staple Mothercare opens its first store as the 'Mother and Child Centre' in Kingston-upon-Thames. For 58 years Mothercare provides childhood necessities to expectant mothers across the country, until the brand comes under administration in 2019.

Portrait stolen
21st August 1961 Bus driver Kempton Bunton steals Goya's *Portrait of the Duke of Wellington* from the National Gallery. Bunton writes to Reuters News Agency demanding £140,000 be donated to a charity providing free television licences to the poor, but his ransom is ignored. Four years later the painting is returned, but whilst Bunton is prosecuted for the theft, he is found guilty only of stealing the frame.

Wales licensing hours
8th November 1961 Welsh counties vote in a referendum on opening hours for public houses. The counties of Anglesey, Cardiganshire, Caernarfonshire, Carmarthenshire, Denbighshire, Merionethshire, Montgomeryshire, and Pembrokeshire all vote to oppose the sale of alcohol on a Sunday.

6 APR 1961 New York Governor Nelson Rockefeller authorises building of World Trade Center.

5 MAY 1961 Alan Shepard becomes first American in space.

27 JUN 1961 Michael Ramsey appointed Archbishop of Canterbury.

1961

More states independent
Sierra Leone, Tanganyika and Kuwait all gain independence from Britain in 1961, though Kuwait requests British military assistance in June to establish its independence from Iraq.

Islands evacuated
10th October 1961 The islands of Tristan da Cunha, a British Overseas Territory, are evacuated thanks to a large volcanic eruption. All 264 inhabitants of the islands are brought to an old RAF base in Hampshire, where they live until able to return in 1963.

Birth control
4th December 1961 Birth control pills become available on the National Health Service for the very first time, causing a revolution in family planning.

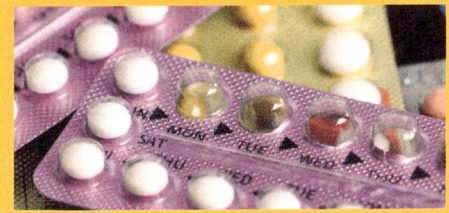

Mass arrests at ban-the-bomb demo
18th September 1961 The biggest CND demonstration yet sees multiple arrests for civil disobedience in and around Trafalgar Square. Up to a thousand people are charged after making sit-down protests on the day on which the USSR has mounted a twelfth nuclear test.

Duke of Kent marries
8th June 1961 Prince Edward, Duke of Kent, marries Katharine Worsley, daughter of baronet Sir William Worsley, at York Minster. The Duke is the son of King George VI's brother Prince George, who was killed in a wartime air crash.

ROYALTY & POLITICS

UK applies for EEC membership

31st July 1961 Although many in his own Conservative Party regard it as a surrender of sovereignty, Harold Macmillan announces that the UK will make a formal application to join the European Economic Community. The Labour Party remains officially opposed.

14 JUL 1961 Huge crowds in London greet Soviet astronaut Yuri Gagarin.

6 AUG 1961 Stirling Moss wins his 16th and final Formula 1 race at the the Nürburgring.

8 SEP 1961 President Charles de Gaulle escapes assassination attempt.

1961

Snowdon made an earl
6th October 1961 Princess Margaret's husband Antony Armstrong-Jones is elevated to the nobility and given the title of 1st Earl of Snowdon in recognition of his family roots in North Wales.

Immigration curbs announced
1st November 1961 The Macmillan government outlines its intention to introduce a Commonwealth Immigration Bill to limit numbers taking up residence in the UK. The new restrictions will become law in July 1962.

FOREIGN NEWS

First man in space
12th April 1961 Soviet space rocket Vostok 1 takes off from Kazakhstan with the first human to reach space on board. Cosmonaut Yuri Gagarin flies 327 kilometers above the planet's surface in an orbit around the Earth at 27,400 km/h. The flight lasts 108 minutes. An engaging personality and unquestionably heroic, Gagarin becomes a poster boy for the Soviet space program and is feted across the world during the following months.

Bay of Pigs
16th April 1961 Having cut all ties with Fidel Casto's regime in Cuba, the newly installed President Kennedy accepts a CIA plan to overthrow Fidel Castro's government using Cuban exiles trained in the US. Some 1,500 exiles led by CIA officers begin the invasion at the Bay of Pigs but encounter the much larger force of the Cuban National Army. Kennedy refuses to use US warships to turn the tide and the invasion is abandoned after three days. The US is humiliated while Castro looks to the Soviet Union for protection.

WWF founded
29th April 1961 One of the world's largest conservation organisations, the World Wildlife Fund (WWF) is founded with an office in Morges, Switzerland. Conceived as an international fundraising organisation in support of existing conservation groups, the WWF becomes a major campaigner on issues relating to the protection of nature, with the backing of many notable figures including Prince Philip, naturalist Peter Scott, biologist Julia Huxley and environmentalist Max Nicholson.

24 OCT 1961 Island of Malta is granted independence by UK.

15 NOV 1961 London landmark the Euston Arch is ordered to be demolished.

21 DEC 1961 John F. Kennedy and Harold Macmillan meet in Bermuda to talk about nuclear policy.

1961

South Africa leaves the Commonwealth
31st May 1961 South Africa votes to leave the British Commonwealth in a whites-only referendum. Elizabeth II is no longer Queen of South Africa and the country becomes a republic.

Destination Moon
25th May 1961 The US may have lost the battle to put the first man in space but President Kennedy sets his sights on the next milestone in space travel. He commits his country to landing a man on the Moon 'and returning him safely to Earth before the end of this decade'. With this, the president gives the green light to the Apollo program.

King of all bombs
30th October 1961 Three days after the stand-off at Checkpoint Charlie, the Soviets flex their muscles once again by testing the 'Tsar Bomba' or 'king of all bombs'. The 50 megaton hydrogen bomb is the largest man-made explosion ever and breaks windows as far away as Finland.

First hatchback
1st July 1961 Renault launches the small family car that will compete with the popular Citroën 2CV and the Volkswagen Beetle: the Renault 4.

Berlin Wall is built
13th August 1961 East Germany begins construction of the Berlin Wall to stop its citizens escaping to the city's western sectors. Since the 1950s, hundreds of thousands have sought refuge in West Germany and the damage to the East German economy and its political credibility is enormous. A 156-kilometer-long barrier of concrete blocks and barbed wire is built around the whole of West Berlin, interrupted by border posts manned by East German troops with orders to shoot anyone who tries to cross. In October, the crisis is heightened when Soviet tanks attempt to take control of Checkpoint Charlie, the Allied crossing point. US and Soviet tanks stand directly opposite each other for sixteen hours until the latter withdraw. One mistake and a third world war could be triggered.

1961

ENTERTAINMENT

Curry in a hurry
Batchelors launch the Vesta Curry, the ultimate in exotic convenience food (actually, the only type of exotic convenience food). Press advertisements stress how a Vesta curry can save on drudgery and reassure cautious Brits that it isn't 'too spicy'. Despite its questionable authenticity, Vesta paves the way for the ready meal revolution.

The Milky Bars are on me!
The Milky Bar Kid, a skinny blond lad in round glasses and Western gear, makes an unconvincing cowboy but his largesse with bars of white chocolate is legendary. The first Milky Bar Kid is played by Terry Brooks who is paid the generous sum of £10 every time an advert is shown. Terry eventually outgrows his costume and leaves the heady world of TV commercials to become an air conditioning engineer in Basildon.

Eyes down
The Betting and Gaming Act leads to a craze for bingo across the country as players can now win big cash prizes. Seaside businesses complain that holidaymakers are addicted to bingo which is diverting money away from their seasonal trade, and landladies insist on cash up front in case guests are spent-up by the end of their stay. Eric Morley, chairman of Mecca dance halls, at the forefront of the bingo movement, tells the *Daily Mirror* that the suggestion that mothers are abandoning their children four or five times a week to indulge their bingo habit is 'nonsense'.

Portraits before a scandal
Numerous portraits of well-known figures and members of the royal family drawn by society osteopath and artist Stephen Ward are published as a series in the respected weekly paper, *The Illustrated London News*. A portrait of the Duke of Edinburgh even appears on the cover. Two years later, Ward is implicated as a key player in the scandalous Profumo Affair.

Yabadabadoooo!
The 'modern Stone Age family', *The Flintstones* are first introduced to British viewers on 5th January when the Hanna-Barbera cartoon airs on ITV. The pure genius of the Flintstones concept, where a typical twentieth-century family sitcom format is transposed to the animated prehistoric town of Bedrock, gives endless scope for storylines featuring Fred and Wilma Flintstone and friends, Barney and Betty Rubble plus the family pet an exuberant, bouncy dinosaur called Dino. It's a vintage year for cartoon debuts as *Yogi Bear* and *Top Cat* also both first appear.

1961

Praise be
The BBC broadcasts the very first episode of *Songs of Praise* from the Tabernacle Baptist Chapel in Cardiff on 1st October, with soprano Heather Harper as guest vocalist.

Dimbleby and the Duke
On 29th May, Prince Philip is the first member of the royal family ever to be interviewed on television when he appears in a pre-recorded twelve-minute slot on *Panorama*. A respectful but visibly nervous Richard Dimbleby questions the Duke about the Commonwealth Technical Training Week, of which he is patron. The royal interviewee seems visibly at ease leading the *Daily Mirror* to comment how he, 'appeared more relaxed than his interviewer'.

Pick of the Pops
Alan 'Fluff' Freeman joins the radio show *Pick of the Pops* on 30th September and every Sunday night takes viewers through the music chart's top tunes. With his free-flowing presentation style, peppered with catchphrases ('Not 'arf!') Freeman becomes the occasionally parodied but much-loved archetypal radio DJ.

Spot the difference
Dodie Smith's 1956 children's novel *One Hundred and One Dalmatians*, is brought to the screen by Disney with Pongo and Missus on a mission to rescue their adorable clutch of puppies from the mad monochromist, Cruella de Vil.

DO YOU REMEMBER THIS?

Tobacco pipe

The Dulux Dog
During the filming of a TV commercial for Dulux paints, the director's Old English Sheepdog, Dash, keeps running into shot to play with the child actors. It is decided that Dash is so photogenic he can appear in the advert and the Dulux Dog is born. He's the first of fourteen different Old English Sheepdogs to be the 'face' of Dulux over the years.

Bedside manner
Richard Chamberlain as young Dr. James Kildare set hearts a-flutter when he begins his internship at Blair General Hospital on 20th October 1961. Chamberlain was by no means the first choice to play the role, which was originally meant for William Shatner, but he is unknown no longer and the medical drama *Dr. Kildare* catapults him to stardom.

Pingwings
The Pingwings, the latest creation from Smallfilms, is shown on ITV through August and September. In the handmade tradition of the company, the bird-like puppets, which approximate to penguins, have been expertly knitted by Peter Firmin's sister, Gloria.

1961

Breakfast at Tiffany's
Audrey Hepburn stars in one of her best roles, as the Midwest girl who reinvents herself as the fun-loving New York socialite, who flirts her way around Manhattan while falling for a struggling writer.

MUSIC

The Rag Trade
Nobody messes with the workers at Fenner's Fashions who will drop everything whenever the familiar order 'Everybody out!' is uttered by shop steward Paddy Fleming. The show, starring Miriam Karlin and Barbara Windsor (photo), is positioned as a comedy but has plenty to say about gender rights and workplace politics.

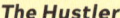

Dylan's in town
24th January 1961 A young singer-guitarist from Minnesota named Robert Zimmerman arrives in New York to play the folk clubs of Greenwich Village. He changes his name to Bob Dylan in tribute to the Welsh poet Dylan Thomas.

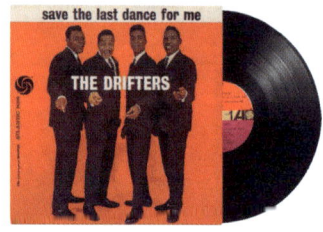

High school hitmakers
30th January 1961 As recent hits prove, New York is the engine room of early 1960s pop. Working for Atlantic Records, producers Jerry Lieber and Mike Stoller have transformed the Drifters' flagging fortunes with Latin-laced hits like *Save the Last Dance for Me* and have launched the group's lead singer Ben E. King on his own career with *Spanish Harlem* and *Stand By Me*. Now they're nurturing a wave of young musical talent from the Brooklyn high schools. When soon-to-be-married school leavers Gerry Goffin and Carole King write the No. 1 *Will You Love Me Tomorrow* for black singing trio the Shirelles, it's just the start of a new era of honest, beautifully crafted and intelligent pop songs about teenage life and love.

The Hustler
Paul Newman brings a magnetic swagger to the screen as 'Fast' Eddie Felson, a talented, small-time pool shark whose self-destructive compulsion to win is played out in the small hours and smoky shadows of America's billiard halls. British audiences are unfamiliar with the game of pool but it matters little when we watch Newman and Jack Gleason play a marathon match with balletic elegance. And when Newman smirks and says, 'You know, all of a sudden, you feel you can't miss?', it's hard not to believe him.

1961

Motown on the march
11th March 1961 Less than a year after it was launched by record producer Berry Gordy, Detroit's Motown label has its first million seller - *Shop Around* by the Miracles, led by William 'Smokey' Robinson. Over in Liverpool, the Beatles are adding Motown songs like the Miracles' *You Really Got a Hold on Me* and the Marvelettes' *Please Mr Postman* to their repertoire and making the label's trademark backbeat part of their sound.

Second place again
18th March 1961 The UK's Eurovision Song Contest entry is *Are You Sure* written and sung by a young Everlys-like duo from Wiltshire called the Allisons. It comes a strong second to Luxembourg's *Nous Les Amoureux*, sung by Jean-Claude Pascal.

Elvis quits live performing
25th March 1961 Elvis Presley proves his pulling power once again with a movie, *GI Blues*, which capitalises on his return from Army service. Its hit song *Wooden Heart* is his seventh UK No. 1. But there is bad news for fans as he performs what manager 'Colonel' Tom Parker insists will be his last live show, in Hawaii. From now on, it will be movies and records only.

Meek and wild
31st August 1960 Biggles actor John Leyton reaches No. 1 in the UK with *Johnny Remember Me* after singing it in in the television soap opera *Harpers West One*, in which he plays wild pop idol Johnny St Cyr.

Happiness for Helen
28th September 1961 Reaching the grand old age of fifteen and free to leave school is Helen Shapiro - and this on the very day that her biggest hit to date, *Walkin' Back To Happiness*, enters the UK chart.

Out of the Shadows
30th September 1961 Just as *Kon-Tiki* is sailing up the charts to No. 1, the Shadows are shaken by the departure of drummer Tony Meehan. Brian Bennett from Marty Wilde's Wildcats takes his place. Meehan's future lies at Decca Records as a producer and talent scout. One of his early tasks at Decca is to turn down the Beatles.

Platform blues
17th October 1961 A fateful meeting happens on a platform at Dartford railway station. Mick Jagger and Keith Richards are both eighteen and last met in primary school. They bond over the Chuck Berry and Muddy Waters albums that Keith is carrying and realise they have a shared love of American blues.

1961

Brian meets the Beatles
9th November 1961 Now regulars at the Cavern Club in Liverpool, the Beatles' lunchtime set attracts Brian Epstein from the nearby NEMS department store. Intrigued, he meets them backstage and within days becomes their manager.

MY FIRST 18 YEARS — TOP 10 — 1961

1. **Please Mr Postman** *The Marvelettes*
2. **Take Five** *Dave Brubeck*
3. **Stand By Me** *Ben E. King*
4. **Midnight in Moscow** *Kenny Ball and his Jazzmen*
5. **Walkin' Back to Happiness** *Helen Shapiro*
6. **Goodness Gracious Me** *Peter Sellers, Sophia Loren*
7. **Will You Love Me Tomorrow** *The Shirelles*
8. **My Kind of Girl** *Matt Monro*
9. **On the Rebound** *Floyd Cramer*
10. **Blue Moon** *The Marcels*

A shore thing
2nd December 1961 Entering the UK chart for a record-breaking 52 weeks without reaching No. 1 is Acker Bilk's *Stranger on the Shore*, the theme tune of a BBC TV serial about a French teenager in Brighton. Best known as a bowler-hatted clarinet-playing jazz man, Acker originally called the melody *Jenny* after his daughter. It fares even better in the US, where it tops the chart and sells a million.

Cliff's new movie
13th December 1961 *The Young Ones* starring Cliff Richard receives a glittering world premiere at the Warner Theatre, Leicester Square. It is Cliff's third film and the first in which he has headline billing.

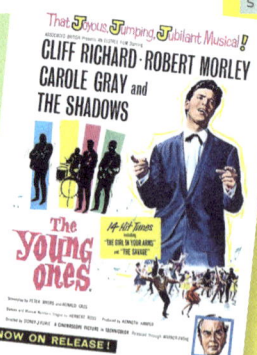

The sound of Fury
The current king of pop impresario Larry Parnes's stable of acts is Billy Fury, a Liverpool boy who as plain Ronald Wycherley once made his living on the Mersey tugboats. As a live performer he's the closest the UK has to Elvis but on disc he's more subdued, preferring ballads rather than rockers. From the hot songwriting team of Gerry Goffin and Carole King *Halfway to Paradise* is his biggest hit yet.

PHOTO CREDITS Copyright 2024, TDM Rights BV.
Photos: **A** Don Morley EMPICS - PA Images - Getty Images / **B** Mirrorpix - Getty Images / **C** John Franks - Hulton Archive - Getty Images / **D** Evening Standard - Hulton Archive - Getty Images / **E** Sovfoto - Universal Images Group Editorial - Getty Images / **F** Bettmann - Getty Images / **G** Nasa - Hulton Archive - Getty Images / **H** Ullstein Bild - Getty Images / **I** Mirrorpix - Getty Images / **J** United Archives - Hulton Archive - Getty Images / **K** Evening Standard - Hulton Archive - Getty Images / **L** Silver Screen Collection - Moviepix - Getty Images / **M** Mirrorpix - Getty Images / **N** AF Archive - Mary Evans / **O** Gai Terrell - Redferns - Getty Images / **P** RB Staff - Redferns - Getty Images / **Q** Sepia Times - Universal Images Group Editorial - Getty Images / **R** Michael Ochs Archives - Getty Images / **S** Hulton Deutsch - Corbis Historical - Getty Images.

1962

MY FIRST 18 YEARS

SPORT

Stanley go out of business
6th March 1962 Financial pressures force the closure of Accrington Stanley, a football club ever-present since 1921. Three months later, Oxford United are elected to take Stanley's place in the fourth division. A re-constituted Accrington Stanley will reclaim a league place in 2006.

A toxic World Cup
10th June 1962 England exit the FIFA World Cup in Chile at the quarter final stage, losing 3-1 to Brazil, the defending champions. Brazil go on to beat Czechoslovakia 3-1 in the final. The tournament is marred by on-field violence, notably in Italy's 2-0 defeat of Chile which earns the epithet of 'the battle of Santiago'. Walter Winterbottom stands down as England manager. He is replaced by Alf Ramsey, who has just guided Ipswich Town to their first ever league championship.

Golden moments at the Games
September - December 1962 Yorkshire-based sprinter Dorothy Hyman is the UK's top performer in the two major international athletics meetings of the year, the European Games in Belgrade and the Commonwealth Games in Perth, Australia. In Belgrade she wins the 100 metres gold and the 200 metres silver before securing bronze in the 4 x 100 metres relay final. Running for England in Perth she takes gold in both the 100 and 200 yard events. There is also European joy for 400 metres winner Robbie Brightwell, 5,000 metres winner Bruce Tulloh, marathon winner Brian Kilby and 20 kilometres walk winner Ken Thompson, putting Great Britain second in the final medal table behind the Soviet Union.

Bangor's European adventure
5th September 1962 British football's unlikely European heroes are tiny Bangor City, who enter the European Cup Winners' Cup as holders of the Welsh Cup and astonish the football world by beating Napoli 2-0 in the first leg of the first round. Napoli win the second leg 3-1 in front of an 80,000 crowd. With the scores level, Napoli win the playoff 2-1 at Arsenal's Highbury ground.

Hill tops in F1
29th December 1962 The last race of the F1 season, the South African Grand Prix, sees an enthralling all-British challenge for the Formula One drivers' championship. When Jim Clark is forced to retire twenty laps from the end, Graham Hill seizes the moment and beats him to the title by twelve points.

16 JAN 1962
Filming begins on *'Dr No'* the first James Bond film.

20 FEB 1962
John Glenn is first US astronaut to orbit the Earth.

29 MAR 1962
Education Act creates system of locally funded tuition fees and grants for undergraduates.

1962

DOMESTIC NEWS

Smallpox outbreak
January 1962 Smallpox strikes Britain as five people with the virus arrive in the UK from an affected area in Pakistan. Two travel to Birmingham, one to Bradford, one to Cardiff and one to London. The outbreak results in six deaths in Bradford, whilst South Wales suffers nineteen. Across the country over a million people receive emergency vaccinations.

Goodbye trolleybuses!
8th May 1962 The last of London's trolleybus or 'Diddler' routes is replaced with a diesel bus service. The new AEC Routemasters now cover all of the 68 trolleybus routes, a network that was once the largest in the world.

Panda crossings
2nd April 1962 The first of the country's new 'panda' crossings opens outside Waterloo station in London, with Guildford and Lincoln receiving them shortly afterwards. The new crossings have triangular patterns rather than stripes, feature red and amber lights for traffic and the command 'cross' for pedestrians.

Britain's first casinos!
2nd June 1962 Britain gets its first legal casinos following the introduction of the Betting and Gaming Act 1960. One of the first opens in Brighton, Sussex, with another, the Clermont Club, opening in London's Mayfair.

Fascist Mosley attacked
31st July 1962 Racial violence once more hits the headlines in July 1962 as race riots break out in Dudley. In contrast, Oswald Mosley, fascist leader of the Union Movement, is attacked and knocked down by protestors intent on stopping him from marching through Manchester on the 29th. Whilst he is rescued by the police, he is pelted with fruit, eggs, coins, and stones, and just two days later, on the 31st, appears at a rally in Dalston, London. Thousands gather, and Mosley and his 'blackshirts' are attacked again, with 54 arrests made.

---

14 APR 1962
Georges Pompidou becomes Prime Minister of France.

25 MAY 1962
Coventry's new cathedral is consecrated.

29 JUN 1962
The Vickers VC-10 long-range airliner makes its first flight.

1962

Space and satellites
14th June 1962 The European Space Research Organisation is formed with Britain joining eleven other countries to create the predecessor to the European Space Agency. Space is beginning to affect the public consciousness, as the Telstar satellite provides the first live transmissions of full-length television shows across the Atlantic.

Iconic cars launched
12th August 1962 The Austin and Morris 1100s launch (photo). Known simply as the "1100" they will go on to become the best-selling cars of the 1960s, selling more than a million vehicles in the UK. The Ford Cortina is also launched in September. but has to wait until the 70s for its heyday, becoming the best-selling car of that decade.

Flavoured crisps!
Flavoured crisps appear on British shelves for the first time as Golden Wonder launch a cheese and onion variety. Previously, crisps have only been available with a small sachet of salt for seasoning, and the launch of flavoured crisps in the UK is a sensation. Other flavours, such as salt and vinegar, follow later in the 60s.

Independence movements gain ground
1962 sees Jamaica, Trinidad and Tobago, and Uganda all gain their independence from Britain.

More motorways
The first phases of the M5 and M6 motorways open, with the M5 connecting Birmingham and north Gloucestershire, and the M6 bypassing Stafford.

DO YOU REMEMBER THIS?

Cigarette case

ROYALTY & POLITICS

Charles at Gordonstoun
1st May 1962 Fourteen-year-old Prince Charles starts at Gordonstoun School near Elgin in Scotland. There has been much discussion in the press about its suitability for the heir to the throne given the austerity of its regime and the school's emphasis on physical education.

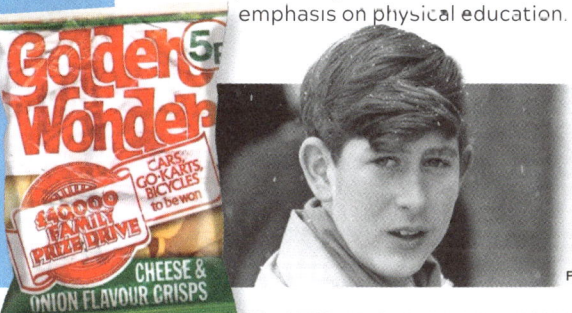

---

12 JUL 1962
Rolling Stones 1st performance (Marquee Club, London).

4 AUG 1962
The Welsh Language Society, is founded as a pressure group campaigning for the protection and promotion of the Welsh language.

25 SEP 1962
Boxer Sonny Liston wins the world heavyweight championship by defeating Floyd Patterson.

1962

No inquiry into thalidomide
17th May 1962 Following harrowing reports of mothers across Britain giving birth to babies with physical deformities, the UK government issues a warning concerning the morning sickness drug Thalidomide. Minister of Health Enoch Powell subsequently refuses to establish a public inquiry into the drug.

Night of the long knives
13th July 1962 In a breathtakingly savage reshuffle of his Cabinet that is widely seen as an attempt to save his own skin as Prime Minister, Harold Macmillan sacks seven of his senior ministers.

Losing an empire, looking for a role?
12th December 1962 In a speech at West Point Military Academy that is directly critical of the Macmillan government, former US Secretary of State Dean Acheson makes his famous statement that 'Great Britain has lost an empire but has not yet found a role'. The speech intensifies a feeling of drift in the 'special relationship' between the UK and US.

FOREIGN NEWS

First limb reattachment
23rd May 1962 The world's first successful reattachment of a severed limb is carried out at a hospital in Boston, Masschusetts, by Dr. Ronald A. Malt. The patient is twelve-year-old Everett Knowles, whose right arm was sliced off at the shoulder by a train.

Eichmann executed
1st June 1962 Nazi henchman Adolf Eichmann is refused clemency and executed in Ramla, Israel, following his conviction on fifteen counts of crimes against humanity, war crimes, crimes against the Jewish people, and membership of a criminal organisation.

Escape from Alcatraz
11th June 1962 Three men escape from the maximum security prison on Alcatraz Island near San Francisco. They place papier-mâché masks in their beds to deceive the guards and flee on a boat made of life jackets stuck together. The men are never seen again.

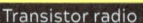

Transistor radio

1 OCT 1962 — Brian Epstein signs a contract to manage The Beatles.

23 NOV 1962 — World's first successful hip replacement operation at Wigan hospital.

22 DEC 1962 — Big freeze begins in UK, lasting until March 1963.

1962

Algeria independent
3rd July 1962 The granting of independence to Algeria by France sees the last gasp of the terror campaign. Three weeks after independence, civil war breaks out between the Provisional Government and the National Liberation Front (FLN). Independence is officially proclaimed on 31st July, with Ahmed Ben Bella as President.

Pop art
9th July 1962 Andy Warhol presents 32 paintings of Campbell's soup cans at the Ferus Gallery in Los Angeles. It is the essence of pop art: mass produced banality on the walls of a gallery. After the sudden death of Marilyn Monroe, Warhol releases a diptych with 50 portraits of the star, based on publicity pictures for the film *Niagara* (1953). The left canvas shows the glamorous movie star while the right canvas depicts her private side and the downside of fame.

Goodbye Norma Jean
5th August 1962 Norma Jean Mortenson - alias Marilyn Monroe - is found dead in her bed at her Los Angeles home, aged 36. An autopsy shows that Monroe died of an overdose of barbiturates, probably intentional. Conspiracy theories surround her death while rumours of entanglement with both John and Robert Kennedy will persist for years.

Mandela in jail
5th August 1962 Nelson Mandela is arrested by the South African authorities. He now leads the military wing of the African National Congress - called Umkhonto we Sizwe (Spear of the Nation) - which carries out acts of sabotage against the apartheid regime. He is jailed for five years, during which time he will be convicted on other charges and sentenced to life imprisonment on Robben Island.

Cuban missile crisis
28th October 1962 The Cold War reaches its most dangerous point during the thirteen days of the Cuban Missile Crisis. After the failed US-backed Bay of Pigs invasion in 1961, Cuban leader Fidel Castro appeals for military assistance from the Soviet Union. Soviet leader Nikita Khrushchev agrees and secretly places nuclear missiles in Cuba, aimed at the US mainland. In September, the missile installations are photographed from US spy planes. President Kennedy demands the immediate removal of the missiles and announces a blockade of Cuba, with US ships ready to stop Soviet ships reaching the island. As the world holds its breath, Kennedy and Khrushchev negotiate in secret. Kennedy offers a compromise - a promise not to attack Cuba and to withdraw US missiles from Turkey if the Soviets dismantle their nuclear base in Cuba. Khrushchev agrees. A devastating nuclear war is narrowly averted.

1962

ENTERTAINMENT

West Side Story in West End cinemas
West Side Story is chosen for the Royal Film Performance on 26th February after which it is shown at the Astoria cinema. In response to rave reviews in America, the cinema has been receiving a deluge of letters and money from film fans hoping to secure a seat in advance and be among the first to see the film version of the electrifying stage musical.

Animal Magic
The first episode of *Animal Magic*, produced by the five-year-old BBC Natural History Unit in Bristol and presented by Johnny Morris, is shown on 13th April. Morris, a natural mimic, would often act as a zookeeper at Bristol Zoo Gardens and give the various animals he encountered their own voices. More scientific intervals of the programme were presented by naturalists such as Tony Soper and Gerald Durrell. *Animal Magic* runs until 1983.

Look and Learn magazine
Fleetway publications launch a new juvenile magazine, *Look and Learn*, on 20th January in which editor David Stone promises readers, 'a treasure house of exciting articles, stories and pictures'. At 26x35cm and with half of the magazine in colour, it stands out against its rivals on the newsstands. *Look and Learn* runs for 1,049 issues until its closure in 1982.

Fab Four Fan Club
Freda Kelly, assistant to Beatles manager Brian Epstein, takes over as secretary of the Fab Four's official fan club and rather naively gives her home address for fan club mail. Inevitably the family home is inundated with letters until she changes it to Epstein's office address.

Just add water
Tang instant orange drink is used during John Glenn's Mercury space flight in February and remains on NASA crews' menus for future space expeditions. Tang, along with the UK powdered orange drink Bird's Apeel or Kellogg's Rise & Shine concentrated juice in a can, enjoy quite a vogue during the 1960s and '70s.

Fundraising frenzy
The first *Blue Peter* fundraising appeal urges viewers to collect used stamps to raise money for homes for homeless people.

Brains of Britain
School swots and student eggheads assemble this year for a classic quiz show on TV. *Top of the Form* successfully migrates from radio (where it's been since 1948) to television on 12th November with a quiz series for school teams.

1962

It's a fair cop
The first episode of *Z-Cars* is broadcast on 2nd January and introduces a new kind of hard-hitting police drama. Rather than the familiar bobby on the beat in the *Dixon of Dock Green* vein, the show follows the officers of a modern police unit in the fictional town of Newtown, whose fight against crime is expedited by their Ford Zephyr police cars. The show hits just the right note and quickly gains 14 million viewers.

Steptoe and Son
On 7th June, the first episode of *Steptoe and Son* is broadcast, with Wilfrid Brambell as the wily, grubby-minded, snaggle-toothed Albert and Harry H. Corbett as Harold, his hapless and downtrodden son, always hoping for better things despite the cynical sneering of his father who he regularly refers to as 'you dirty old man'. Audiences love their bickering partnership and at the height of its popularity, *Steptoe and Son* attracts 28 million viewers.

A nation of DIY-ers
Barry Bucknell's mission to teach the country how to 'do-it-yourself' gets more ambitious when he presents *Bucknell's House* and take viewers through a step-by-step renovation of a dilapidated house in Ealing, west London. Bucknell contributes to a huge DIY boom during which magazines like *Do-It-Yourself* and *Practical Householder* also provide instruction on how to renovate and modernise.

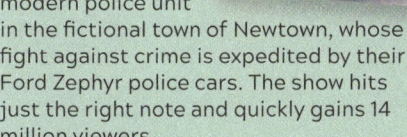

Saint Roger
As the suave and unruffled Simon Templar, who is a kind of mid-century Robin Hood, using unconventional means and over-stepping law to bring about justice, Roger Moore's stint as *The Saint* is something of a dry run for the role of James Bond. He part-purchases the rights to *The Saint* which is a canny business moves as it switches to colour in 1966 and is syndicated around the world.

The Jet(son) Set
With the Space Race well and truly underway, Hanna-Barbera capitalises on the success of *The Flintstones* but instead of the Stone Age, catapult their next cartoon family into the Space Age. *The Jetsons* is a tongue-in-cheek look at the future as the Jetsons of Orbit City drive around in bubble-topped spaceships and get help at home from a robot called Rosey.

1962

Satire on screen
Satire is to be a defining feature of the 1960s comedy scene, and *That Was The Week That Was*, broadcast first on 24th November, leads the way. Never afraid to court controversy, *TWTWTW* lampoons politicians, mocks public figures and even has a go at the royal family, drawing complaints regularly but doing no damage whatsoever to viewing figures. Hosted by David Frost, the show opens each week with a new song based on the week's news sung by Millicent Martin, and a rolling roster of cast members include Willie Rushton, Roy Kinnear, Lance Percival and cartoonist Timothy Birdsall.

Lawrence of Arabia
10th December 1962 Peter O'Toole was director David Lean's choice to play T. E. Lawrence in this retelling of *Lawrence of Arabia*, even though Montgomery Clift, Albert Finney and Marlon Brando were all considered. Filmed on a huge scale with a cast of thousands, Lean's masterpiece wins six Academy Awards including Best Picture and Best Director. It is the benchmark by which future directors will measure their own work.

To Kill a Mockingbird
Gregory Peck is cast as morally upstanding lawyer Atticus Finch in this faithful film version of Harper Lee's bestselling, Pulitzer-Prize-winning novel about the small-town bigotry in Depression-era Alabama, exposed by Finch's defence of a black man falsely accused of raping a white woman. Peck wins an Oscar for his role as does the playwright Horton Foote, for his sensitive and authentic adapted screenplay.

 ## MUSIC

Make or break for the Beatles
1st January 1962 A make or break year for the Beatles begins with an audition for Decca Records, where ex-Shadows drummer turned Decca producer Tony Meehan opts to sign another group auditioning that day, Brian Poole and the Tremeloes. Manager Brian Epstein's last throw of the dice is to call on George Martin at Parlophone, who finally gives the boys a contract. Insisting that they record one of their own songs rather than the plodding *How Do You Do It*, their first release is *Love Me Do*. By this time Ringo Starr has replaced Cavern club favourite Pete Best on drums and John Lennon has married Cynthia Powell.

Cribbins on class
February - July 1962 The great British comedy song is alive and well and living at Parlophone Records. Label boss George Martin has already recorded Peter Sellers, the *Beyond the Fringe* team and Flanders and Swann. Now he has brought comic actor Bernard Cribbins to Abbey Road to make two hilarious if macabre commentaries on class differences - *Hole in the Ground* and *Right Said Fred*.

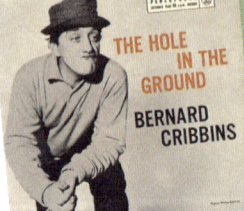

1962

Another record for Cliff
11th January 1962 Cliff Richard's success story hits another level. In another 'first' for the singer, *The Young Ones* receives pre-release orders of 524,000 - a British record for advance sales. It is only the fourth record ever to reach No. 1 during its first week of release.

Seeger is free
19th May 1962 After a protracted legal process, folk singer and activist Pete Seeger has his 1955 conviction for contempt of Congress overturned. He had refused to answer questions about his political affiliations during anti-communist hearings.

American idols on tour
Among the US teen idols touring the UK this year is Neil Sedaka, who gave up a concert career for pop music. Neil is a former classmate of Carole King and writes with high-school pal Howie Greenfield. Sedaka hits like *Happy Birthday Sweet Sixteen* and *Breaking Up Is Hard To Do* are notable for their multi-tracking, as Neil harmonises with himself on cascades of 'dooby-downs' and 'tra-la-las'. Also on tour is Bobby Vee, who has come a long way since filling in for Buddy Holly following the air crash that claimed Buddy's life.

Steaming to No. 1
21st July 1963 Songs by Carole King and Gerry Goffin are everywhere this year. *The Locomotion* is a No. 1 in the US for Little Eva, who babysits their daughter, while *Up on the Roof* is a charming, evocative hit for the Drifters. To cap it all, Carole is now releasing a record of her own - *It Might As Well Rain Until September*, a song of summer separation that treads similar ground to that other seasonal hit of 1962, Brian Hyland's *Sealed with a Kiss*.

Jersey boys' joy
15th September 1962 Two successive US chart toppers - *Sherry* and *Big Girls Don't Cry* - herald the arrival of a New Jersey vocal group whose music will still be celebrated in the 21st century by a much loved Broadway show. The Four Seasons are four streetwise Italian-American boys who draw on the writing and production talent of Bob Crewe and Bob Gaudio. Theirs is a black-influenced vocal sound built around one of the wonders of the early 1960s music scene, the phenomenal falsetto of Frankie Valli.

The name is Bond
Just as *Dr No* kicks off one of the most lucrative franchises in movie history, so its soundtrack sets a fantastic new precedent in movie music making. *The James Bond Theme* is composed by Monty Norman, orchestrated by John Barry and features an unforgettable guitar solo from Vic Flick - and it proves so iconic that it is incorporated into every subsequent Bond film.

Ray goes country
12th July 1962 Musically speaking, Ray Charles is a law unto himself. Following his stunning, genre-busting combinations of gospel, jazz and blues rhythms, he is now bringing his touch to the unfashionable world of country music with the album *Modern Sounds in Country and Western Music*. Contradicting predictions that it might damage his career, it's a huge seller, with its standout track - Ray's soulful version of the Don Gibson ballad *I Can't Stop Loving You* - topping the US and UK chart.

1962

Soul brother No. 1
24th October 1962 Starring at the legendary Apollo Theatre in Harlem, New York City, is the self-styled 'soul brother number one', James Brown. A truly historic night of incredible physical and vocal gymnastics is recorded for posterity, and the subsequent album *Live at the Apollo* will remain on the US rhythm and blues chart for an unprecedented 66 weeks. Brown's breakthrough to the mainstream follows in June 1963 with a pleading revival of a 1940s Perry Como number - *Prisoner of Love*.

MY FIRST 18 YEARS TOP 10 — 1962

1. **Come Outside** *Mike Sarne*
2. **Can't Help Falling in Love** *Elvis Presley*
3. **Telstar** *The Tornados*
4. **Dream Baby** *Roy Orbison*
5. **Hey Baby** *Bruce Channel*
6. **Run to Him** *Bobby Vee*
7. **He's a Rebel** *The Crystals*
8. **A Picture of You** *Joe Brown*
9. **The Young Ones** *Cliff Richard and the Shadows*
10. **Up on the Roof** *The Drifters*

Open | Search | Scan

Telstar spans the globe
4th October 1962 Taking its title from the telecommunications satellite launched in July, *Telstar* by the Tornados begins a five-week stay at the top of the British chart before repeating the feat across the world, including the US.

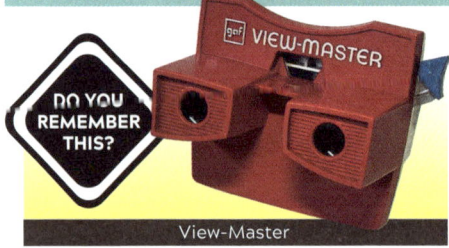

DO YOU REMEMBER THIS?
View-Master

Perfectly Frank
8th November 1962 Voice of the year is Frank Ifield, a UK-born Australian who adds a country twang, a yodel and a fetching harmonica to vintage songs like *I Remember You* and *Lovesick Blues*, both of them No. 1s.

Dusty goes solo
Playing their own brand of country-folk music on hits like *Island of Dreams*, the Springfields have made a big impression. Tom Springfield writes the songs and his sister Dusty is the focal point - until she goes solo in October and changes her whole look and style. Adopting a bouffant hairdo and Motown-like backing, she makes an instant mark with *I Only Want to be with You*.

PHOTO CREDITS Copyright 2024, TDM Rights BV.
Photos: **A** Bernard Cahier - Hulton Archive - Getty Images / **B** PA Images - Getty Images / **C** Mirrorpix - Getty Images / **D** Hulton Archive - Getty Images / **E** Ron Case - Hulton Archive - Getty Images / **F** Stan Meagher - Hulton Royals Collection - Getty Images / **G** Les Lee - Hulton Archive - Getty Images / **H** Tom Szczerbowski - Getty Images / **I** Donaldson Collection - Moviepix - Getty Images / **J** API - Gamma-Rapho - Getty Images / **K** Universal History Archive - Universal Images Group - Getty Images / **L** Ronald Grant Archive - Mary Evans / **M** The Land of Lost Content - Mary Evans Picture Library / **N** BBC - Ronald Grant Archive - Mary Evans / **O** The Land of Lost Content - Mary Evans / **P** Studiocana Films LTD - Mary Evans / **Q** Hanna Barbera - Ronald Grant Archive - Mary Evans / **R** Ronald Grant Archive - Mary Evans / **S** AF Archive - Mary Evans / **T** Gilles Petard - Redferns - Getty Images / **U** David Redfern - Redferns - Getty Images / **V** David Redfern - Redferns - Getty Images.

1963

MY FIRST 18 YEARS

SPORT

Football in the freezer
The UK's terrible winter plays havoc with the football fixtures, forcing a twelve-week shutdown and the creation of the Pools Panel by the football pools operators to predict what the scores would have been. Everton eventually beat Spurs to the league championship and Manchester United win the FA Cup by beating Leicester 3-1. But the most spectacular day in the football year is Boxing Day which delivers a series of unbelievable scorelines including Fulham beating Ipswich 10-1. An incredible 66 goals are scored in ten first division games.

Spurs win in Europe
15th May 1963 Tottenham Hotspur win the European Cup Winners Cup in fine style, beating Atletico Madrid 5-1 in Rotterdam. It is the first trophy for a British side in European competition.

Cooper v. Clay
18th June 1963 British heavyweight champion Henry Cooper boxes the fight of his life at Wembley Stadium against world championship contender Cassius Clay. Against all expectations he puts a taunting Clay (later Muhammad Ali) on the canvas at the end of the fourth round, but Clay recovers and wins on a technical knockout when Cooper is forced to retire with a cut eye. Cooper's gallant challenge makes him a national hero overnight.

First ever Gillette Cup
7th September 1963 The Gillette Cup, English cricket's first one-day competition, climaxes with a final between Sussex and Worcestershire at Lord's. Led by England captain Ted Dexter, Sussex win by 14 runs.

Two auspicious debuts
The year sees two notable footballing debuts. In May, West Ham's Bobby Moore is Alf Ramsey's choice to lead his new-look England team and makes his first appearance as captain in a 1-0 victory over Czechoslovakia. In September, seventeen-year old Belfast boy George Best plays for Manchester United for the first time in a first division fixture against West Bromwich Albion.

Chester the champion
5th June 1963 Essex teenager Chester Barnes becomes the youngest ever winner of the England table tennis championships. He goes on to win the next three championships in a row and remains synonymous with UK table tennis until his retirement in 1975.

14 JAN 1963
Legendary locomotive *Flying Scotsman* is withdrawn from service.

9 FEB 1963
Maiden flight of Boeing 727 aircraft.

16 MAR 1963
Death of William Beveridge, pioneer of welfare state in UK.

43

1963

DOMESTIC NEWS

Big freeze
January - March 1963 Britain's 'Big Freeze' continues as snow blankets the country. January sees an average temperature of -2.1 degrees centigrade, and in some areas even the sea freezes. February sees a 36-hour blizzard and winds of up to 81 miles per hour, before the country finally starts to thaw in March.

The Great Train Robbery!
8th August 1963 A gang of men waylay a Royal Mail train heading from Glasgow to London on the West Coast Mainline and steal the £2.6 million carried on board. The police offer a £10,000 reward for information, which leads to the thieves being identified, but not before they go to ground. Eight are arrested and seven found guilty at trial in 1964, with a further five arrested at later dates. There seem to be at least four others involved who are never caught.

Nuclear in the news
6th April 1963 The UK agrees to purchase Polaris nuclear missiles from the United States, leading to protests across the country. The CND's annual Aldermaston to London march sees numbers swell to over 70,000 on the 15th April.

Hillman Imp launched
2nd May 1963 The Hillman Imp goes into production at the new Rootes Group car plant in Linwood in Scotland. The Imp is designed specifically to compete with the Mini Cooper and features both rear-wheel drive and a rear engine layout. It also makes the most of its small size with a rear bench seat that folds down. The Imp would later become a successful rally car.

All change in the leadership
In a tumultuous political year, Labour leader Hugh Gaitskell dies on 18th January and is succeeded by Harold Wilson. The tawdriness of the Profumo affair undermines Harold Macmillan's government and he resigns as Prime Minister in October. Foreign Secretary Lord Home leaves his seat in the House of Lords to succeed him. By the end of the year, the whole political climate has changed.

---

7 APR 1963
Yugoslavian leader Tito made President for life.

15 MAY 1963
Weightwatchers slimming company founded in New York.

16 JUN 1963
Soviet cosmonaut Valentina Tereshkova is the first woman in space.

1963

Say hello to Sindy!
September 1963 Pedigree Dolls and Toys launch their famous 'Sindy' fashion doll. Designed as the British answer to Barbie, which was not particularly popular in the UK at the time, Sindy was designed with the British audience in mind. Instead of Barbie's American glamour, Sindy was given a more 'girl-next-door' style that appealed to UK consumers, and she would become the best-selling toy of 1968 and 1970.

Dartford Tunnel opens
18th November 1963 The Dartford Tunnel finally opens after the completion of a 57-year construction project disrupted by the Second World War. The toll is two shillings and sixpence.

DO YOU REMEMBER THIS?

Glass Coca Cola bottle

The Profumo affair
25th September 1963 The Denning Report on the Profumo affair is published, concluding that there have been no security breaches and that government ministers and security services acted 'appropriately'. The scandal saw John Profumo, Secretary of State for War, have an affair with Christine Keeler, a nineteen-year-old model, who was also involved with a Soviet naval attaché, creating a love-triangle that was potentially damaging for national security.

Kenya and Zanzibar
Kenya and Zanzibar become the latest countries to gain independence from Britain, Kenya on 12th December, and Zanzibar on the 19th.

Lava lamps
Edward Craven-Walker, and his lighting company Mathmos, launch the 'Astro' lamp. These extraordinary lamps, featuring a wax mixture floating inside an illuminated, transparent liquid, become a design sensation. Also known as 'lava' lamps, they develop associations with hippie culture and remain a feature of fun-loving British shelves to this day.

ROYALTY & POLITICS

Macmillan signs test ban treaty
7th October 1963 A treaty banning the testing of nuclear weapons in the atmosphere is signed by the leaders of the US, USSR and UK. Harold Macmillan later refers to the signing of the treaty as the biggest achievement of his premiership.

---

30 JUL 1963
Kim Philby confirmed as Soviet spy now living in Moscow.

1 AUG 1963
Arthur Ashe becomes the first African-American tennis player in the US Davis Cup team.

15 SEP 1963
Bombing of Baptist Church in Birmingham, Alabama, kills four black children.

1963

De Gaulle says *Non*
14th January 1963 In what is a personal humiliation for Prime Minister Harold Macmillan, President de Gaulle rejects the UK's application to join the Common Market. He claims that the UK's membership would be at odds with her Commonwealth links and that the UK would always value her relationship with the US over Europe.

FOREIGN NEWS

Beeching slashes the railways
27th March 1963 Dr Richard Beeching's report into 'modernising' the UK's railways is published, recommending the shutting down of half the existing railway lines and over 2,000 stations. The report is accepted by the government and closures are expected to begin within two years.

White smoke
3rd June 1963 The death of Pope John XXIII sparks a wave of condolence for the simple farmer's son whose appeals for unity among all Christians, together with his humour and spontaneity, made him one of the twentieth century's best-loved religious leaders. On 21st June, after a two day papal conclave, the famous white smoke appears and Cardinal Giovanni Battista Montini succeeds him as Pope Paul VI (photo).

Princess Alexandra weds
24th April 1963 Princess Alexandra, cousin of the Queen and daughter of the late Duke of Kent, marries businessman Angus Ogilvy at Westminster Abbey. Princess Anne is chief bridesmaid. The televised wedding is watched by an estimated 200 million worldwide.

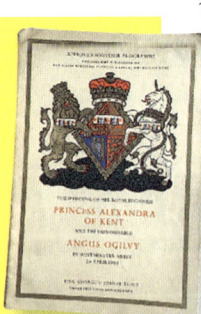

Communication line
30th August 1963 'The quick brown fox jumped over the lazy dog's back 1234567890' is the first message sent on the new teleprinter hotline between Washington and Moscow. Having a direct line of communication between the White House and the Kremlin is intended to prevent future escalations of the Cold War.

Dam catstrophe
9th October 1963 After heavy rainfall and landslides, a wave of water over 100 metres high flows over the Vajont Dam in Italy, killing 3,700 people in the towns and villages below.

30 OCT 1963
Lamborghini motor company founded in Italy.

15 NOV 1963
Valium is approved in the US and becomes the most prescribed drug in the world between 1969 and 1982.

12 DEC 1963
Kenya gains independence.

1963

'Ich bin ein Berliner!'
26th June 1963 West Berlin has been a western enclave inside East Germany for eighteen years. In a powerful speech in front of the City Hall in West Berlin, President John F. Kennedy delivers words of hope to beleaguered peoples everywhere: 'All free people, wherever they live, are citizens of Berlin, and therefore I, as a free man, am proud to be able to say: 'I am a Berliner!'

Nuclear-free space
15th October 1963 Almost a year on from the Cuban Missile Crisis, the US and Soviet Union agree to a United Nations resolution banning the placing of nuclear bombs in space.

'I have a dream!'
28th August 1963 In the largest demonstration ever seen in the US, more than a quarter of a million demonstrate for 'jobs and freedom' for African Americans in Washington DC. The masses gather at the Lincoln Memorial, where Mahalia Jackson, Bob Dylan and Joan Baez perform *We Shall Overcome* and *Blowin' in the Wind* and numerous speakers take the floor. Rev. Martin Luther King Jr. shares his dream of a world without racism with the words: 'I have a dream that one day my four little children will live in a nation where they will not be judged by the colour of their skin but by the content of their character. I have a dream today.' King's 'I Have a Dream' speech becomes a huge source of inspiration for the civil rights movement and is considered one of the finest speeches ever made.

Kennedy assassinated
22nd November 1963 In Dallas, Texas, to bolster support for his re-election, President John F. Kennedy is driven through the city in an open limousine accompanied by his wife Jackie and Texas governor John Connally and his wife Nellie. When the car passes the Texas School Book Depository, Kennedy is shot in the back and head. Lee Harvey Oswald, an ex-marine who once lived in Moscow, is arrested around 90 minutes later. On Air Force One, Vice President Lyndon B. Johnson is sworn in with Jackie Kennedy, still in her blood-stained pink dress, looking on. Oswald denies the murder and is himself shot and killed two days later by a known Mafia associate, Jack Ruby, as he is escorted out of Dallas police headquarters. A month of national mourning begins. The subsequent Warren Commission investigations produce more questions than answers and conspiracy theories remain. Was Castro or the KGB responsible? Did the CIA secretly prepare the assassination attempt? Was the Mafia behind it all? More than 60 years later, the debate goes on.

1963

Exit Adenauer
16th October 1963 In West Germany, the fourteen-year reign of Chancellor Konrad Adenauer comes to an end. Adenauer has turned the country into a reliable and very successful Western nation after the war. Adenauer is succeeded by Ludwig Erhard, under whom Germany experiences a period of low inflation and enormous industrial and economic growth.

Snap happy
Kodak release their Instamatic 50 camera in the UK in February, an instant-loading, point and snap camera that even the most technically inept person can use. Film manufacturers can barely keep up with demand.

ENTERTAINMENT

Diana
DC Thomson launches *Diana* magazine, which runs until 1976 (when it merges with *Jackie*). *Diana*'s target audience is girls from around 11 to 14, and its picture stories include *Jane - Model Miss*, *Mary Brown's Schooldays* and the sci-fi strip cartoon, *The Fabulous Four*. *Diana* also publishes *The Avengers* comic strip from issues 199 to 224 to coincide with the popular television series.

Ready Steady Go!
Ready Steady Go! bursts on to screens on ITV at 6pm on Friday 9th August, a new music show that quickly becomes the TV embodiment of the Swinging Sixties. With the introductory catch-phrase, 'the weekend starts here' *Ready Steady Go!* (or *RSG!*) attracts all the best pop acts and fills the studio with the most fashionable crowd of hip dancers, invited after being scouted in the nightclubs of London. Anchoring the show is Cathy McGowan - Queen of the Mods - who was plucked from obscurity to front the show along with Radio Luxembourg DJ Keith Fordyce.

National treasure
The National Theatre Company, destined to be the official dramatic company allied to the National Theatre on the South Bank, open their first season at the Old Vic, which the company leases while their permanent home is under construction. The first play is *Hamlet* with Peter O'Toole, fresh from his success in *Lawrence of Arabia* and only available for 27 performances due to prior filming commitment.

Sharp cut
Snipper du jour Vidal Sassoon cuts American actress Nancy Kwan's long hair into a sharp, glossy bob prior to her filming *The Wild Affair*. Kwan is so nervous during the haircut she plays chess with her manager to distract her. The result is a sensation.

1963

Ruling the air waves
Plans are well under way for the launch of Radio Caroline from a converted merchant vessel anchored off Felixstowe, just outside the UK's territorial limit. As a pirate radio station, Caroline will offer the wall-to-wall pop music that BBC radio does not, besides becoming the launchpad for many future stars of mainstream radio such as Tony Blackburn, Johnnie Walker and Dave Lee Travis. Caroline finally takes to the air on 28th March 1964.

Doctor who?
On 23rd November, *The Unearthly Child*, the first episode of a new science-fiction drama called *Doctor Who*, is shown on the BBC, starting eighty seconds behind schedule due to the news reporting on the assassination of President Kennedy. William Hartnell plays 'The Doctor, a humanoid alien who travels through time and space in a shape-shifting spaceship, the TARDIS. Due to a malfunction the TARDIS is permanently in the form of a police call box, but miraculously is vast inside despite its compact exterior dimensions.

Busman's holiday
Cliff Richard is Britain's most bankable star when he appears in *Summer Holiday*, his fifth film since 1959. Cliff plays Don, a mechanic at London Transport's service bus depot, who along with his pals, borrows a London double-decker bus and drives through Europe, meeting girls and singing and dancing along the way. It's no surprise that the film is a hit (coming only second to the Bond film *From Russia with Love* this year), and it generates four no. 1 singles, *Bachelor Boy*, *The Next Time*, *Foot Tapper* (for the Shadows) and the title track, *Summer Holiday*.

Ooh, you are awful!
After his role in TV's *The Army Game*, Dick Emery fronts his own BBC comedy sketch show, *The Dick Emery Show*. Emery's parade of characters become household favourites, from the hopeless Bovver Boy (whose long-suffering dad is played by Roy Kinnear) to Mandy, a flirtatious blonde who can't help but read sexual innuendo into every conversation, usually leading her to nudge her interviewer and utter the words, 'Ooh, you are awful!'.

Tom Jones
Many of actor Albert Finney's roles to date, from the film *Saturday Night, Sunday Morning*, or the Royal Court play, *Luther*, have been of the challenging and introspective nature, but in *Tom Jones*, Finney breaks the mould and has the time of his life as the pony-tail wearing, rambunctious womaniser roistering around the hostelries and haystacks of eighteenth-century England. As the posters state, 'Everybody loves Tom Jones!'

Mint mouthful
After Eight Wafer Thin Mints are new from Rowntree and Company and marketed as the ultimate in dinner party sophistication, guaranteed to 'turn any event into an occasion'.

Five o'Clock Club
150 kids form the raucous audience for twice a week show *Five o' Clock Club* which is first shown on ITV on 1st October. *Five o' Clock Club* mixes segments on hobbies such as pets, model-making and cooking, with puppets Fred Barker (a woolly dog) and a Liverpudlian owl Ollie Beak a music act in every show.

1963

Save your stamps
Tesco offers its shoppers the chance to collect Green Shield stamps at its stores. It's one of Green Shield Stamps' most important partnerships, and one of the first loyalty schemes introduced by a major retailer in the UK. At the end of each shop, stamps are issued which are stuck into a saver book and later exchanged for products in the Green Shield Stamps catalogue.

The Great Escape
Of the seventy-six POWs who attempted to escape from Stalag Luft III, fifty were shot on the orders of Hitler, and only three successfully made it home. The Great Escape takes a considerable amount of artistic licence in re-telling the original story, not least the inclusion of American soldiers in the escape attempt, done to appeal to US audiences, nevertheless it is an enthralling tribute to the bravery of those who lost their lives in a bid for freedom.

Jason & the Argonauts
Released in the US on 15th August, Ray Harryhausen's pioneering stop-motion visual effects are the real star of this mythological fantasy, from the merciless bronze giant Talos to the chilling sword-wielding skeletons that Jason and the Argonauts must battle. Harryhausen said it was the film he was most proud of almost thirty years later, when he was honoured with a Lifetime Achievement Award at the Academy Awards.

The Birds
It's a mystery why birds begin viciously attacking the people of Bodega Bay in Hitchcock's avian horror, released in the UK on 10th September, but the puzzling nature of the attack is perhaps why the film is so unsettling. Tippi Hedren is reportedly close to breakdown during filming due to Hitchcock's unrelenting demands. As for cinema audiences, nobody looks at a flock of starlings in the same way again.

MUSIC

The Stones start to roll
14th May 1963 Still smarting from passing up the Beatles, Decca Records sign a group that is well placed to challenge them. The Rolling Stones have cut their teeth in London's rhythm and blues clubs and play the music of Chuck Berry, Howlin' Wolf, Jimmy Reed et al with authenticity and insolence. They're managed by ex-Beatles publicist Andrew Oldham, whose strategy is to portray them as the anti-Beatles, with longer hair, a hard blues-based sound and lots of threat.

Beach Boys catch a wave
3rd August 1963 Surfin' USA marks the first appearance of a soon to be regular name on the UK record chart - the Beach Boys. In the US, 'surf' music is all the rage, a marriage of clanky guitars and high-voiced harmonies that's redolent of sun-kissed beaches, high waves, tanned muscle men and bikini-clad girls. Brian Wilson is the chief songwriter of the group and bases the song on Chuck Berry's *Sweet Little Sixteen*. Berry responds with a writ.

Freewheelin' Bob
27th May 1963 Bob Dylan already has one album under his belt but it's *The Freewheelin' Bob Dylan* that is really turning heads. It's the outcome of a burst of songwriting activity encouraged by girlfriend Suze Rotolo, who is pictured with Bob on the iconic album cover.

Beatlemania begins
As the year dawns, the Beatles are a little-known Liverpool group with one small hit to their name. Twelve months later, they are not just the biggest group in UK music but an all-consuming part of British life and culture. The journey starts with the No. 2 hit *Please Please Me*, showing off their harmonies and the songwriting skills of Lennon and McCartney. An LP follows, a collection of their stage numbers, then a first No. 1 with *From Me to You*, a second with the style-defining *She Loves You*, and a summer of 'Beatlemania' - girls swamping city centres wherever the Fab Four perform, boys sent home from school to get their hair cut, night after night of concerts where the band cannot hear themselves for screams, and press report after press report where they emerge as intelligent, funny spokesmen for a generation of post-war kids that has found a voice at last. Come the autumn there's another LP, *With the Beatles*, packed with John and Paul originals, plus a fifteen-minute performance on the Royal Variety Show that sends the country's love affair with the Fab Four into overdrive. Could an unwitting US be next for conquest?

Twelve-year-old genius
24th August 1963 Stevie Wonder becomes the first ever artist to top the US singles, LP and R&B charts during the same week. Stevie makes his first visit to the UK during December, where word about Motown is spreading fast, helped by the Beatles' LP versions of Smokey Robinson and Barrett Strong hits.

Epstein builds his stable
Not content with managing the greatest thing ever to happen to the UK music industry, Brian Epstein builds a stable of Liverpool talent. Gerry and the Pacemakers achieve what even the Beatles couldn't with three consecutive No. 1s with their first three releases, while John and Paul supply songs to Billy J. Kramer and the Fourmost. The Swinging Blue Jeans, one of the first Liverpool bands to switch from skiffle to rock, also score with *Hippy Hippy Shake* and *Good Golly Miss Molly*. Epstein does miss out on the Searchers who by common consent are the most musically gifted group on Merseyside. They have two years of hits but lack the songwriting ability to keep them at the top.

Patsy Cline RIP
5th March 1963 Tragedy strikes deep at the heart of country music with the death in a plane crash near Nashville of singing legend Patsy Cline.

1963

Spector reveals his 'wall of sound'
19th October 1963 In Los Angeles, sharp-shooter producer and label owner Phil Spector is making his reputation by loading his productions for the Crystals and the Ronettes with what becomes known as a 'wall of sound' - layer after layer of earthquake-inducing drums and strings. Best of the lot is *Be My Baby* for the Ronettes, featuring his future wife Ronnie Bennett on lead vocal. It's said to be the Beatles' favourite record of the year. Spector spends the whole summer recording a Christmas album featuring all his groups, then withdraws it after President Kennedy is assassinated on its day of release.

MY FIRST 18 YEARS — TOP 10 — 1963

1. She Loves You *The Beatles*
2. If You Gotta Make a Fool ... *Freddie and the ...*
3. Summer Holiday *Cliff Richard*
4. Dance On *The Shadows*
5. Be My Baby *The Ronettes*
6. Da Do Ron Ron *The Crystals*
7. Do You Love Me *Brian Poole and the Tremeloes*
8. Do You Want ... *Billy J. Kramer and the Dakotas*
9. Come On *The Rolling Stones*
10. You'll Never Walk Alone *Gerry and the Pace...*

Open | Search | Scan

The little sparrow is dead
14th October 1963 The death is announced of the legendary singer Edith Piaf, following a long period of illness, aged 47 years. Three days later, a crowd of over 40,000 gather in Paris for the funeral of 'the little sparrow'. Her tiny frame, powder keg voice and heart-churning songs of passion and tragedy made her the single most influential vocal talent ever to come out of France.

From *Carousel* to the Kop
31st October 1963 After two No. 1s, Gerry Marsden of Gerry and the Pacemakers pleads with producer George Martin to release *You'll Never Walk Alone* as a single. Martin isn't convinced but trusts Gerry's hunch that this arms-in-the-air highlight of their stage act can give him a third chart topper. As a hymn-like Rodgers and Hammerstein song from the show *Carousel*, it is hardly classic Merseybeat, yet Gerry's soaring vocal and George's rolling strings turn it into an anthem for the ages - and one that is swiftly adopted by the famous Kop at Liverpool FC on their way to championship glory.

PHOTO CREDITS Copyright 2024, TDM Rights BV.
Photos: **A** Mirrorpix - Getty Images / **B** PA Images - Getty Images / **C** Osorio Artist - Shutterstock / **D** Evening Standard - Hulton Archive - Getty Images / **E** Evening Standard - Hulton Archive - Getty Images / **F** Evening Standard - Hulton Archive - Getty Images / **G** Moore - Hulton Archive - GettyImages / **H** Ullstein Bild - Getty Images / **I** Bettman - Getty Images / **J** Historical - Corbis Historical - Getty Images / **K** Bettmann - Getty Images / **L** The Land of Lost Content Collection - Mary Evans Picture Gallery / **M** Ronald Grant Archive - Mary Evans / **N** Michael Ochs Archives - Getty Images / **O** Dalek by Colin Smith - / **P** Studiocanal Films Ltd - Mary Evans / **Q** Mirrorpix - Getty Images / **R** Ronald Grant - Alfred J Hitchcock Productions - Mary Evans / **S** Michael Ochs Archives - Getty Images / **T** Michael Ochs Archives - Getty Images / **U** Hulton Archive - Getty Images / **V** Mirrorpix - Getty Images / **W** Michael Ochs Archives - Getty Images / **X** GAB Archive - Redferns - Getty Images / **Y** GAB Archive - Redferns - Getty Images.

1964

MY FIRST 18 YEARS

SPORT

Paddy wins at Monte Carlo
21st January 1964 Driving for the British Motor Corporation, Paddy Hopkirk and co-driver Henry Liddon win the Monte Carlo Rally in a Mini Cooper S. The win cements the Mini in the affections of the UK public and gives a massive boost to its overseas reputation and sales.

DO YOU REMEMBER THIS?
Ken (Barbie) doll

Lifetime ban for Swan
13th April 1964 A match-fixing scandal unveiled by *The People* newspaper leads to the banning of Sheffield Wednesday and England international Peter Swan for life and his imprisonment for four months for fraud. Club teammates Tony Kay and David Layne receive similar punishments. All are convicted for placing bets on the outcome of their club's match against Ipswich Town in December 1962. The bans last until 1972, when Swan returns to playing and managing in the lower leagues.

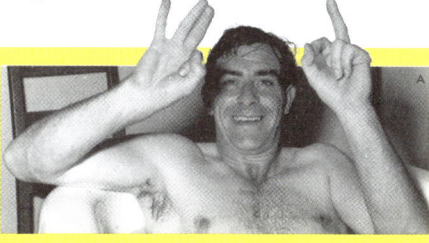

300 up for Fred
15th August 1964 While bowling for England against Australia in the fifth Test match, Fred Trueman becomes the first player to take 300 Test wickets. It is one of the few bright spots in a disappointing Test series in which Australia retain the Ashes.

Clay defeats Liston
25th February 1964 In one of boxing's biggest shocks, brash contender Cassius Clay takes the world heavyweight boxing title from the seemingly immovable Sonny Liston. The fight drips with controversy and the outcome is in doubt until the start of the seventh round, when Liston claims a shoulder injury and fails to come out of his corner. Clay is declared the winner by a technical knock-out. The fight marks the real beginning of the Cassius Clay/Muhammad Ali legend, as he joins the Nation of Islam movement two days later and adopts his new name in early March.

27 JAN 1964
Mary Whitehouse launches Clean Up TV campaign.

3 FEB 1964
Warren Commission convenes to investigate Kennedy assassination.

27 MAR 1964
Great Train Robbers are sentenced.

1964

Olympics in Tokyo
10th - 24th October 1964 In an Olympic Games in Tokyo that reaches more people across the world than ever before thanks to new satellite technology, the UK team achieves some notable successes. Its four golds go to long jumpers Lynn Davies and Mary Rand, Ken Matthews in the 20-kilometre walk and Ann Packer in the 800 metres, who also wins silver in the 400 metres. Ann is one half of Britain's golden couple of the Games: her husband Robbie Brightwell wins silver in the 4 x 400-metre relay.

Mods and Rockers
30th March 1964 Britain becomes embroiled in a culture war as two opposing groups, 'Mods' and 'Rockers', clash. The first physical conflicts occur at Clacton Beach and Hastings over Easter, followed by more disturbances in Brighton in May. 'Mod' culture focuses on a clean-cut image, with members wearing suits and riding scooters, listening to jazz and soul. 'Rockers' in contrast wear leather jackets and ride motorcycles, favouring rock 'n' roll and R&B.

DOMESTIC NEWS

Springtown march
28th January 1964 Families living in the Springtown Camp in Derry, Northern Ireland, march through town to demand they are rehoused. Around 400 families have been living in the camp, in buildings made largely from corrugated iron, since the 1940s. The failure of the Protestant local authority to rehouse the predominantly Catholic families in proper houses gives rise to several civil rights protests in Northern Ireland.

Hello Habitat!
11th May 1964 The very first Habitat store is opened by designer Terence Conran in London. The Fulham Road store becomes famous for its modern aesthetic, featuring whitewashed brick walls and spotlights. The brand grows quickly and is soon found across the country.

Chunnel go ahead!
6th February 1964 Proposals to create a Channel tunnel connecting Britain to the continent are agreed upon by the British and French governments. The new rail tunnel is to pass 31 miles under the sea and connect Folkestone to Coquelles. Whilst an agreement is reached in 1964, studies and planning mean construction will not start for another decade.

21 APR 1964 — BBC2 is launched.

28 MAY 1964 — The Palestine National Congress forms the PLO in Jerusalem.

8 JUN 1964 — Christine Keeler released from prison.

1964

Shopping undercover!
29th May 1964 A new building opens at the Bull Ring, Birmingham. Alongside traditional outdoor market stalls, a large indoor shopping centre is developed, the first of its kind in the country.

More Moors murders
17th June 1964 Moors Murderers Ian Brady and Myra Hindley claim their third victim, twelve-year-old Keith Bennett, who is snatched on his way to his grandmother's house. Bennett's body is never found. In December their fourth victim, ten-year-old Lesley Ann Downey, is taken from a fairground near her home. It would be another year before their crimes would be uncovered.

Brook Advisory Centres
July 1964 The first Brook Advisory Centre is opened by Helen Brook, offering contraception and sexual health advice to teenagers. Other services, such as the Family Planning Association, had served only married, or soon-to-be-married, women. The Brook Centres play an important role in preventing teenage pregnancy and became synonymous with the sexual revolution of the 60s. By 1969 they are advising more than 10,000 young people.

Malawi, Malta and Zambia
6th July 1964 Malawi gains its independence from Britain, followed on 21st September by the island of Malta. On 24th October, Northern Rhodesia also gains independence and becomes the Republic of Zambia.

TV Innovations
1964 sees changes in the British television experience as BBC2 launches, with technical difficulties, in April. The 60s has seen television ownership rocket, with 90% of households now owning a set.

Forth Road Bridge
4th September 1964 The Forth Road Bridge opens across the Firth of Forth, and becomes the longest steel suspension bridge in Europe. The bridge replaces a centuries-old ferry service carrying 1.5 million passengers annually, and significantly cuts the journey time between Edinburgh and Fife.

Japanese cars
Japanese motor company Daihatsu launch their Compagno model car in Britain, becoming the first Japanese carmaker to export their vehicles to Europe. Despite curiosity in Japanese products, they do not welcome much sales success until the 1980s.

14 JUL 1964 — Jacques Anquetil of France wins fourth consecutive Tour de France.

12 AUG 1964 — Death of Ian Fleming, creator of James Bond.

4 SEP 1964 — Forth Road Bridge opens in Scotland.

1964

ROYALTY & POLITICS

Sir Alec gives way to the Beatles
12th February 1964 Sir Alec Douglas-Home makes his first visit to the US as UK Prime Minister and meets President Johnson for talks. Extraordinarily, the talks were scheduled for a week earlier but were postponed due to the Beatles' visit to New York.

Prince Edward born
10th March 1964 Prince Edward is born at Buckingham Palace. He is the fourth child of the Queen and the Duke of Edinburgh and is third in line to the throne. According to reports, his is the first royal birth to be witnessed by his father.

Wilson is Prime Minister
15th October 1964 One of the most anticipated general elections this century leads to the Conservatives losing power and the first Labour government for thirteen years, under the stewardship of Prime Minister Harold Wilson. The majority of just four seats over all other parties gives the new government little room for manoeuvre in its plans for legislation.

Churchill retires
27th July 1964 Sir Winston Churchill announces that he is retiring from Parliament after serving as MP for the constituency of Woodford since 1945. He is now 89 years old and in ill health.

Capital punishment suspended
21st December 1964 Four months after the last execution by hanging, Parliament votes to end the death penalty by 355 votes to 170. The vehicle for abolition is a Private Member's Bill proposed by Sydney Silverman MP which will reach the statute book in a year's time. No executions are carried out in the meantime.

FOREIGN NEWS

Tobacco warning
11th January 1964 A report commissioned by the US Surgeon General from leading scientists warns that smoking is a hazard to bronchial and cardiac health. Cigarette consumption in the US drops by almost twenty per cent during 1964 as a direct result.

---

14 OCT 1964
Philips begins experimenting with colour TV.

18 NOV 1964
FBI director J. Edgar Hoover calls Martin Luther King Jr. a 'most notorious liar'.

22 DEC 1964
Denis Law wins award for best European football player, the Ballon d'Or.

1964

Primitive mouse
US engineer Douglas Engelbart invents the computer mouse. He demonstrates the device at a conference in San Francisco in 1968 and obtains a patent two years later. The primitive mouse is a wooden box with a thick electrical cord and two metal wheels that allow the X/Y position to be displayed on the screen.

Nehru is dead
27th May 1964 Jawaharlal Nehru, Prime Minister of India since partition in 1947 and a creator of the Non-Aligned Movement, dies in New Delhi.

Mandela's defence
12th June 1964 Nelson Mandela is sentenced to life imprisonment on Robben Island for organising a guerrilla war against South Africa's apartheid regime. At the start of his defence he speaks for three hours about an ideal society in which everyone lives together in harmony and with equal opportunities. His speech ends with the historic words 'My Lord, if needs be, it is an ideal for which I am prepared to die.'

Gulf of Tonkin incidents
2nd - 4th August 1964 Two incidents in the Gulf of Tonkin precipitate a major escalation of the Vietnam conflict. US Congress approves President Johnson's use of war powers to combat attacks, clearing the way for the rapid intensification of US involvement.

Khruschev deposed
15th October 1964 There is an unexpected change of the guard in the Kremlin. Soviet leader Nikita Khrushchev is deposed by the Politburo, partly because of the loss of face that the Soviet Union suffered over the Cuban Missile Crisis. Khrushchev is placed under house arrest as the more conservative Leonid Brezhnev (photo) replaces him as the new Communist Party leader and Alexei Kosygin is made Prime Minister.

A second emancipation
2nd July 1964 The historic Civil Rights Act is signed into law by President Johnson. It abolishes racial segregation in schools, hotels and transport, and makes discrimination in employment on grounds of race illegal. Martin Luther King Jr describes it as 'a second emancipation'. The Act comes just over a year after his 'I have a dream' speech in Washington DC.

LBJ re-elected
8th November 1964 As his campaign slogan goes, it's 'all the way with LBJ'. Lyndon Johnson is re-elected President of the US, defeating his Republican challenger Senator Barry Goldwater with a record 61 per cent share of the popular vote.

1964

King recognised
10th December 1964 Dr Martin Luther King Jr becomes the youngest ever recipient of the Nobel Peace Prize, which is awarded to him in recognition of his work in leading non-violent resistance to racial discrimination in the US.

ENTERTAINMENT

Lest we forget
The Great War, a landmark, 26-part documentary marking the fiftieth anniversary of the outbreak of the First World War, begins on the BBC on 30th May. The series, which is narrated by Michael Redgrave, includes interviews with a number of veterans who had responded to requests in the press, and attracts an average audience of eight million per episode.

Jackie
DC Thomson launch *Jackie* magazine, packed with features on fashion and make-up, advice on boys and splashes about the latest teen pop stars. Its agony aunts, Cathy and Claire, prove to be a lifeline for teenage girls negotiating the complexities of love and teenage angst. The first issue on 11th January features (who else but?) Cliff Richard on the cover.

Power shifts on Fleet Street
In the world of newspapers, the *Daily Herald*, a paper which had begun in 1912 as an organ in support of the trade union and Labour movement, closes and relaunches as *The Sun*, although *The Sun*'s circulation is, for a time, even lower than its ailing predecessor. It is purchased by Rupert Murdoch in 1969 for £800,000, with a promise to publish an 'honest, straightforward newspaper'. In time, Murdoch's *Sun* will have radically opposed political views to the original *Daily Herald*, and he remarks on 'the ease with which I entered British newspapers'.

A Hard Day's Night
Beatlemania is reaching a crescendo when *A Hard Day's Night* premieres at the Pavilion Theatre on 6th July and several hundred perspiring policemen battle to hold back 12,000 screaming fans who have descended on Leicester Square to see their heroes in the flesh. Directed by Richard Lester, who also directs *Help!* the following year, it's a nimble, off-beat mockumentary in which the band members play themselves, helped (or rather hindered) by Paul's on-screen grandfather, Wilfred Brambell. A critical as well as commercial success, the boys' screen debut is widely praised.

On the ball
Match of the Day, television's first regular football programme, is transmitted on BBC2 on 22nd August, kicking off the 1964-5 football season, but the BBC agree with the Football League to keep the match chosen (Arsenal v. Liverpool) secret until 4pm for fear fans will stay at home rather than attend in person.

1964

Play School

'Here's a house, here's a door. Windows: 1, 2, 3, 4. Ready to knock? Turn the lock. It's Playschool.' For pre-school children of the next three decades, *Playschool*, which is first shown on 21st April, is part of their daily routine, a show in which presenters sing songs, dance, tell stories and urge you to guess which shaped window (the round, the square or the arched) will be showing the day's film. *Playschool* has a pool of presenters who, if not already well-known, will go on to become so due to their association with the show; actor Paul Danquah is television's first black children's presenter, then there is Johnny Ball, Chloe Ashcroft, Floella Benjamin, Toni Arthur and the loose-limbed Derek Griffiths. At his audition, Brian Cant, who presents the show for twenty-one years, used a box to pretend he was rowing out to sea. The real stars of course are the toys, Humpty; the dolls, Jemima and Hamble; Big and Little Ted.

Apology accepted

I'm Sorry, I'll Read That Again is first broadcast on the BBC Home Service (later Radio 4) on 3rd April. Derived from a sketch show created by members of the Cambridge University Footlights Revue, the cast includes  John Cleese, Graeme Garden, Tim Brooke-Taylor and Bill Oddie. The show's title, referencing the apology given by announcers when fluffing lines on live radio, set the tone for its irreverent and off-the-cuff brand of humour.

Charlie and the Chocolate Factory

Roald Dahl's timeless tale of Charlie Bucket and his eventful trip to the marvellous chocolate factory of Mr Willy Wonka is published in the UK by Allen and Unwin on 23rd November, with illustrations by Faith Jacques.

Top of the Pops

ITV has *Ready Steady Go!* and now it's time for BBC to get down with the kids. *Top of the Pops* is first broadcast on New Year's Day from a converted church in Dickenson Road, Rusholme, Manchester and fires a salvo to the competition with a prestigious line-up of music makers; Dusty Springfield is the first act to perform in a show that also boasts the Rolling Stones, the Hollies, the Swinging Blue Jeans and the Dave Clark Five. With music performances introduced by popular DJs of the day and a studio full of shimmying local audience members, *Top of the Pops* becomes the UK's longest-running music programme and hosts some of pop and rock's greatest moments.

Seven Up

Aristotle's challenge, 'Give me a child when he is seven and I will show you the man' is the premise for this ambitious and groundbreaking social experiment as documentary, in which fourteen children from different backgrounds are selected to be filmed every seven years. The first, *Seven Up* introduces audiences to the seven-year-olds including Tony, the east end lad with ambitions to be a jockey and sweet Liverpudlian, Neil, who wants to be an astronaut, but audiences must wait until 1973 to meet them again.

1964

Bond strikes gold

Agent 007, played with unerring sang-froid by Sean Connery, comes into his own when *Goldfinger*, the third in the series of film adaptations of Ian Fleming's novel opens at the Odeon Leicester Square on 17th September. Goldfinger's budget is more than that of *Dr. No* and *From Russia with Love* combined, and for the first time, MI6 gadgetry and technology become an essential part of Bond's arsenal as he globetrots around the world determined to outwit Auric Goldfinger while wearing a succession of immaculate Anthony Sinclair suits.

Meccano makes it

Construction toy Meccano has been part of children's toy cupboards since it was first introduced in 1898, but the company fall into financial difficulties and is purchased by Lines Brothers, who operate under the brand name, Tri-Ang. Under its new owners, Meccano undergoes a revamp with pieces now made in black and yellow to mirror the colour scheme of most construction vehicles.

Doolittle vs. Poppins

Despite her huge success in the Broadway and West End productions of *My Fair Lady*, Warner Brothers boss Jack Warner thinks Julie Andrews isn't a big enough name to play Eliza Doolittle in the film version, and casts Audrey Hepburn (albeit with her songs dubbed by Marni Nixon). Andrews instead lends her cut-glass British accent and impressive vocal cords to Disney in *Mary Poppins* and scoops an Academy Award, while Hepburn doesn't even receive a nomination for *My Fair Lady*.

MUSIC

Here's the Tottenham sound!

16th January 1964 After Merseybeat, what price the Tottenham sound? The Dave Clark Five are the resident quintet at a ballroom in Tottenham, North London, who mix organ, guitar, saxophone and stomping drums with the half-shouted vocals of singer Mike Smith. Their No. 1 with *Glad All Over* is enough to cause a flutter of worry in the Beatle ranks that they might have a serious rival.

The Beatles invade!

7th February 1964 The Beatles land in New York where astute promotion has helped *I Want to Hold Your Hand* become the fastest-ever million seller in US history. Over 73 million tune in to *The Ed Sullivan Show* for their first glimpse of the group two days later. By the end of the month they have five singles in the US Hot 100 and three LPs in the album chart. The Beatles' impact on the home of rock'n'roll is seismic as they open the floodgates for a other UK groups to rush through - most controversially, the Rolling Stones. So complete is the 'British invasion' that home-grown bands have to look and sound British to get noticed.

1964

Bachelor boys
20th February 1964 In the middle of a beat group bonanza, who should sit at No. 1 in the UK but a trio of cardigan-clad Irishmen with *Diane*, a song from 1927. The Bachelors - brothers Con and Dec Cluskey and their pal John Stokes - will finish the year as Decca Records' top chart act, ahead of even the Rolling Stones.

Cilla has a heart
27th February 1964 Cilla Black is the fourth of Brian Epstein's acts to reach No. 1, with her George Martin produced cover of Dionne Warwick's *Anyone Who Had a Heart*. Cilla (real name Priscilla White) was formerly the cloakroom girl at the Cavern. *You're My World* gives her another No. 1 during May.

Bluebeat comes to Britain
14th March 1964 Determined to bring the bluebeat and ska sounds of his native Jamaica to the world, Chris Blackwell created his Island label in 1959 to record local artists and license the discs overseas. Millie Small's delightful *My Boy Lollipop* is the international breakthrough that Jamaican music has been waiting for.

Girl power 1960s style
21st May 1964 Following the trail blazed by Dusty Springfield and Cilla Black, pint-sized fifteen-year-old Lulu arrives with a sizzling cover of the Isley Brothers' *Shout*. Glaswegian Lulu (real name Marie McDonald Lawrie) has not even left school yet. Also waving the flag for 1960s girl power is Dagenham's Sandie Shaw who raids the Dionne Warwick songbook for *Always Something There To Remind Me* and upsets Britain's chiropodists by performing in her bare feet.

Mancs on the march
Now that London's record labels have raided Liverpool of its groups they turn their attention to Manchester, 30 miles east. The wacky Freddie and the Dreamers are the first scalps, followed by the Hollies, Mindbenders and Herman's Hermits, whose toothy lead singer Peter Noone once played a scallywag in *Coronation Street*.

The Stones roll on
16th July 1964 The bad boys of UK pop score their first No. 1 with *It's All Over Now*, a song by Bobby and Shirley Womack of the Valentinos that they recorded at Chess studios in Chicago, home of their blues heroes Chuck Berry and Muddy Waters. So far they have no original material, but that changes when Andrew Oldham locks Mick and Keith in a kitchen and tells them to write a song for new protégé Marianne Faithfull. As Tears Go By is the result. For the moment, they're sticking to covers for singles, with Willie Dixon's *Little Red Rooster* the next in line for No. 1.

1964

Animal tracks
9th July 1964 UK pop's hottest producer is Mickie Most, who's behind hits for Herman's Hermits (*I'm Into Something Good*), Lulu (*Shout*) and Newcastle blues band the Animals. The combination of Eric Burdon's coalmine-deep blues voice and Alan Price's swirling organ playing make *House of the Rising Sun* one of the grittiest No. 1s ever - and, at well over four minutes, one of the longest.

Sam Cooke shot dead
11th December 1964 Sam Cooke is shot dead in a Los Angeles motel. Originally the handsome, honey-voiced lead man of gospel group the Soul Stirrers, he left to find pop success with *Only Sixteen*, *Wonderful World* and *Another Saturday Night*. The recent *A Change is Gonna Come*, a powerful plea for black civil rights, signalled a shift towards the gospel/rhythm and blues blend pioneered by Ray Charles.

Hitsville USA
Motown's releases this year include such imperishable pop classics as Mary Wells' *My Guy*, Martha and the Vandellas' *Dancing in the Street* and the Supremes' *Baby Love*, all the products of a crack team of musicians, writers and producers in a Detroit studio working under the shrewd eye of owner Berry Gordy. The Motown sound oozes glamour and gospel-like feeling - and it's only just getting started.

MY FIRST 18 YEARS TOP 10 — 1964

1. **Baby Love** The Supremes
2. **Can't Buy Me Love** The Beatles
3. **I Get Around** The Beach Boys
4. **A World Without Love** Peter and Gordon
5. **Goldfinger** Shirley Bassey
6. **It's All Over Now** The Rolling Stones
7. **You Really Got Me** The Kinks
8. **Oh Pretty Woman** Roy Orbison
9. **The Times They Are A' Changin'** Bob Dylan
10. **Dancing in the Street** Martha and the Vandellas

Open | Search | Scan

The big O
British pop's US invasion isn't all one way. In a class all his own is Roy Orbison, once a label mate of Elvis at Sun Records and latterly the purveyor of unbearably sad self-composed ballads. Famously static in live performance, his towering falsetto and dark glasses give 'the big O' an almost ghostly stage presence. Roy's two No. 1s of 1964 are the angst-laden *It's Over* and the frankly lascivious *Oh Pretty Woman*.

1965 — MY FIRST 18 YEARS

SPORT

An American first
27th March 1965 It's an all-American triumph in the 119th running of the Grand National. Crompton 'Tommy' Smith becomes the first American jockey to win the race, on the US-owned and trained horse Jay Trump, who defeats Freddie in a close finish at 100/6.

DO YOU REMEMBER THIS?

Ministeck

Arise, Sir Stanley
1st January 1965 Stanley Matthews becomes the first ever professional football player to receive a knighthood. He will be 50 years old in February, shortly before he plays his last competitive match for Stoke City.

Dawn Fraser banned
1st March 1965 Triple Olympic gold medal-winning Dawn Fraser is suspended by Australia's Amateur Swimming Association for ten years for misconduct during the previous year's Olympic Games in Tokyo. It is punishment for her decision to march in the opening ceremony against their instructions, and for an incident in which she was alleged to have stolen a flag from outside Emperor Hirohito's palace.

Double triumph for Clark
31st May 1965 Jim Clark is the first non-American driver in 49 years to win the Indianapolis 500. Two months later he wins the German Grand Prix at Nürburgring to take the second of his Formula One World Drivers' Championships, so becoming the only driver in history to win the Indy 500 and the Formula One championship in the same year.

Ali v Liston
25th March 1965 In a rematch to decide the world heavyweight championship, Muhammad Ali (formerly Cassius Clay) beats Sonny Liston once again. Liston falls to the canvas after two minutes of the second round and does not get up.

20 JAN 1965
Lyndon Johnson inaugurated as US President for second term.

23 FEB 1965
Death of Stan Laurel, one half of Laurel and Hardy comedy team.

7 MAR 1965
US Marines arrive in Vietnam as conflict intensifies.

1965

Football firsts
The end of the 1964-65 season sees Manchester United win the league championship for the first time since the 1958 Munich air crash that decimated their playing squad. Liverpool beat Leeds United 2-1 to win the FA Cup for the first time, this in a match that sees Albert Johanneson of Leeds become the first black player to grace a cup final. Debuting in the European Cup Winners' Cup, West Ham beat 1860 Munich 2-0 in the final. An innovation for the 1965-66 season is the allowance of one substitution per side per game, the very first player to take the field as a 'sub' being Keith Peacock (Illustration) of Charlton Athletic. After all these firsts there is a last: the very last Christmas Day fixture is played in England, a derby match between Blackpool and Blackburn Rovers. From now on festive games will be restricted to Boxing Day

DOMESTIC NEWS

NHS charges end
31st January 1965 The Labour government ends charges for prescriptions available on the National Health Service. The charge had been 2 shillings, but for the next three years prescriptions are free to all, before charges are reintroduced in 1968.

Goldie the Eagle
11th March 1965 The nation is gripped as the infamous 'Goldie the Eagle is finally recaptured by his London Zoo keepers after eleven days on the run'. Goldie's brief bid for freedom dominates the news for a fortnight, after his escape during a routine cage clean. Goldie wasn't done with his life on the run, however, escaping again for five days in December.

Famous foods
1965 sees the launch in the UK of several famous brands, including the very first Pizza Express restaurant, a British brand, which opens in Soho, London, on 27th March. American brand KFC launches in Preston, Lancashire, in May, and in the same month the Asquith brothers launch their new supermarket chain with Associated Dairies, taking the 'As' from Asquith and the 'Da' from dairies to create British brand 'ASDA' (photo).

6 APR 1965
UK government's TSR-2 bomber aircraft project is abandoned.

12 MAY 1965
West Germany and Israel establish diplomatic relations.

1 JUN 1965
The first Certificate of Secondary Education (CSE) examinations take place.

1965

Little Baldon air crash
6th July 1965 Tragedy strikes as a Handley Page Hastings crashes shortly after take-off from RAF Abingdon. The flight is carrying 41 service personel on a parachute training mission and comes down in Little Baldon with no survivors.

Ronnie Biggs escapes!
8th July 1965 Ronnie Biggs, one of the thieves convicted of the Great Train Robbery, escapes from Wandsworth prison. Biggs is on the run for 36 years, spending time in Australia and South America, before returning to the UK, and prison, in 2001.

No smoking adverts
1st August 1965 Advertisements for cigarettes are banned from British television, forming the first step in measures designed to curb the nation's smoking habit. Anti-smoking campaigners must wait until the 1990s for further restrictions to be enacted.

Moors Murderers caught
7 October 1965 Ian Brady is charged with the murder of seventeen-year-old Edward Evans. Over the next month the police arrest Brady's girlfriend, Myra Hindley, and 150 police officers comb Saddleworth Moor, looking for the bodies of further victims. Eventually the remains of Lesley Ann Downey and John Kilbride are discovered, along with tape recordings of the murders, and a horrified nation learns the extent of the pair's crimes.

Television morality fears
13th November 1965 Theatre critic Kenneth Tynan becomes the first person to clearly say the F-word on British television. The live debate he is partaking in discusses issues relating to censorship in the theatre, and morality in entertainment becomes a hot topic in 60s Britain.

Sea Gem collapses
27th December 1965 The Sea Gem oil rig collapses in the North Sea killing thirteen people. The rig is in the process of being moved to a new location when two of its ten legs collapse, sending men and equipment into the cold North Sea.

Mary's minis!
The world of fashion gets mini skirt fever as designer Mary Quant introduces her shockingly short designs to London's streets. Her shop on the King's Road in Chelsea, 'Bazaar', does a roaring trade and soon the mini skirt becomes synonymous with the 'Swinging' Sixties.

19 JUL 1965
Mont Blanc Tunnel is opened between France and Italy.

5 AUG 1965
A five month war begins between India and Pakistan.

27 SEP 1965
Death of Clara Bow, icon of the silent movie era.

1965

ROYALTY & POLITICS

Hand mixer

DO YOU REMEMBER THIS?

Churchill is dead
24th January 1965 Britain's wartime Prime Minister Sir Winston Churchill dies at his London home at the age of 90. He is accorded a huge state funeral at St Paul's Cathedral six days later and is buried in Bladon churchyard in Oxfordshire.

Sir Alec resigns
2nd July 1965 Alec Douglas-Home surprises even his closest colleagues by resigning as Conservative Party leader. Attention turns immediately towards his successor. For the first time Conservative MPs will be able to choose their own leader by secret ballot. The winner is Edward Heath (photo), the first Conservative leader not to have had a public school education.

Death of the Princess Royal
28th March 1965 Mary, Princess Royal, dies at her home, Harewood House in Yorkshire, aged 67. The only daughter of King George V and Queen Mary, sister of King Edward VIII and King George VI and aunt of Queen Elizabeth II, she was known for her strong advocacy of higher education for women.

Race Relations Act
8th December 1965 The Race Relations Act comes into force making it a civil offence to discriminate against people on grounds of colour, race or ethnic or national background.

Government agenda
May - July 1965 With the partial nationalisation of the steel industry narrowly secured, the Labour government's legislative programme includes a promise to introduce a blood alcohol limit to combat drink driving. Further measures include the introduction of a 70 mph speed limit on UK roads and, after the appointment of Roy Jenkins as Home Secretary in December, a raft of social reforms including the planned decriminalisation of homosexuality.

---

7 OCT 1965
Post Office Tower opens in London.

27 NOV 1965
First major anti-Vietnam war protest in Wahington DC.

22 DEC 1965
Barbara Castle becomes Minister of Transport.

1965

FOREIGN NEWS

Arafat's new force
1st January 1965 Palestine Liberation Movement leader Yasser Arafat announces the formation of a military wing to pursue a guerilla war against Israel.

Rolling Thunder begins
22nd March 1965 Operation Rolling Thunder begins - aerial bombing of North Vietnam on a daily basis. Over 55,000 missions will be mounted over the next three years and will bring an end to the war no closer. In October, the war escalates with the US bombing of Viet Cong positions in neighbouring (and neutral) Cambodia.

Dolby system
At his London laboratory, US engineer Ray Dolby develops a system to suppress tape noise that will become a movie and recording industry standard.

Malcolm X shot dead
21st February 1965 Black Power leader Malcolm X is assassinated in New York. Formerly an advocate of black separatism and a member of the Nation of Islam, his formation of the Organisation of Afro-American Unity and his growing advocacy of world brotherhood made him a hate target for black militants.

War in Kashmir
5th August 1965 Pakistan sends thousands of troops disguised as civilians into India and sparks conflict in Kashmir that will lasts five months.

First space walker
18th March 1965 Soviet cosmonaut Alexei Leonov is the first man to walk in space. He floats outside Voskhod 2 for twelve minutes. 'You just can't comprehend it. Only there can you feel the grandeur, the enormous scale of everything around us,' he says later.

Voting Rights Act
6th August 1965 President Johnson signs the Voting Rights Act into law, removing obstacles such as literacy tests that disqualified African-Americans from voting.

Watts aflame
11th August 1965 Mass rioting breaks out in Watts, a poor black neighbourhood of Los Angeles, following a minor traffic incident. The riots last for six days and cause 34 deaths and over a thousand injuries.

1965

 ## ENTERTAINMENT

Short life for London Life
London Life magazine is launched on 9th October by the Thomson organisation, intended as a hip and happening replacement for the *Tatler*. Contributions include fashion advice from Terence Stamp and Jean Shrimpton, Marc Bolan writes the music reviews one issue, photographs are by Terence Donovan and Duffy, and artwork is supplied by a young artist called Ian Dury. By the end of 1966, staff turn up to work one day to be told the title is closing with immediate effect.

Pipe Up
Unusual pipes and long cigarette holders are all the rage with mods in London this year, who keep one 150-year-old Soho tobacconist in business with their demand for strange smoking accoutrements, or 'kinky gear'.

The hills are alive…
Nuns! Nazis! Lederhosen! Singing siblings! It's all here in what many consider the ultimate musical as Julie Andrews takes on the career-defining role of Maria, a novice nun whose restless character leads the Mother Superior at her Austrian convent to send her to become governess to the motherless offspring of gruff disciplinarian Captain von Trapp (Christopher Plummer). Rodgers and Hammerstein's sing-a-long score seals the film's reputation as a future classic.

Big move for Biba
Around sixty models and well-known personalities, including *Ready, Steady Go!* presenter Cathy McGowan and singer Cilla Black, help the cult London fashion store Biba move premises from Abingdon Road to Kensington Church Street in what is a carefully orchestrated publicity stunt.

Magic Roundabout
Adapted from the stop-motion animation French original, the psychedelic world of *The Magic Roundabout* is first introduced to the British public on 18th October. When the programme is moved the following year, from its slot before the 6 O' clock News to an earlier time, the BBC receives a flood of complaints from adults who are unable to get home from work in time to watch it, proving the cross-generational appeal of Florence, Zebedee, Dougal and Brian the Snail.

Ladybird, ladybird
Ladybird is one of the best-selling childrenswear brands in the 1960s and most children will be dressed in at least one or two Ladybird garments, whether it's dresses and coats for Sunday best, or vests, baby clothes, pyjamas and playsuits from the more affordable Woolworth's range.

1965

Round the Horne
Created by Barry Took and Marty Feldman, radio sketch show *Round the Horne* is first broadcast on 7th March and includes a number of the cast from its predecessor show, *Beyond our Ken*, among them Kenneth Williams and Hugh Paddick. Blazing a trail for shows such as *The Goodies* and *Monty Python's Flying Circus*, *Round the Horne's* cast of nonsensical characters has the urbane straight man Kenneth Horne at its centre, whose smooth patter is liberally laced with innuendo.

Exterminate!
With *Doctor Who* now firmly established as essential viewing, Whovian playthings are in demand from miniature replicas of the Doctor's most dangerous foe to the AstroRay Dalek Gun made by Bell Toys, essential for keeping at one's side while hiding behind the sofa.

Up the Junction
The launch of *Wednesday Playhouse* the previous year provides a platform for some of the decade's most influential dramas, including *Up the Junction* written by Nell Dunn and directed by Ken Loach who shoots it in a drama-documentary style. Following the lives of three female friends from south London, *Up the Junction* tackles some challenging themes, notably back-street abortion, and after it is broadcast on 3rd November, the BBC receives 400 complaints.

Call My Bluff
Call My Bluff, the much-loved panel game in which participants attempt to explain the meaning of an obscure word in the English dictionary, with only one definition actually true, is broadcast for the first time on 17th October. Debonair wit Frank Muir captains one team, while the magisterial Robert Morley heads the other; the host is Robin Ray, later succeeded by Robert Robinson. For viewers, the show's lasting appeal is not only the amusing banter among contestants but the chance to expand one's vocabulary with a wondrous array of new words from hickboo to ablewhacket.

Telling tales
The very first story - Cap of Rushes - is told on Jackanory on 13th December by Lee Montague. *Jackanory's* simplicity is also its power. Storytellers, recruited from the realms of theatre, film and literature, sit in a chair in front of the camera as they read the autocue and captivate kids with their energetic and characterful readings of stories old and new. Over the years, Kenneth Williams, Michael Hordern, Alan Bennett and Rik Mayall are just some who sit in the Jackanory chair, with Bernard Cribbins (photo) boasting a record-breaking 111 appearances.

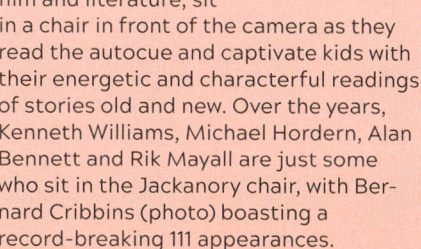

1965

A Bright Future
Wannabe science boffins (and anyone quite simply interested in new technology) gets their first taste of *Tomorrow's World* presented by Raymond Baxter on the BBC on 7th July 1955.

Darling Julie
Julie Christie, gorgeous and gifted, is swiftly becoming the 'it' girl of sixties cinema. This year she stars as Lara opposite Omar Sharif, Tom Courtenay and Geraldine Chaplin in *Dr Zhivago*, David Lean's sweeping, Russian revolution romance based on Boris Pasternak's novel. But it's the John Schlesinger film *Darling*, in which she plays a model and actress juggling the attentions of two older men, that bags her an Academy Award. *Darling* has its finger on the pulse of swinging London and Julie Christie is at its beating heart.

Sex a-Peel
Diana Rigg joins the cast of *The Avengers* as Emma Peel, replacing Honor Blackman's Cathy Gale (who leaves to film *Goldfinger*). In partnership with Patrick Macnee's Steed, she's a brilliant secret agent and martial arts expert, rescuing him from a succession of scrapes wearing the best outfits any crime-fighting heroine could wish for.

Thunderbirds are GO!
Tracy Island in the Pacific Ocean is the base for International Rescue, headed by Jeff Tracy whose five sons, Scott, Virgil, John, Gordon and Alan (aided by brilliant scientist Brains) can scramble their high-performance Thunderbird craft at a moment's notice to rescue those in need. Created by Gerry Anderson, also renowned for supermarionation productions *Captain Scarlett*, *Joe 90* and *Stingray*, the Thunderbirds' special British agent, the glamorous Lady Penelope Creighton-Ward, is voiced by Sylvia Anderson, Gerry's wife and co-creator of the show.

Charlie Girl
Singing star Joe Brown co-stars with Anna Neagle in the musical *Charlie Girl*, which opens at the Adelphi Theatre on the 15th December. The show is one of the most successful of the 1960s, running for 2,202 performances until March 1971.

MUSIC

The Byrds take flight
20th January 1965 By setting an acoustic song to a rock accompaniment, California band the Byrds create a whole new style called folk-rock. The song is Dylan's *Mr Tambourine Man*, which former folk singer and twelve-string guitarist Roger McGuinn has embellished with gorgeously dense harmonies. The record tops the US and UK charts and encourages Dylan to embrace rock.

1965

The best of British blues
14th January 1965 In the wake of the Rolling Stones, London's rhythm and blues club scene is awash with talent. Scoring the year's first new No. 1 are Georgie Fame and the Blue Flames, resident band at the Flamingo in Soho, with the Mose Allison song *Yeh Yeh*. Manfred Mann, with Jagger's pal Paul Jones on vocals, are already Top Ten regulars. Cream of the crop are the Yardbirds, whose guitarist Eric Clapton (photo) joined from John Mayall's Bluesbreakers and has an almost messianic following. He leaves the group in March rather than promote what to him is the distastefully commercial *For Your Love*. Another much-talked-about guitar hero, Jeff Beck, joins in his place.

A righteous No. 1
4th February 1965 Produced and co-written by Phil Spector, the Righteous Brothers' *You've Lost That Lovin' Feelin'* spotlights the cavernous bass voice of Bill Medley and the high counter singing of Bobby Hatfield, who make the most convincing 'white soul' sound yet heard in pop music.

Jones the voice
13th March 1965 New at No. 1 in the UK is Pontypridd-born Tom Jones with *It's Not Unusual*. Tom's steamroller voice and Presley-like movements stand out in a group-saturated music scene.

Stones across the water
18th March 1965 After a series of covers, the Rolling Stones finally hit No. 1 with a Jagger-Richards song. They record *The Last Time* with Phil Spector guesting on acoustic guitar but it's just the appetiser for *(I Can't Get No) Satisfaction* on which Jagger rages with frustration and Keith Richards plays a fuzz-toned guitar riff to die for.

Beatles work it out
Another non-stop Beatle year finds Liverpool's best receiving MBEs from the Queen at Buckingham Palace, filming *Help!* in the Bahamas and meeting Elvis at Graceland. The joyless title of the *Beatles for Sale* LP suggests that some world weariness is creeping in, but their music is evolving, influenced by Bob Dylan's iconoclasm and the new musical adventurism of the Byrds and the Beach Boys. Paul even spreads his wings with *Yesterday*, soon to become the most recorded song in history. On the *Rubber Soul* album they start to edge away from boy-girl love songs to reflective pieces like *In My Life* and *Nowhere Man*, while augmenting their instrumentation with piano, organ and even a sitar.

A world of their own
2nd December 1965 Voted best new group by *New Musical Express* readers are an Australian folk group without an electric guitar in sight. The Seekers have had two UK No. 1s so far - *I'll Never Find Another You* and *The Carnival is Over*.

1965

Provincial pop
What Liverpool, Manchester and London can do, so can the rest of Britain. As a full scale Beatles- and Stones-stoked music boom gathers pace, the Moody Blues (photo) and the Spencer Davis Group emerge from the Midlands. From Hertfordshire come the Zombies - bigger stars in the US than in the UK - and Unit Four Plus Two with the chart topping *Concrete and Clay*. Every town and city seems to have its own group scene, making the future of British pop music look very bright indeed.

MY FIRST 18 YEARS TOP 10 — 1965

1. **Tears** Ken Dodd
2. **It's Not Unusual** Tom Jones
3. **The In Crowd** Dobie Gray
4. **Concrete and Clay** Unit Four Plus Two
5. **Subterranean Homesick Blues** Bob Dylan
6. **You've Lost That Lovin' Feelin'** Righteous Bros
7. **Mr Tambourine Man** The Byrds
8. **Satisfaction** The Rolling Stones
9. **Go Now** The Moody Blues
10. **Get Ready** The Temptations

Open | Search | Scan

Doddy beats the Beatles
30th September 1965 The biggest selling single of the year - now at No. 1 for the first of five weeks - is not a Beatles track but the gushing *Tears* by another famous Liverpudlian export, comedian Ken Dodd.

Dylan goes electric
25th July 1965 The Newport Folk Festival witnesses an electrifying moment in every sense. Bob Dylan, enfant terrible of folk music, takes to the stage with a rock band, plugs in and lets rip with *Maggie's Farm* and the rambling but unignorable *Like a Rolling Stone*. Crowd reaction is split between bemused and enraged, someone cuts the power supply but there's no going back.

Protest pop
28th August 1965 A vogue for protest pop begins when Dylan soundalike Barry McGuire of the New Christy Minstrels tops the US chart with *Eve of Destruction*, which rants about everything from segregation to fallout shelters. Almost simultaneously, Sonny and Cher - Phil Spector acolyte Sonny Bono and backing singer Cherilyn Sarkisian - dress like anti-war protesters and declare their mutual besottedness to the world in *I Got You Babe*.

PHOTO CREDITS Copyright 2024, TDM Rights BV.
Photos: **A** PA Images - Getty Images / **B** Bettmann - Getty Images / **C** Heritage Images - Hulton Archive - Getty Images / **D** Keystone - Hulton Archive - Getty Images / **E** Topical Press Agency - Hulton Archive - Getty Images / **F** Evening Standard - Hulton Archive - Getty Images / **G** Hulton Deutsch - Corbis Historical - Getty Images / **H** Reg Burkett - Hulton Archive - Getty Images / **I** Bettmann - Getty Images / **J** Pictures from History - Universal Images Group Editorial - Getty Images / **K** Universal History Archive - Universal Images Group Editorial - Getty Images / **L** - Ronald Grant Archive - Mary Evans / **M** Illustrated London news ltd - Mary Evans / **N** Evening Standard - Hulton Archive - Getty Images / **O** - Ronald Grant Archive - Mary Evans / **P** Derek Berwin - Hulton Archive - Getty Images / **Q** MGM - Ronald Grant Archive - Mary Evans / **R** ABC Studiocanal - Mary Evans / **S** Carlton International - Ronald Grant Archive - Mary Evans / **T** David Redfern - Redferns - Getty Images / **U** Bob Haswell - Hulton Archive - Getty Images / **V** GAB Archive - Redferns - Getty Images / **W** Avalon - Hulton Archive - Getty Images / **X** GAB Archive - Redferns - Getty Images.

1966

MY FIRST 18 YEARS

SPORT

Billie Jean's at our door
1st July 1966 Having defeated reigning champion Margaret Smith in the semi-final, Billie Jean King of the US wins the first of her six Wimbledon tennis championships at the age of 22. She beats Brazilian Maria Bueno 6-3 3-6 6-1.

European gold
30th August - 7th September 1966 Great Britain's only two medals in the European Athletics Championships in Budapest are both golds and go to Lynn Davies in the long jump and Jim Hogan in the marathon.

Ali v. the Brits
Reigning world heavyweight boxing champion Muhammad Ali takes on two British opponents during the course of the year. May sees a rematch with Henry Cooper, who three years earlier had put the then Cassius Clay on the canvas before losing to a technical knockout. Ali wins the fight at Arsenal's Highbury stadium by a sixth round technical knockout. while August finds Ali pitched against Geordie fighter Brian London at Earl's Court. The outclassed London lasts for nearly three rounds before succumbing to a knockout punch.

England's greatest day
30th July 1966 On the greatest day in England's football history, the national team defeat West Germany 4-2 at Wembley to win the FIFA World Cup. England are the tournament hosts and overcome Argentina 1-0 in the quarter final and Portugal 2-1 in the semis to reach the final. The star of the final is striker Geoff Hurst who scores a hat trick, his last goal coming at the very end of extra time. As BBC television commentator Kenneth Wolstenholme famously tells the watching millions, 'Some people are on the pitch, they think it's all over ... it is now.' Manager Alf Ramsey will be rewarded with a knighthood in the New Year honours list.

12 JAN 1966
Lyndon B. Johnson says US should stay in South Vietnam until communist aggression ends.

3 FEB 1966
Unmanned Luna 9 is first spacecraft to make rocket-assisted landing on the Moon.

8 MAR 1966
An IRA bomb damages Nelson's Pillar in Dublin.

1966

DOMESTIC NEWS

Action Man launched!
30th January 1966 Palitoy launches 'Action Man' a British licensed version of the American toy 'G.I. Joe'. This posable, dressable soldier doll initially comes in three versions, 'Action Soldier', 'Action Sailor', and 'Action Pilot'.

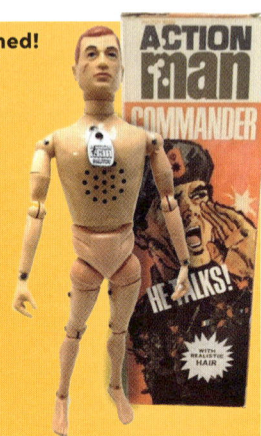

Panda on a plane
11 March 1966 London Zoo's panda Chi Chi makes the news as she is flown to Russia to mate with An An at Moscow Zoo. Sadly, the two do not take to each other and the attempts are unsuccessful. Chi Chi proves one of the most popular animals at London Zoo, and her image is immortalised as the logo of the World Wildlife Fund.

Britain goes on safari!
11th April 1966 Britain gets its first safari park as the Marquess of Bath opens one on his estate at Longleat. It is the first such experience, outside of Africa, in the world and allows visitors to drive their cars through enclosures containing the 'Longleat lions' and other animals.

Murderers convicted
6th May 1966 The Moors Murderers Ian Brady and Myra Hindley are finally brought to justice for their crimes following a trial that grips and revolts the nation. Both killers receive multiple concurrent life sentences and are never released, Hindley dying in jail in 2002, and Brady in 2017.

Barclaycard launches
29th June 1966 The Barclaycard is launched as Britain's first creditcard. Initially it is a 'charge' card, meaning the balance must be paid in full every month to avoid penalties, but by the end of 1967 it becomes a full credit card. This allows shoppers to purchase items throughout the month and pay their bills on payday, revolutionising shopping.

Pickles saves World Cup!
27th March 1966 Pickles the dog is applauded as a national hero as he sniffs out the stolen FIFA World Cup trophy. The Jules Rimet trophy had been stolen seven days before whilst on display. With the World Cup just four months out, the search is desperate, and Pickles is the hero of the hour as he finds the trophy under a hedge in South London.

---

6 APR 1966 — Cross-Channel hovercraft service inaugurated between Ramsgate and Calais.

30 MAY 1966 — Graham Hill wins the Indianapolis 500.

30 JUN 1966 — France leaves NATO.

1966

Independence spreads
More former British colonies and territories gain independence, as British Guiana becomes Guyana, the Bechuanaland Protectorate becomes Botswana, Basutoland becomes Lesotho, and Barbados becomes a Commonwealth realm.

Wage freezes and unemployment
20th July 1966 The government's Prices and Incomes Board gets the legal power to control wages, announcing the beginning of a six-month wage and price freeze. The country's economic troubles continue as unemployment rises by around 200,000 between September and November.

Plaid Cymru's first seat
14th July 1966 A by-election in Carmarthen occasioned by the death of sitting MP Megan Lloyd George brings Gwynfor Evans, leader of the Welsh Nationalist party Plaid Cymru, to Parliament. He defeats his Labour opponent and becomes Plaid Cymru's first ever Member of Parliament. The result is a catalyst for the growth of Plaid as a party and suggests that Labour's hold on its heartland of Wales may be under threat.

Shepherd's Bush murders
12th August 1966 The country is rocked by the murder of three Metropolitan Police officers. The officers are shot dead in East Acton as they approach a suspicious vehicle. The murderers go on the run. Whilst two are apprehended a few days later, one of them evades a large manhunt that lasts until November, when he is finally apprehended. All three receive life sentences of 30 years.

Pirate radio to be outlawed
27th July 1966 The government introduces the Marine etc Broadcasting Offences Bill to make illegal the unlicensed pirate radio stations operating around the UK coast. It will become law in a year's time. The move is unpopular, given the high broadcasting figures that stations such as Radio Caroline and Radio London attract.

ROYALTY & POLITICS

Labour landslide
31st March 1966 With the Labour government's majority reduced to two by recent by-elections, Prime Minister Harold Wilson calls a general election. It is the last to be held with a minimum voting age of 21. Labour returns with a landslide victory over Edward Heath's Conservatives, gaining 48 seats and achieving a majority of 98.

---

31 JUL 1966 — 31 drown as pleasure cruiser MV Darlwyne sinks off Cornish coast.

22 AUG 1966 — London's Centre Point office block completed and left empty for ten years.

6 SEP 1966 — South African premier Hendrik Verwoerd assassinated.

1966

The Queen at Aberfan
29th October 1966 The Queen visits Aberfan in South Wales, eight days after the village school is engulfed by a coal tip landslide causing over 140 deaths, the majority of them children.

France leaves NATO
30th June 1966 Having withdrawn French forces from NATO's Mediterranean fleet and refused to place American nuclear weapons on French soil, President Charles de Gaulle makes good his threat to leave NATO, which is now obliged to move its headquarters from Paris to Belgium.

Democratic fashion
15th September 1966 Having set the tone in haute couture during the 1950s with his trapeze dress with a free waist, Yves Saint Laurent opens a Paris boutique to sell ready-made clothes aimed at democratising fashion, challenging the assumption that London is now the centre of the fashion world thanks to Carnaby Street, Mary Quant and the mini skirt.

FOREIGN NEWS

Nigerian coup
15th January 1966 The government of Nigeria is overthrown and its Prime Minister murdered in a military coup. In July, a different section of the military seizes power under General Yakubu Gowon. A bloody civil war soon erupts as the eastern province of Biafra fights for independence.

Gandhi elected
19th January 1966 Indira Gandhi, daughter of the late Jawaharlal Nehru, is elected Prime Minister of India in succession to Lal Bahadur Shastri, who died nine days earlier after signing the Tashkent peace agreement with Pakistan.

Let's twist again
Twister, the game where humans are the pieces, and bodily entanglement is an unavoidable result of taking part, is launched this year. Store buyers are initially reluctant, expressing concerns the game is too risqué but the following year, *Twister* (which was originally called Pretzel) sells three million units.

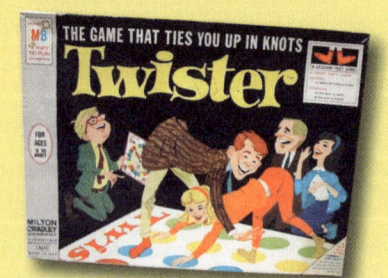

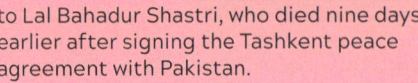

22 OCT 1966 Soviet spy George Blake escapes from prison and is next seen in Moscow.

4 NOV 1966 Devastating floods strike Florence and Venice.

15 DEC 1966 Death of animation pioneer Walt Disney.

1966

Emperor Cannibal?
1st January 1966 Colonel Jean Bodel Bokassa leads a military coup in the Central African Republic and declares himself President. Although he seems to have good intentions for the people of the poverty-stricken country, he soon has opponents eliminated and enriches himself and a small group of associates. A rumour then circulates that Bokassa feasts on the flesh of his political opponents.

Cultural Revolution
16th May 1966 An inflammatory article in the *Chinese People's Daily* calls for the destruction of 'all monsters and demons'. Chinese leader Mao Zedong demands that the country must be cleansed of any form of bourgeoisie and begins the Cultural Revolution, though which Mao, following Lenin's example, aims to secure total power. At least half a million are killed during the revolution, which lasts until Mao's death in 1976.

Pogles' Wood
First introduced to viewers as *The Pogles* in the TV programme *Clapperboard* in 1965, *Pogles' Wood* from Smallfilms begins a new series on 7th April under the *Watch with Mother* banner. Created in the barn belonging to Oliver Postgate, Mr and Mrs Pogle, along with their adopted son Pippin and Tog the squirrel, live in a tree hollow. Postgate narrated the series which usually began with the question, 'Now where will we find the Pogles?'

LSD is outlawed
6th October 1966 The drug LSD - lysergic acid diethylamide - is outlawed in California, though it will continue to be manufactured clandestinely and widely used within the state's hippie communities.

ENTERTAINMENT

DO YOU REMEMBER THIS?

Fondue set

The Frost Report
The Frost Report premieres on BBC1 on 10th March 1966 with writers and performers from the cream of British comedy talent, including John Cleese, Eric Idle, Graham Chapman, Terry Jones and Michael Palin, who find their Python writing style while working on the show.

77

1966

Till Death Us Do Part
Alf Garnett, a bald, bigoted racist, railing against practically everything in modern Britain, is introduced to an unsuspecting public on 6th June and within two days, the Conservative Party have asked for a copy of the script due to Alf (played to perfection by Warren Mitchell) referring to Edward Heath as, 'a grammar school twit'. Scriptwriter Johnny Speight smartly turned Garnett into a parody of himself, exposing him as a character that embodies the worst aspects of the British.

It's a Knockout
From 7th July 1966, the battle for regional supremacy of the UK is thrashed out on BBC every Saturday evening as amateur athletic teams from around the country don outsized cartoon costumes and tackle obstacle courses, slippery slopes and avoid buckets of slime in a series of baffling races. Still, there is nothing the British population like better than seeing their fellow citizens making fools of themselves, and the slapstick carnage of *It's a Knockout* is regularly watched by 19 million viewers.

On the Margin
Alan Bennet writes and performs this satirical sketch show with the support of a regular cast including future BBC political commentator John Sergeant, and guest appearances from Michael Hordern and Prunella Scales. Bennett's sardonic comedy is contrasted with more serious poetry readings and, unusually, archive clips of nostalgic music hall performances.

Alfie
A serial womaniser, Alfie knocks around London, loving and leaving a trail of sexual conquests in his wake, until events cause him to examine his self-centred behaviour with a sense of remorse. Michael Caine, unconventionally but mesmerizingly handsome, breaks the fourth wall and talks to the camera and with that laconic expression and chipper attitude, you can see how he's such a successful seducer.

Cathy Come Home
Ken Loach directs another *Wednesday Playhouse* play, *Cathy Come Home*, a dramatic exposé highlighting the inhumanity of a social system in which one young woman finds herself trapped. *Cathy Come Home* follows the devastating descent of one couple into poverty and homelessness, as Cathy finds her marriage destroyed and her children taken from her. The searing impact of the film on the British public means huge support for the charity Shelter which forms shortly afterwards.

1966

Icon of an era
Model Lesley Hornby is 'discovered' when her photograph by Barry Lategan, sporting a chic cropped hairdo by the hairdresser Leonard, is seen by *Daily Express* journalist Deirdre McSharry and published under the headline, 'The Face of 1966'. Aged just 16, Twiggy's androgynous look with her inimitable, gangly frame, freckles, saucer eyes and spider lashes, becomes synonymous with the Swinging Sixties.

Holy smoke Batman!
DC Comics superhero Batman and his sidekick Robin first hit TV screens in America on 12th January. Adam West dons the cape as Bruce Wayne/Batman with Dick Grayson/Robin played by Burt Ward. Together they run around Gotham City fighting crimes committed by an inordinate number of dastardly villains. The series has its tongue firmly in its cheek and Batman's comic-book roots are never forgotten. Lines are delivered with hammy drama and the fight scenes cut with cartoon graphics of punch-up noises. Wham! Ker-pow!

Born Free
Virginia McKenna and Bill Travers play real-life couple George and Joy Adamson, who attempt to introduce an orphaned lion called Elsa back into the wild in Kenya. For McKenna and Travers, the film has a life-changing effect and they go on to become wildlife campaigners, and found the Born Free Foundation. John Barry's song, *Born Free*, sung by Matt Munro with lyrics by Don Black, wins an Academy Award for best original song.

Carry on Screaming
The *Carry On* juggernaut continues with *Carry On Screaming*, the franchise's thirteenth film: a barely-disguised parody of the Hammer Horror genre in a riff on the Frankenstein story.

Live long and prosper
The multi-racial, multi-species crew of the 23rd-century starship, USS *Enterprise*, led by Captain James T. Kirk (William Shatner) are on a mission to 'boldly go where no man has gone before' patrolling the galaxies as a kind of inter-planetary peace-keeping force, but with groovier coordinated uniforms. *Star Trek* ensures that beneath the action and sci-fi kitsch, is a moral and philosophical message in storylines that act as metaphors for current global issues like feminism or the Vietnam War. *Star Trek* gains a cult following and flowers into one of the most successful TV and film franchises of all time.

1966

Prehistoric pin-up
Nobody seems to care much that prehistoric man and dinosaurs are co-existing in *One Million Years B.C.* a fantasy adventure which is released on 25th October, even though dinosaurs died out about 65 million years before early man made an appearance. All eyes instead are on Raquel Welch, who strides around with only a fur bikini cladding her voluptuous frame. The image of Welch as the ultimate in sexy prehistoric womanhood becomes a cultural phenomenon.

What's it all about?
22nd February 1966 Composer Burt Bacharach is a name on everyone's lips. He and lyricist Hal David record mainly with their discovery Dionne Warwick, but Dusty Springfield (*Wishin' and Hopin'*), the Walker Brothers (*Make It Easy on Yourself*) and Tom Jones (*What's New Pussycat?*) have all had hits with their songs. Now Bacharach is in London to oversee Cilla Black's recording of the title song of the film *Alfie*.

Beatles quit performing
These are momentous months for the Beatles. In the middle of an exhausting US tour, John Lennon's opinion that 'we are more popular than Jesus now' provokes an anti-Beatle backlash, convincing the group that they should stop live performing altogether. Their last ever concert is at Candlestick Park in San Francisco in August. The plan now is to focus exclusively on making music in the studio, with a big project in mind that will eventually take shape as *Sgt Pepper*.

MUSIC

Sounds of Simon
1st January 1966 Paul Simon, who is touring UK folk clubs as a singer-songwriter, discovers that a track he made in New York with best pal Art Garfunkel called *The Sound of Silence* is sitting at the top of the US charts. Except it's not quite the same track: someone has added a rock backing to it. Within days he is back in the US and recording again with Art as avatars of the new folk-rock.

James Brown's solo show
11th March 1966 ITV's must-see music show *Ready Steady Go!* departs from its standard format to showcase the inimitable James Brown. The doyen of 60s soul music, Brown receives a Grammy for *Papa's Got A Brand New Bag*, while *It's A Man's Man's Man's World* tops the US R&B chart in May.

1966

In praise of swinging England
16th April 1966 That the UK represents everything that is hip, young and swinging is confirmed by a famous article in *Time* magazine. On cue, Roger Miller's *England Swings* depicts the old country as a place of rosy-cheeked children and friendly bobbies. The tongue-in-cheek song is a gift to the tourist trade and confirms the current American passion for all things British.

Frank and Nancy
2nd June 1966 After several years of absence from the singles chart, Frank Sinatra is back with *Strangers in the Night*. He tops both US and UK charts, as does his daughter Nancy with the proto-feminist anthem *These Boots Are Made for Walkin'*, featuring the most famous descending bassline in pop music.

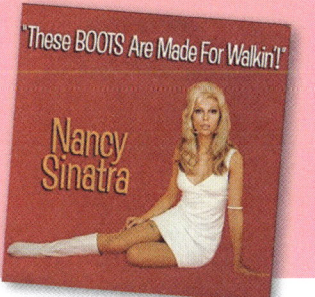

Spector's masterpiece
25th June 1966 Phil Spector has created another masterpiece. Credited to Ike and Tina Turner but with only Tina heard on the track, *River Deep Mountain High* is the ultimate 'wall of sound' record, made with over twenty musicians in multiple takes over many days.

Kink commentaries
7th July 1966 The Kinks came out of London's Muswell Hill in 1964 playing a primitive kind of heavy metal on the chart topping *You Really Got Me*. Gradually their sound has mellowed and leader Ray Davies's lyrics have become more observational and satirical, typified by the Carnaby Street send-up *Dedicated Follower of Fashion* and the lament of a bored rock star, *Sunny Afternoon*. Few songs better evoke the long, hot, enervating British summer of 1966.

Comings and goings
1st August 1966 Can groups survive the loss of key members? Paul Jones leaves Manfred Mann to go solo and is replaced by Mike D'Abo from Band of Angels, while Jimmy Page joins the Yardbirds in place of Paul Samwell-Smith. Meanwhile the Animals, having already lost Alan Price and Chas Chandler, break up altogether in September, though Eric Burdon keeps the band name with a new line-up.

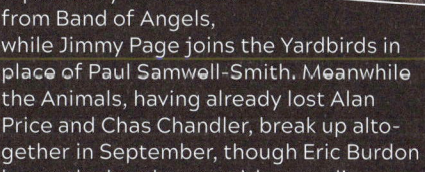

1966

Beach Boy brilliance
7th November 1966 Some call it the record of the year and even the decade. It may even be the record of the millennium. The UK's new No. 1 is *Good Vibrations* by the Beach Boys, who are now creating the most imaginative soundscapes in pop history. The genius behind this and the head-turning *Pet Sounds* LP is Brian Wilson, who roots the group's sound in sun-kissed harmonies and production techniques learned from Phil Spector.

MY FIRST 18 YEARS — TOP 10 — 1966

1. **Summer in the City** The Lovin' Spoonful
2. **My Generation** The Who
3. **Wouldn't it be Nice** The Beach Boys
4. **Reach Out, I'll Be There** The Four Tops
5. **Sunny Afternoon** The Kinks
6. **Eleanor Rigby** The Beatles
7. **Semi-Detached Suburban...** Manfred Mann
8. **The Sun Ain't Gonna S...** The Walker Brothers
9. **Homeward Bound** Simon and Garfunkel
10. **Walk Away Renee** The Left Banke

Open | Search | Scan

Talkin' about their generation
Mod fashions and iconography are all over British pop at the moment, but one band in particular seems to have truly authentic Mod credentials. From the Mod heartland of Shepherds' Bush, the Who have a restless and questioning resident songwriter in Pete Townshend, whose songs like *My Generation*, *Substitute* and *I'm a Boy* distil the Mod experience. Such is the band's aggression on stage that their performances usually end with them destroying their equipment.

Folk-rock evolves
Out of the folk music hub of Greenwich Village burst the Lovin' Spoonful, with good-time songs like *Daydream* and *Do You Believe in Magic* written by John Sebastian and a style evoking old-time jug bands. Sebastian's chum John Phillips forms the Mamas and the Papas who decamp to Los Angeles to add the sweetest of boy-girl harmonies to *Monday Monday* and *California Dreamin'*. Back in the UK, Donovan (photo) evolves from a guitar-playing troubadour with a Bob Dylan cap into a creator of whimsical, fey and faintly psychedelic hits such as *Sunshine Superman* and *Mellow Yellow*.

PHOTO CREDITS Copyright 2024, TDM Rights BV.
Photos: **A** Hulton Deutsch - Corbis Historical - Getty Images / **B** Hulton Archive - World Cup Hurst - Getty Images / **C** Harry Benson - Hulton Archive - Getty Images / **D** Mirrorpix - Getty Images / / **E** Mirrorpix - Getty Images / **F** Mirrorpix - Getty Images / **G** Bettmann - Getty Images / **H** Photo 12 - Universal Images Bokassa Group - Getty Images / **I** BBC - Ronald Grant Archive - Mary Evans / **J** Associated London Films Columbia Pictures - Ronald Grant Archive - Mary Evans / **K** AF Archive - Paramount Pictures - Mary Evans / **L** - Ronald Grant Archive - Mary Evans / **M** Bettmann - Getty Images / **N** Columbia Pictures - Ronald Grant Archive - Mary Evans / **O** Studio Canal Films Ltd - Mary Evans / **P** Hulton Archive - Archive Photos - Getty Images / **Q** Sunset Boulevard - Corbis Historical - Getty Images / **R** Archive Photos - Moviepix - Getty Images / **S** GAB Archive - Redferns - Getty Images / **T** Mirrorpix - Getty Images / **U** David Redfern - Redferns - Getty Images / **V** GAB Archive - Redferns - Getty Images / **W** GAB Archive - Redferns - Getty Images / **X** Charlie Gillett Collection - Redferns - Getty Images / **Y** Michael Ochs Archives - Getty Images / **Z** Keystone - Hulton Archive - Getty Image.

1967 — MY FIRST 18 YEARS

SPORT

Arise Sir Alf
1st January 1967 Alf Ramsey, manager of the victorious 1966 World Cup-winning England side, is recognised with a knighthood in the New Year honours list. The England captain, Bobby Moore, receives an OBE.

100/1 outsider wins the Grand National
Foinavon, ridden by John Buckingham, is a rank outsider at 100/1 at the start of the 1967 Grand National steeplechase at Aintree on 8th April. But the racing gods are smiling on him and when numerous horses and riders fall at the 23rd fence, Buckingham avoids the melee and takes the lead and romps home to victory.

Grand Slam queen
American Billie Jean King wins the second of her six Wimbledon singles titles against British player Ann Jones, as well as scooping the women's doubles and mixed doubles titles at the tournament.

Arise Sir Francis
Francis Chichester sails his yacht, the *Gipsy Moth IV*, back into Plymouth harbour on the evening of 28th May, 226 days and 28,500 miles after departing. In recognition of his achievement in becoming the first person to sail solo around the world from west to east, he is knighted by the Queen at Greenwich.

Knocked out
9th May 1967 Muhammad Ali is stripped of his World Heavyweight Champion titles and banned from boxing after refusing to be drafted into the US Army at the height of the Vietnam War. Ali argues that as a black Muslim, he is a conscientious objector, but his moral stand comes at great personal cost.

Our 'Enry
Heavyweight boxer Henry Cooper becomes the first person to win three Lonsdale belts outright after his victory over Billy 'Golden Boy' Walker on 7th November. A few weeks later, he wins the first of his two BBC Sports Personality of the Year Awards.

12 JAN 1967
Britain's latest new town is to be built on a 22,000-acre site in Buckinghamshire and called Milton Keynes.

2 FEB 1967
Nicotine-free Bravo cigarettes, made from cured lettuce, go on sale in Tesco supermarket in Brixton.

30 MAR 1967
Photographer Michael Cooper shoots the Peter Blake-designed album artwork for The Beatles' *Sgt. Pepper's Lonely Hearts Club Band*.

1967

DOMESTIC NEWS

Campbell killed
4th January 1967 Donald Campbell, pioneering racing driver, is killed in an attempt to break his own Water Speed World Record in his craft Bluebird. A serial record breaker, Campbell heads to Coniston Water in the Lake District to attempt 300 mph but is killed as Bluebird lifts out of the water and backflips.

European Economic Community
15th January 1967 Britain enters negotiations to discuss joining the European Economic Community. Italy and the Netherlands signal their support for Britain's membership, and a formal application is made from the United Kingdom in May. However, President Charles de Gaulle of France vetoes the move in November.

Outer Space Treaty
27th January 1967 The Outer Space Treaty is signed by the UK, United States, and the Soviet Union in a landmark agreement to prohibit nuclear weapons in space and ensure that no country can claim sovereignty of part of the cosmos. It is also agreed that celestial bodies such as the moon can be used only for peaceful purposes. In light of these agreements, the British launch their Ariel 3 satellite in May, the first satellite to be developed outside either the Soviet Union or the United States.

***Torrey Canyon* Disaster**
18th March 1967 The oil tanker SS Torrey Canyon runs aground off Land's End near the Scilly Isles and begins shedding its cargo of crude oil. 170 miles of British and French coastline are contaminated in one of the world's most serious spills.

Stockport air disaster
4th June 1967 British Midland Flight G-ALHG crashes in Stockport killing 72 passengers and crew in one of Britain's worst air disasters. The crash occurs as the plane is heading into land at Manchester Airport, when two of its engines cut unexpectedly. 12 people survive thanks to the brave efforts of members of the public and police.

New Look Stamps
5th June 1967 British stamps receive a new look as the General Post Office unveils the new 'Machin' series of stamps, replacing the old Wilding series. The new stamps are much simpler than previous designs, and feature Arnold Machin's sculpture of the Queen.

APR 1967
Marion Boyers and John Calder are prosecuted under the Obscene Publications Act for publishing the novel, *Last Exit to Brooklyn*.

MAY 1967
Bird's launch *Angel Delight*, an instant dessert made by magically whipping a sachet of flavoured powder into milk.

27 JUN 1967
The UK's first cash machine opens at a branch of Barclay's Bank on Enfield High Street.

1967

Gay and women's rights
4th July 1967 Following on from the Wolfenden Report's 1957 recommendations, acts of consensual male homosexuality between consenting adults are decriminalised in England and Wales. This first step in gay rights comes just a few months before the Abortion Act is passed in October, legalising abortions up to the 28th week of pregnancy.

Welsh Language Act
27th July 1967 The introduction of the Welsh Language Act takes a step towards protecting Welsh speakers, by enshrining their right to use Welsh in legal proceedings and in official documents in Wales. Alongside the protection of the Welsh language, the Act also importantly repeals an Act from 1746 which defines Wales as part of England.

Britain abroad
10th September 1967 A referendum held on British sovereignty in the Crown colony of Gibraltar returns a huge majority in favour of remaining a British territory. Of the island's 12,000 voters, only 44 vote to become part of Spain. In contrast, in November, British troops finally leave the State of Aden after 128 years, leading to the formation of the republic of Yemen.

Hither Green rail crash
5th November 1967 49 people are killed when the evening express from Hastings to London Charing Cross hits a broken rail and leaves the tracks at the Hither Green Depot.

Scooter

BBC radio changes
8th November 1967 A month after the BBC renames all its radio networks to accommodate its new pop music station, Radio 1, it launches a new local radio service, starting with BBC Radio Leicester. Both Radio 1 and these local radio stations are designed to replace the newly outlawed 'pirate' radio stations. Eight experimental local stations launch initially, with services to the rest of the country rolled out in the 1970s.

Pound devalued
19th November 1967 The deepening sterling crisis in the UK leads to Prime Minister Harold Wilson taking the drastic action of devaluing the pound by 14%, from $2.80 US dollars to $2.40. The decision is controversial, and Wilson attempts to reassure the nation, stating in a broadcast that the 'pound... in your pocket' will not be affected.

17 JUL 1967
The Keep Britain Tidy campaign launches a dedicated Anti-Litter Week.

2 AUG 1967
A second, southbound bore of the Blackwall Tunnel under the River Thames in east London is opened.

20 SEP 1967
The Queen names the new passenger ship, *Queen Elizabeth 2 (QE2)* at Clydebank.

1967

ROYALTY & POLITICS

FOREIGN NEWS

A royal reconciliation?
7th June 1967 Queen Elizabeth, the Queen Mother meets the Duke and Duchess of Windsor for the first time since the 1936 abdication after they had been invited to London for a dedication ceremony for a memorial plaque to Queen Mary at Marlborough House.

Moved to say sorry
On the 11th October, pop group the Move are obliged to issue a formal apology in the High Court to Prime Minister Harold Wilson after they had featured a caricature of the P.M. in the nude on a promotional postcard for their single, *Flowers in the Rain*. The band are ordered to pay all royalties from the single to a charity of the Prime Minister's choice.

Flower power's first shoots
14th January 1967 Something is brewing in San Francisco, where a 'Human Be-In' takes place in Golden Gate Park. It's a gathering of hippies who live in the city's bohemian district of Haight-Ashbury and reject what they see as the bourgeois, well-behaved lifestyle of their parents' generation. The hippie movement has its roots in the nomadic west coast community led by Ken Kesey, author of *One Flew Over the Cuckoo's Nest*. Many hippies believe in free love, communal living and the mind-expanding drug LSD. They're against capitalism, materialism, and war. Their music as played by groups like the Grateful Dead and Jefferson Airplane is free form, unruly, loud and mind expanding. Everything is set for a legendary 'summer of love', as radio vibrates to the sounds of the Frisco bands and the cult of flower power goes international.

The student prince
9th October 1967 Prince Charles begins his first term as an undergraduate student at Trinity College where he reads Archaeology and Anthropology in his first year, followed by two years of History. Arriving in true sixties style as a passenger in a red Mini, the bashful eighteen-year-old is met by a crowd of vocal well-wishers and the inevitable flashbulbs of the press.

8 OCT 1967
Death of Clement Attlee, Britain's Prime Minister from 1945 to 1951.

27 NOV 1967
John Noakes gamely models a chest wig on Blue Peter while Valerie Singleton tells young viewers they are all the rage in the US.

4 DEC 1967
The Royal Smithfield Show opens at Earl's Court with no animals and mechanical exhibits only, due to an outbreak of foot-and-mouth disease.

1967

Astronaut deaths
27th January 1967 A tragic setback in the space race: three astronauts are killed in a fire in their Apollo spacecraft during a test launch. Designated Apollo 1, this was to be the first attempt at a manned crew mission. Crewed flights are suspended for twenty months.

Oppenheimer dies
18th February 1967 Robert Oppenheimer dies of throat cancer aged 62. The director of the Manhattan Project that created the atom bomb, his concerns over nuclear proliferation and his earlier left-wing political affiliations led to the removal of his security clearance in 1954.

Svetlana defects
9th March 1967 In one of the Cold War's most surprising twists, Svetlana Aliluyeva, daughter of Joseph Stalin, defects to the west at the US Embassy in New Delhi.

Coup in Greece
21st April 1967 A military coup in Greece ousts Prime Minister Andreas Papandreou. The new regime headed by Colonels George Papadopoulos and Stylianos Pattakos imposes martial law, suspends democracy and even outlaws beards and mini skirts. The infamous Colonels rule until 1974.

Six-Day War
5th - 10th June 1967 To prevent encirclement by the Arab states, Israel launches what becomes known as the Six-Day War against Egypt, Syria, Iraq and Jordan. Virtually all of the Arab air defences are destroyed on the first day and Israeli forces sweep into Sinai and the West Bank. The war ends when Israel and Syria agree to a UN-mediated truce.

Che is dead
8th October 1967 Revolutionary leader Che Guevera, whose relations with Fidel Castro's Cuban regime have cooled, is captured and executed by government forces in Bolivia.

First heart transplant
3rd December 1967 In Cape Town, a team of surgeons led by Christiaan Barnard performs the first heart transplant. A 57-year-old Polish immigrant named Louis Washkansky receives the heart of a young woman who died in an accident. He will die eighteen days later from pneumonia due to a weakened immune system.

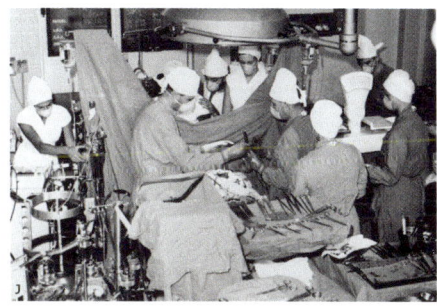

1967

Ceaușescu in power
9th December 1967 Nicolae Ceaușescu becomes Chairman of the Romanian State, with dictatorial powers. Initially his regime seems liberal and mild compared to the rest of the Soviet Bloc, but by the late 1970s Ceaușescu is the strictest of Stalinist dictators running the most repressive regime in Eastern Europe.

Holt disappears
17th December 1967 Australian Prime Minister Harold Holt disappears while swimming near Portsea, Victoria. His body is never found.

ENTERTAINMENT

Eurovision winner
8th April 1967 After nearly a decade of trying, the UK finally wins the Eurovision Song Contest with *Puppet on a String* by Sandie Shaw. Sandie (real name Sandra Goodrich) has been a chart regular for three years and secretly feels that this song is beneath her, yet it is her most lucrative record ever.

Top *Trumpton*
The stop-animation children's series *Trumpton* first airs on 3rd January 1967, with gentle stories from Trumptonshire, a place originally introduced to young viewers in *Camberwick Green* the previous year. Pivotal to each episode, narrated by Brian Cant, is an emergency call-out by Trumpton's trusty fire brigade led by Captain Flack, whose team dutifully responded to their memorable roll call of 'Pugh, Pugh, Barney McGrew, Cuthbert, Dibble, Grub.'

Derring done
Since its launch in 1879, the *Boy's Own Paper* has fed successive generations of young men with a diet of stirring tales of derring-do, public school stories and advice on wholesome, practical pursuits. But in 1967, its publisher decides a paltry circulation of 24,000 (compared to 190,000 in its 1890s heyday) cannot justify its continuation in a vastly changed market.

The Jungle Book
Disney's full-length animation based loosely on the 1894 stories of Rudyard Kipling opens in the UK on 17th November 1967. With its lush artwork and uplifting jazz tunes including the toe-tapping *Bare Necessities*, *The Jungle Book* is a critical and commercial success.

1967

Monkee business
It is Beatlemania all over again when manufactured pop foursome The Monkees touch down at Heathrow on 28th June to perform in Britain for the first time. They are greeted by what one news report describes as 'a highly trained team of hysterical mini-skirters' as Manchester-born frontman Davy Jones is rugby tackled by one particularly determined lovestruck fan. The following day, Davy, Peter, Mike and Mickey are woken to a dawn chorus of hundreds of screaming girls outside the Royal Garden Hotel in Kensington.

The test card girl
When BBC engineer George Hersee asks his daughter Carole to pose for photographs with a blackboard and her clown doll, Bubbles, little does she know it will make her one of the most recognisable faces in British television history. Her picture subsequently becomes the test card image for the BBC and it is Carole (and the rather sinister Bubbles) who viewers see on-screen until 1998.

Calamity the Cow
Children's Film Foundation release *Calamity the Cow*, which stars a terribly well-spoken teenage Phil Collins three years before he joins prog-rock band Genesis.

Battleship is launched
Budding naval strategists can test out their skills with the launch of the board game *Battleship*. The aim of the game for two players is to hunt, sink or destroy your opponent's (imaginary) fleet of ships, using nothing more than a plastic board with pegs.

BBC2 embraces colour
Television viewers begin to see the world in glorious technicolour on 1st July 1967 when BBC2 is the first channel in Europe to show programmes in colour, starting with its coverage of the Wimbledon Lawn Tennis Championships. But with just 5,000 colour television sets in circulation among the population it will be a few more years before colour TV becomes the norm.

Just a Minute
22nd December 1967 Three months after the launch of Radio 4, a new panel show, *Just a Minute*, takes to the airwaves, hosted by Nicholas Parsons. The show's insanely simple format - that contestants should speak on any given topic, 'without hesitation, repetition or deviation' proves to be a winning formula. Parsons remains the host until shortly before his death in 2020 at the age of 96.

Fiddler on the Roof
Fiddler on the Roof opens at Her Majesty's Theatre on 16th February 1967 starring Israeli actor Topol in the role of Tevye; he would later be nominated for an Academy Award for playing the same role in the 1971 film adaptation. The £80,000 production is the hit of the year, eventually running for 2030 performances.

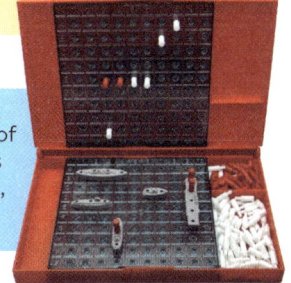

1967

Fashion on film
Two major films of 1967, *Far from the Madding Crowd* starring Julie Christie, Alan Bates and Terence Stamp, and *Bonnie and Clyde* with Faye Dunaway and Warren Beatty, have a major influence on fashion, as trim silhouettes and mini skirts give some ground to hippyish Victoriana and Depression-era style dresses.

Blow Up!
For his first English-speaking film, Michaelangelo Antonioni plunges headfirst into a strange and sometimes seedy world of swinging London with a tale about a fashion photographer, played by David Hemmings, who thinks he witnesses a murder. The film's fashionable themes and sexual content quickly make it into a cult classic, with its racy reputation enhanced by a scene with Jane Birkin, in which female pubic hair is glimpsed for the first time in mainstream cinema.

Sixties comedy favourite
Not in Front of the Children becomes one of the year's most popular sitcoms. Wendy Craig stars as Jennifer Corner in her first sitcom, playing the role of a harassed, middle-class wife and mother, a 'type' in she which comes to excel. *Not in Front of the Children* runs for 39 episodes over 4 series until 1970 and wins Craig a BAFTA for Best Actress in 1969.

Dee Time
Radio disc jockey Cyril Nicholas Henty-Dodd, better known as Simon Dee, attracts 18 million viewers with his early evening chat show *Dee Time* on BBC1. In a scene that is to become something of a sixties cliché, at the end of each programme, Dee is filmed driving off in a white E-type Jaguar beside blonde model Lorna Macdonald.

It happens in Monterey
16th - 18th June 1966 Monterey in California is the site of the first true rock festival, which showcases not just star names like the Who and the Byrds but also acts from the mushrooming San Francisco scene who haven't even signed with a record label yet. Janis Joplin (photo) and her band get a big-money deal, while Jefferson Airplane, the Grateful Dead, Moby Grape and a jaw-dropping Jimi Hendrix seize the chance to launch themselves on a bigger stage. Ending with Scott McKenzie singing his 'summer of love' hippie anthem *San Francisco*, Monterey is the start of a new rock era in which the music is louder, druggier and more provocative than ever.

1967

Britain's Summer of Love
Between the 26th and 28th August, the Festival of the Flower Children takes place at Woburn Abbey in Bedfordshire, seat of the Duke of Bedford, where acts include the Small Faces, the Bee Gees and Eric Burdon from The Animals. Britain's Summer of Love is centred largely in London, where clubs like the UFO (where Pink Floyd play) or The Middle Earth Club attract hippies and musicians who embrace drug culture, psychedelic sounds and 'flower power'. While the Beatles and the Rolling Stones become steeped in the scene, for most young people, the Summer of Love is a news story in which they are observers rather than participants.

Beatles in Pepperland
Two very different but complementary songs about their Liverpool childhoods, *Penny Lane* and *Strawberry Fields Forever*, launch the Beatles as an exclusively studio-based band. Two months of recording produce *Sgt. Pepper's Lonely Hearts Club Band*, an all-bells-and-whistles, LSD-tinged album of songs inspired by news stories (*A Day in the Life*, *She's Leaving Home*), comic characters (*Lovely Rita*, *When I'm 64*) and even a child's drawing (*Lucy in the Sky with Diamonds*). The LP sets new standards in production and packaging and inspires all manner of bands to create their own *Pepper* equivalent. After this peak, the late-summer suicide of Brian Epstein leaves the band rudderless, while their self-made television movie *Magical Mystery Tour* is poorly received.

MUSIC

It's a mystery
One of the biggest records of the year is surely among the most mysterious in chart history. Based on a Bach organ fugue with lyrics referencing Chaucer and Greek mythology, *A Whiter Shade of Pale* is the first hit for Procol Harum (photo), who were once an Essex beat group called the Paramounts.

Hendrix unveiled
11th January 1967
At a press reception in Soho, ex-Animal Chas Chandler reveals his new discovery, blues guitarist Jimi Hendrix. Jimi is an instant sensation and charts with *Hey Joe* and *Purple Haze* before touring the UK as the Jimi Hendrix Experience. *Are You Experienced* is one of the albums of the year, while Jimi's festival-stealing appearance at Monterey shows his native US what they have been ignoring. A second album, *Axis Bold as Love*, keeps up the momentum in December.

1967

MY FIRST 18 YEARS
TOP 10 — 1967

1. **Paper Sun** *Traffic*
2. **See Emily Play** *Pink Floyd*
3. **Respect** *Aretha Franklin*
4. **Heroes and Villains** *The Beach Boys*
5. **Matthew and Son** *Cat Stevens*
6. **Excerpt from a Teenage Opera** *Keith West*
7. **Waterloo Sunset** *The Kinks*
8. **Don't Sleep in the Subway** *Petula Clark*
9. **Itchycoo Park** *Small Faces*
10. **Flowers in the Rain** *The Move*

Open | Search | Scan

Stones are busted
12th February 1967 Mick Jagger and Keith Richards are arrested on drugs charges at Redlands, Keith's home. At the subsequent court hearing, Richards is sentenced to a year in prison while Jagger gets three months. On appeal, Richards' conviction is quashed and Jagger's sentence is reduced to a conditional discharge. In a separate case, Brian Jones is sentenced to three months, reduced on appeal to three months' probation. Even *The Times* voices disquiet over the apparent police witch hunt against the Stones.

Brothers in harmony
24th February 1967 The Bee Gees arrive from Australia sounding very like their Beatle idols. Managed by Brian Epstein associate Robert Stigwood, harmonising brothers Barry, Robin and Maurice Gibb debut with *New York Mining Disaster 1941* and close out the summer with the chart-topping *Massachusetts*.

Engelbert emerges
4th March 1967 Keeping the Beatles' *Penny Lane* off No. 1 and staying there for six weeks is *Release Me* by Gerry Dorsey - or, as he has renamed himself, Engelbert Humperdinck. His country-tinged ballads are aimed squarely at an older female audience. He has more weeks on the chart in 1967 than any other artist.

Otis killed in air crash
10th December 1967 Five months after winning legions of hippie fans at Monterey, Otis Redding is killed with four members of his backing group the Bar-kays in an air crash in Wisconsin. His last record, made just three days before his death, is *Sittin' on the Dock of the Bay*, a departure from his usual style and a sign of his wish to develop a broader audience.

EMI think pink
July 1967 One of EMI's first 'progressive' signings, Pink Floyd enjoy a meteoric rise. Originally a blues band, they surface in London's underground clubs with an expansive, electronics-driven approach and eccentric Syd Barrett songs. They record debut LP *The Piper at the Gates of Dawn* at Abbey Road with ex-Beatles engineer Norman Smith, though by year end there is increasing concern about Syd's mental state and LSD intake.

PHOTO CREDITS Copyright 2024, TDM Rights BV.
Photos: **A** Mirrorpix - Getty Images / **B** PA Images - Getty Images / **C** Bundesarchiv Steiner - Egon - / **D** Ullstein bild - Getty Images / **E** Mirrorpix - Getty Images / **F** Alper Barbara - Archive Photos - Getty Images / **G** Eric Brissaud - Gamma-Rapho - Getty Images / **H** Hulton Archive - Archive Photos - Getty Images / **I** Lee Lockwood - The Chronicle Collection - Getty Images / **J** Bettmann - Getty Images / **K** - Ronald Grant Archive - Mary Evans / **L** Bettmann - Getty Images / **M** Silver Screen Collection - Moviepix - Getty Images / **N** Larry Ellis - Hulton Archive - Getty Images / **O** Estate of Keith Morris - Redferns - Getty Images / **P** David Cairns - Hulton Archive - Getty Images / **Q** PYMCA:Avalon - Hulton Archive - Getty Images / **R** Mirrorpix - Getty Images / **S** Avalon - Hulton Archive - Getty Images / **T** Michael Ochs Archives - Getty Images / **U** Hulton Archive - Getty Images.

1968

MY FIRST 18 YEARS

SPORT

Manchester United best in Europe
On 29th May, Manchester United face Benfica of Portugal in the European Cup final at Wembley Stadium. Three goals in extra time, from George Best, Brian Kidd and Bobby Charlton, secure a 4-1 victory and make Manchester United the first English team to win the title. On 24th December, Best is awarded the Ballon D'Or as European player of the year.

Tragedy at Hockenheim
32-year-old Scottish farmer and racing driver Jim Clark, Formula One World Champion in 1963 and 1965, and winner of 25 Grand Prix races, is killed at Hockenheim race circuit when his Lotus-Cosworth somersaults off the track and into woods at 170 mph.

Winning on equal terms
Billie Jean King wins her third Wimbledon ladies' singles title, her first of the Open era, and receives a cheque for £750 compared to the £2,000 received by the men's champion, Rod Laver. The disparity triggers King's crusade to achieve parity of earnings for women in the game.

What a flop
American high jumper Dick Fosbury revolutionises the high jump event at the Olympic Games by adopting a 'back first' technique which will become known as the Fosbury Flop.

Hemery hurdles to gold
David Hemery wins the Olympic gold medal in 400m hurdles in Mexico City on 15th October. Commentator David Coleman (photo), in a frenzy of excitement as Hemery nears the finish line, neglects to notice his GB teammate John Sherwood gets bronze, and utters words he will long regret: 'Hemery takes the gold, in second place Hennige and who cares who's third? It doesn't matter.'

Black Power salute at Mexico Olympics
On 16th October, during the medal ceremony for the men's 200 metres at the Mexico Olympic Games, American athletes Tommie Smith and John Carlos, who have won gold and bronze medals respectively, each raise a black-gloved fist during the playing of the *Star Spangled Banner*.

---

15 JAN 1968
'Irretrievable breakdown of marriage' becomes legal grounds for divorce in the UK.

13 FEB 1968
Escaping discrimination in newly independent Kenya, up to 1,500 Kenyan Asians are arriving in Britain each week.

21 MAR 1968
Road deaths in the UK have fallen by 23% after introduction of breathalyser tests in January 1966.

1968

DOMESTIC NEWS

Ford launch the Escort
January 1968 Ford announce their replacement for the Ford Anglia, the 'Escort', which, like the Anglia, will be manufactured at the Halewood plant. The two-door base model features rear-wheel drive, but headlights are an additional extra, included in the De Luxe model.

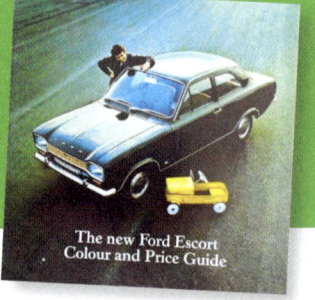

Dagenham ladies strike!
7th June 1968 Sewing machinists go out on strike to protest their classification as 'unskilled' workers. Labelled as such, they earn only 85% of what male 'skilled' employees at the plant earn. The strike is successful, leading to their pay being increased to 92% of the men's earnings, and sets in motion events that will lead to the 1970 Equal Pay Act.

DO YOU REMEMBER THIS?

Vacuum cleaner

Mining ends in Black Country
2nd March 1968 300 years of coal mining in the Black Country come to an end as the Baggeridge Colliery near Sedgley closes. Whilst a handful of open-cast mines survive, the way of life that had fuelled the Industrial Revolution, and earned the area its nickname, is on the decline in what was once its heartland.

Dust falls
1st & 2nd July 1968 England and Wales are struck by severe 'dust' storms that combine mineral dust from the Sahara with cold and wet weather. Some areas are thrown into near total darkness by the clouds, and the UK suffers one of its worst and most widespread hailstorms on record. Three people are struck by lightning and one person drowns in flood water.

Five and ten pence
23 April 1968 The country wakes with new coins in its pockets, as it moves toward the decimalisation of the currency. New five and ten pence pieces are introduced, replacing the shilling and the florin, in an attempt to get the public used to the new currency before the process is completed in 1971.

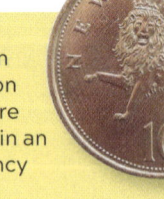

18 APR 1968
New London Bridge, opened 1831, is sold to US millionaire Robert McCulloch for £1 million.

16 MAY 1968
15-year-old Alex Smith becomes Britain's first lung transplant patient but dies 12 days later.

24 JUN 1968
Comedian Tony Hancock dies in Sydney after taking an overdose, aged 44.

1968

Last steam service
11th August 1968 The very last of British Rail's steam locomotives makes its final journey from Liverpool to Carlisle, signalling an end to the age of steam. From now on the only operating steam trains in the UK are on heritage railways or special services.

The Great Flood of 1968
15th September 1968 Severe storms lead to the worst floods in the Home Counties in over 100 years as large parts of the south east are affected. In Edenbridge Railway Station, the service from London's Charing Cross become stranded by flood water, with passengers stuck on board for 12 hours.

Second-class post
16th September 1968 The General Post Office launches a change in services, splitting post into first and second class for the first time. New second-class stamps cost 4d, while first class is 5d.

Derry march
5th October 1968 400 people gather to march through Derry in protest at discrimination in housing. They are supported by the fledgling Northern Ireland Civil Rights Association and the march is attended by several prominent MPs. Trouble breaks out when the Royal Ulster Constabulary use batons to drive the crowd across the river and engage violently with young people. Many are injured, and the extensive media presence leads to images of police brutality being shared widely across the country.

Race Relations Act
26th November 1968 Building upon the Race Relations Act of 1965, the new Act makes it illegal to discriminate against people on racial grounds in issues relating to employment, housing, or public services.

Hong Kong flu
December 1968 Cases of the Hong Kong flu, present in Britain since August, begin to rise in the country. The pandemic will last into 1970, claiming millions of lives globally and around 80,000 within the UK.

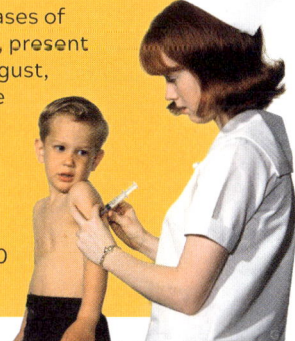

---

9 JUL 1968
The Queen opens the Brutalist Hayward Gallery on London's South Bank.

8 AUG 1968
Princess Margaret makes the inaugural journey on board the Mountbatten-class hovercraft from Dover to Boulogne.

1 SEP 1968
The first section of the London Underground's Victoria line opens between Walthamstow and Highbury & Islington.

1968

ROYALTY & POLITICS

Anti-Vietnam demo
In a year characterised by protests around the world, on 17th March, demonstrators protesting against the United States, involvement in the Vietnam War, and Britain's support of US action, converge on Grosvenor Square where many clash with riot police outside the American embassy.

Rivers of Blood
20th April 1968 Shadow Secretary for Defence Enoch Powell makes his infamous 'Rivers of Blood' speech when addressing a meeting of the Conservative Political Centre in Birmingham. The speech is in opposition to the proposed Race Relations Act and immigration from the Commonwealth and proves enormously controversial both for its theme and its rhetoric.

Death of Princess Marina
Princess Marina, Duchess of Kent, dies at Kensington Palace on 27th August aged 61, a month after being diagnosed with an inoperable brain tumour.

FOREIGN NEWS

Prague Spring
4th January 1968 In Czechoslovakia, newly appointed Communist Party secretary Alexander Dubček pushes for 'socialism with a human face'. His political and social reforms are too much for the country's Soviet masters whose tanks invade on the night of 20th August. Dubček is replaced by hardliner Gustav Husak and 'the Prague Spring' comes to an abrupt end as.

Thatcher on track
Margaret Thatcher gives her first House of Commons speech as shadow transport minister this year, arguing for investment in British Rail. More than two decades later, in a premiership that had implemented the privatisation of most state-owned services, when Thatcher resigns as Prime Minister, British Rail is the only one that remains. It too is finally privatised under John Major's government.

18 OCT 1968
US athlete Bob Beamon sets an astonishing world record of 8.90m in the long jump at the Mexico Olympics.

28 NOV 1968
Death of prolific children's author Enid Blyton.

30 DEC 1968
Judy Garland begins a residency at the Talk of the Town in London in what will be her final performances.

1968

Horror photo
1st February 1968 The most horrifying photograph of the Vietnam War is published, catching the moment a Viet Cong prisoner is executed by a South Vietnamese police chief.

Gagarin killed
27th March 1968 Yuri Gagarin, the first man in space, is killed on a training flight near Kirzhach in Russia. His ashes are interred in the walls of the Kremlin.

Baader-Meinhof
2nd April 1968 A new anarchist group announces itself with bomb attacks on department stores in Frankfurt. Andreas Baader and Ulrike Meinhof give their name to the gang, which is soon regarded as the biggest terrorist threat to mainland Europe. Also known as the Red Army Faction, these anti-imperialist urban guerrillas will get progressively more daring – and lethal – with assassinations and kidnappings before the leaders' capture in 1977.

King and Kennedy
4th April 1968 Martin Luther King Jr is murdered in Memphis, Tennessee. The killing of the most articulate and charismatic of civil rights leaders ignites days of rioting across the US. In Indianapolis, New York Senator Robert Kennedy calms his audience with a call for peace between the races. Presidential candidate Kennedy is cultivating young and disaffected voters with a promise to end the Vietnam War and plans for deep rooted social change. Two months later, following victory in the Californian Democratic primary, he is shot by Palestinian immigrant Sirhan Sirhan. He dies in hospital the next day. Millions line the route as a funeral train brings his body west for burial in Arlington Cemetery, Washington DC, where his brother was laid to rest five years before.

Slide projector

May '68 revolt
3rd May 1968 Inspired by a global wave of anti-war and anti-capitalist dissent, student protests erupt and bring France close to revolution. On 13th May, a million march through the streets of Paris. By the last week of May, two-thirds of French workers are on strike in sympathy, paralysing the world's fifth largest economy. On 30th May, with the government on the brink of collapse, President de Gaulle dissolves the National Assembly, promises reforms and calls an election. His gamble works: some normality returns and de Gaulle's party increases its majority. But while he holds the country together (just), his own days as leader are numbered.

1968

Pope rejects birth control
25th July 1968 In an encyclical that dismays many, Pope Paul VI signals no change to the Catholic Church's position on artificial birth control. Catholics are advised to exercise abstinence and restraint. Sex is for procreation not recreation.

Nixon is President
5th November 1968 Republican candidate Richard Milhous Nixon, who after losing the presidential election to John Kennedy in 1960 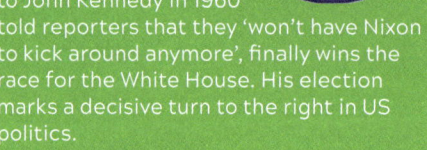 told reporters that they 'won't have Nixon to kick around anymore', finally wins the race for the White House. His election marks a decisive turn to the right in US politics.

Greetings from the Moon
25th December 1968 Apollo 8 is the first manned spacecraft to orbit the Moon. On Christmas Day a quarter of the world's population, at this point the largest television audience ever, watch the three astronauts deliver a seasonal message. Apollo 8's  mission is to search for landing sites for future missions to the Moon. President Kennedy's promise that the US will put the first man on the Moon before the end of the decade is close to being realised.

ENTERTAINMENT

One for sorrow, two for joy
Magpie airs for the first time on 30th July as ITV's answer to the BBC's *Blue Peter*. *Magpie* is a bit more hip than its wholesome rival. It covers music and fashion, has a rock-tinged theme song based on the traditional rhyme about magpies and presenters like Mick Robertson (who joins in 1972 and looks a bit like Brian May) and Jenny Hanley find their faces pinned up on teenage bedroom walls.

Garden greats
TV gets out in the garden this year. The first episode of *Gardener's World*, presented by Ken Burras from the Oxford Botanical Gardens, is broadcast on 5th January. The following year, Percy Thrower (photo) takes over as presenter with filming taking place in his own garden, The Magnolias in Shrewsbury. *The Herbs*, which debuts on BBC1 on 12th February, has Parsley the Lion, Dill the Dog, Tarragon the Dragon et al living in the walled kitchen garden of a country house. The magical password to gain entry to this horticultural wonderland? Herbidacious.

1968

Home front humour
The members of Walmington-on-Sea's Local Defence Volunteers make their first appearance on 31st July. *Dad's Army*, penned by David Croft and Jimmy Perry, is a comic tribute to those who served in the Home Guard during the Second World War. Arthur Lowe plays pompous bank manager and self-appointed leader of the group, Captain Mainwaring, who heads a superb cast that deliver Croft and Perry's lines with immaculate timing and create some of British comedy's finest moments. The interaction between Mainwaring and Ian Lavender's hapless innocent, Private Pike ('You stupid boy') is particularly memorable.

Going ape
Hollywood make-up artist John Chambers is given a budget of $50,000 to transform Roddy McDowell, Maurice Evans and cast into unnervingly  convincing simian overlords for the film, *Planet of the Apes*, adapted from Pierre Boulle's novel *La Planète des singes*. Charlton Heston, who spends most of the film in a loin cloth, is in the minority as a human, one of three astronauts who crash land on a planet where they discover, to their alarm, man is subjugated by monkey. Chambers is awarded an honorary Oscar for his work on the film.

Twinkle
The first issue of *Twinkle*, 'a picture paper for little girls', comes out on 27th January, with a free bracelet and St. Christopher charm on the cover to tempt buyers.

Hair at last
The 1968 Theatres Act is given royal assent on 26th July and finally ends censorship in the theatre. One of the first shows to benefit from the lifting of restrictions is the rock musical *Hair*, which contains nudity and profanities. Hair opens at the Shaftesbury Theatre on 27th September with a cast that includes Paul Nicholas, Elaine Paige, Marsha Hunt, Tim Curry and Richard O'Brien. *Hair* runs for 1,997 performances, closing when the roof of the Shaftesbury Theatre collapses.

Chocs away
Cadbury's Milk Tray show their first TV advertisement in which actor and model Gary Myers is the thoughtful action man who thinks nothing of beating avalanches or plunging into waves in his bid to secretly deliver a box of chocolates, 'all because the lady loves Milk Tray'.

Chitty Chitty Bang Bang
After a heart attack in 1961, Ian Fleming's wife confiscates his typewriter in an attempt to force him to rest. So he simply writes a children's novel, *Chitty Chitty Bang Bang - The Magical Car* in longhand. In 1967, Albert R. Broccoli decides the story has potential as a film and recruits Dick Van Dyke to play inventor Caractacus Potts, while Sally Anne Howes stars as Truly Scrumptious. But perhaps more terrifying than any Bond villain is ballet dancer Robert Helpmann as the evil Childcatcher. *Chitty Chitty Bang Bang* goes on to become a children's classic.

1968

It's The Basil Brush Show – Boom boom!
After appearances of the garrulous Basil Brush on magician David Nixon's shows, *The Basil Brush Show* begins on BBC on 14th June. Basil is a talkative fox with an upper-class accent, a terrible habit of interrupting, and a tendency to laugh hysterically at his own jokes. In his traditional tweeds and cravat, he's a typical English gent (if you don't count the fact he's actually a fox AND a puppet) and charms the guests who willingly appear on his show. Ivan Owen, who provides Basil's voice, models it on the actor Terry-Thomas.

Wacky Races
Hanna-Barbera's latest cartoon features the wackiest motor racing competition in the world as an unusual set of competitors line up on the grid every episode, with some using more underhand means to win than others. *Wacky Races* introduces us to miniature gangsters the Anthill Mob, pink-loving southern belle Penelope Pitstop and moustache-twirling arch-villain Dick Dastardly and his snickering asthmatic sidekick Muttley.

Festival first
A year before Woodstock happens, 10,000 people descend on Ford Farm, Godshill for the first Isle of Wight festival. Among the acts on the bill are Jefferson Airplane, the Move, Smile and Fairport Convention. The following year, Bob Dylan plays the festival after a long absence and in 1970, the festival has swelled to such a size, the island is overrun with 100,000 festival-goers.

(Morecambe and) Wise move
Eric and Ernie's move to the BBC, after seven successful years in ATV's *Two of a Kind*, is driven by the comedy duo's desire to have their show in colour at a time when BBC2 is still the only channel transmitting in colour. The first episode of the *Morecambe and Wise Show* airs on 2nd September, and soon becomes the jewel in the BBC's light entertainment crown, with up to 28 million people settling down to watch their annual Christmas Day shows.

Hop to it
The Spacehopper hits UK shops in the spring of this year. Originally called 'Pon-Pon', this large inflatable with ball with ribbed horns to use as handles is manufactured by Corgi-Mettoy in the UK and soon streets, driveways, parks and cul-de-sacs are overrun with kids hopping about on them. The fact the Spacehopper has a fearsome face etched on its front and is possibly the most exhausting and inefficient way to get from A to B does little to dent its popularity.

1968

Cilla
Cilla is broadcast on BBC1 on 30th January and marks the beginning of Cilla Black's transition from singing star to TV personality, in a deal brokered by Brian Epstein shortly before his premature death; *Cilla* will run for eight series until 1976.

Oliver!
Lionel Bart's 1960 stage musical comes to cinema screens in this big, loud and colourful adaptation of Dickens' *Oliver Twist*. Ron Moody, anxious to distance his character Fagin from the anti-semitic stereotype of the novel, plays the role with a light mischievous touch, while Jack Wild's Artful Dodger is full of chirpy confidence, Oliver Reed as Bill Sikes glowers with brooding menace and Mark Lester is guileless innocence in the title role. Add to that a bulging songbook of sensational tunes, and it's no surprise that *Oliver!* wins six Academy Awards.

MUSIC

Petula breaks a taboo
2nd April 1968 America's favourite British music star of the moment is former child star Petula Clark. Thanks to hits like *Downtown* and *Don't Sleep in the Subway* and the movies *Goodbye Mr Chips* and *Finian's Rainbow*, she now has a top-rated prime-time TV show. During a duet on the show with Harry Belafonte, she takes his arm and breaks an unwritten ban on interracial touching on US TV. The show sparks uproar but Petula is unrepentant.

Changes for the Beatles
15th May 1968 As the Beatles put the extravagances of *Sgt. Pepper* behind them to navigate life without Brian Epstein, they set up Apple Corps, to release Beatle records and promote new talent. George persuades the others to join him in India for a transcendental meditation course run by Maharishi Mahesh Yogi. Although they no longer write collaboratively, a positive of the trip is the number of songs which John and Paul create. Many appear on a double album with a plain white cover simply titled *The Beatles*.

Small Faces, big sound
24th May 1968 A fine Mod band always slightly in the shadow of the Who and the Kinks, the Small Faces make Ogden's *Nut Gone Flake*, with a circular sleeve in the style of a tobacco tin. It includes *Lazy Sunday*, a comic take on their East London roots and a sequel to 1967's *Itchycoo Park*.

The king is back
3rd December 1968 Heralding Elvis Presley's re-emergence after years of so-so movies and records is the one-off television special *Elvis*. Singing live on stage for the first time since 1960, he looks lean and lithe and in great voice.

Cream goes sour
26th November 1968 After a productive but fretful year, Cream play their last gig to a packed Royal Albert Hall. Eric Clapton and Ginger Baker form another supergroup in Blind Faith (photo) with Stevie Winwood from Traffic.

1968

Cliff does Eurovision
6th April 1968 The UK hosts the Eurovision Song Contest, with hopes pinned on Cliff Richard and the bouncy *Congratulations*. Cliff comes second by one point to Spain's entry, *La La La* by Massiel.

MY FIRST 18 YEARS TOP 10 1968

1. **Hey Jude** *The Beatles*
2. **Nights in White Satin** *The Moody Blues*
3. **What a Wonderful World** *Louis Armstrong*
4. **Classical Gas** *Mason Williams*
5. **Everlasting Love** *Love Affair*
6. **Fire** *The Crazy World of Arthur Brown*
7. **Where Do You Go to My Lovely** *Peter Sarstedt*
8. **The Mighty Quinn** *Manfred Mann*
9. **Cinderella Rockefella** *Esther and Abi Ofarim*
10. **Build Me Up Buttercup** *The Foundations*

Open | Search | Scan

Mary's opportunity
4th May 1968 Eighteen year old-Welsh folk singer Mary Hopkin appears on the ITV talent show *Opportunity Knocks* and is noticed by Paul McCartney, who's looking for artists to sign to Apple Records. He chooses a song for her based on a Russian folk tune, *Those Were the Days*, which is at No. 1 within weeks.

Here's to you, Mrs Robinson
1st June 1968 Contracted to supply songs to the movie *The Graduate*, Paul Simon writes one verse of *Mrs Robinson* for use on the soundtrack. Fully fleshed out and released as a Simon and Garfunkel single, the song is a satirical put-down of status-conscious middle America just as a wave of student protests hits its peak.

Led Zeppelin formed
7th July 1968 The Led Zeppelin story starts here with the break-up of the Yardbirds and Jimmy Page's formation of a new hard rock band - initially called the New Yardbirds - with Chris Dreja, John Paul Jones and Robert Plant. Debuting live in October and signing a massive deal with Atlantic Records, they record their hugely influential self-titled first album for release in January.

Fleetwood Mac
6th July 1968 Adding a third guitarist to an already much talked-about line-up is the most outstanding new British blues band in years, Fleetwood Mac. Danny Kirwan joins ex-John Mayall's Bluesbreakers Peter Green and Jeremy Spencer, drummer Mick Fleetwood and bassist John McVie completing the band.

Dusty in Memphis
24th November 1968 US TV's *Ed Sullivan Show* plays host to Dusty Springfield, fresh from recording in Memphis under top soul producer Jerry Wexler. It's a marriage made in heaven that yields the album *Dusty in Memphis* and possibly the greatest single ever by any white soul singer, *Son Of A Preacher Man*.

1969

MY FIRST 18 YEARS

SPORT

Sir Matt Steps back
Sir Matt Busby, who has managed Manchester United since 1945, announces his retirement on 14th January. During his time in charge of the club he has collected thirteen trophies including five league championships and the European Cup but finds he is not quite ready for his pipe and slippers. As well as becoming a director of Manchester United he has one final stint in charge, as interim manager in the first half of 1971 after Wilf McGuinness is sacked in December 1970.

Grand Slam greats
Rod Laver defeats fellow Australian Tony Roche in the US Open Men's Singles final on 9th September and in doing so, becomes one of only a handful of players to win all four Grand Slam titles in a single year. In tennis news closer to home, Birmingham-born Ann Jones becomes the Wimbledon Ladies' Singles champion after beating Billie Jean King in the final and goes on to also win the mixed doubles title with Australian Fred Stolle. As a result of her achievements, she is voted Sports Personality of the Year for 1969.

Gentleman Jack
In a Ryder Cup competition riven with animosity between the two sides, in the final round at the Royal Birkdale Golf Club in Southport, Jack Nicklaus concedes a three-foot putt to Britain's Tony Jacklin, meaning the tournament ends in a tie (although America retain the Cup). Nicklaus's gesture is viewed as the pinnacle of decent sportsmanship.

Stewart wins at Silverstone
Jackie Stewart is victorious at the British Grand Prix at Silverstone on 19th July, putting more than a lap between him and the other drivers. He dominates the 1969 Formula One season and becomes World Champion.

King Eddie
Belgian cycling supremo Eddy Merckx utterly dominates this year's Tour de France, and gives a historic, superhuman performance in the mountainous seventeenth stage from Louchon to Mourenx, stretching his lead by another eight minutes.

24 JAN 1969
Ford unveil their sporty new saloon, the Capri at the Brussels Motor Show.

19 FEB 1969
The High Court awards compensation to children born with deformities caused by thalidomide drug.

13 MAR 1969
Scientists at Cambridge University announce that human eggs have been fertilised in a test tube.

1969

Pot Black
Snooker is a fairly niche sport in Britain until David Attenborough, in his role as BBC2 controller, sees the potential in showing a game with coloured balls as a way to promote the channel's colour broadcasts. The first *Pot Black* tournament is recorded at the BBC's Birmingham studios and broadcast on 23rd July. Unlike traditional snooker tournaments, *Pot Black* is fast-paced with each match played in just one frame. Ray Reardon emerges the winner out of the eight competitors.

First B&Q store opens
March 1969 Richard Block and David Quayle launch their first 'B&Q' DIY superstore in Southampton. The one-stop shop for all things home improvement proves enormously popular and shapes the do-it-yourself home improvement craze of the 70s.

Reggie Kray

Ronnie Kray

Kray twins guilty
4th March 1969 Notorious gangsters and celebrity nightclub owners, the Kray twins, are found guilty of murdering George Cornell and Jack 'the Hat' McVitie and are sentenced to life imprisonment with a minimum term of 30 years. Ronnie and Reggie become almost legendary characters, celebrated and despised by their community in equal measure.

DOMESTIC NEWS

Northern Ireland
1969 sees an increase in violence in Northern Ireland, as marches and protests are broken up by police and, from April, British troops. August witnesses a three-day riot known as the Battle of the Bogside, with trouble continuing for several days. The Irish Taoiseach calls for a United Nations peacekeeping force on 13th August, and more British troops are deployed. In October, the British government accepts the recommendation to abolish the Ulster Special Constabulary.

Victoria line opens
7th March 1969 London's new underground line, named for Queen Victoria, becomes the first new tube line in over 60 years. The section from Walthamstow to Victoria is formally opened by the Queen, with the extension to Brixton not completed for a further two years.

22 APR 1969
Sailor Robin Knox-Johnson becomes the first person to make a solo, non-stop circumnavigation of the world.

7 MAY 1969
The Cunard liner *Queen Elizabeth 2* (*QE2*) sails into New York harbour for the first time.

14 JUN 1969
The Queen's black horse, Burmese, makes his first appearance at Trooping the Colour and will continue to take part in the ceremony until 1986.

1969

Harrier jump jet
1st April 1969 The RAF announce their acquisition of the new Hawker Siddeley Harrier 'jump jet'. The jet is ground-breaking in its ability to take off and land vertically and becomes a popular image of British Aerospace innovation.

Welsh bombings
30th June 1969 The Movement for the Defence of Wales, Mudiad Amddiffyn Cymru, continues the bombing activity that has seen tax offices, water pipes and conference centres damaged. The day before the investiture of Prince Charles as Prince of Wales, two members are killed when the bomb they are attempting to plant explodes prematurely. Two bombs are also planted on the day of the investiture, one of which seriously injures a ten-year-old boy.

Concorde prototype
9th April 1969 The prototype for Concorde, the very first supersonic passenger jet, makes its maiden British flight just a few weeks after the French test theirs in March. The project is a joint endeavour between the British and the French governments and will enter service in 1976, revolutionising cross-Atlantic travel.

Raleigh Chopper
April 1969 The Raleigh 'Chopper' bike is launched in the UK. Available in five colours, the bike proves to be a cultural icon for decades, featuring in television and films such as the *Back to the Future* movies. It is the most desired bike of the 70s, and remains so until overtaken by the BMX in the 1980s.

DO YOU REMEMBER THIS?
Standing ashtray

More currency changes
1st August 1969 The halfpenny, in circulation since 1717, ceases to be legal tender as the country takes another tentative step towards decimalisation. In October, the new 50 pence piece is introduced. This seven-sided coin is to replace the ten-shilling note and leaves much of the public sceptical.

3 JUL 1969
Swansea is granted city status to mark the investiture of Prince Charles.

8 AUG 1969
Iain Macmillan photographs the Beatles on the zebra crossing near the Abbey Road studios for their new album cover.

28 SEP 1969
'Book 'em, Danno'. American crime series *Hawaii 5-0* is broadcast for the first time on ITV Yorkshire.

1969

London Street Commune evicted
21st September 1969 Police move in and evict the squatters of the London Street Commune, who have been occupying 144 Piccadilly for several days. Earning the street the nickname 'Hippy-dilly', the protesters are calling for improvements to housing, after homelessness charity Shelter announces 3 million people are living in poor conditions across the country.

ROYALTY & POLITICS

Ballot Box Babies
On 17th April, the Representation of the People Act lowers the voting age in the UK from 21 to 18.

Devlin becomes youngest MP
Twenty-one-year-old Bernadette Devlin wins the Mid Ulster by-election and becomes the young M.P. to take a seat in the House of Commons, taking the Oath of Allegiance on 22nd April, and shortly afterwards making her maiden speech.

Royal family on film
The royal family's experimentation with publicity finds its full expression when they star in a fly-on-the-wall documentary, *Royal Family*, stirring up voyeuristic interest among the Queen's subjects. When it is transmitted on BBC1 on 21st June, viewing figures estimate that 68 per cent of the British population tune to see previously private moments like the Queen buying Prince Edward an ice cream in the shop near Balmoral, or the royals preparing for a family barbecue.

Investiture of the Prince of Wales
Investiture of the Prince of Wales takes place at Caernarfon Castle on 1st July, in a ceremony that has its roots in the medieval age but is beamed into the country's living rooms through modern technology.

15 OCT 1969
Media tycoon Rupert Murdoch purchases the *Sun* newspaper.

25 NOV 1969
In protest at the British government's involvement in Biafra and support of the Vietnam War, John Lennon returns his MBE.

18 DEC 1969
The House of Lords vote to abolish the death penalty in England, Scotland, and Wales.

1969

FOREIGN NEWS

Jan Palach
16th January 1969 Czech student Jan Palach sets himself on fire in Wenceslas Square in Prague in protest against the reversed reforms of the Prague Spring. He dies three days later from his injuries.

Bed-in for peace
25th March 1969 Five days after John Lennon marries avant-garde artist Yoko Ono, the couple honeymoon in Amsterdam and take over the presidential suite of the Hilton hotel. Welcoming the world press, John and Yoko spend the entire time in bed and talking peace.

Exits and entrances
28th March 1968 As the US says a final goodbye to former President Dwight D. Eisenhower (photo), the year sees far-reaching changes in leadership elsewhere. Also in March, Golda Meir becomes the first female Prime Minister of Israel. In April, Charles de Gaulle steps down as President of France when a referendum goes against him and is succeeded by Georges Pompidou. In September, North Vietnam's President Ho Chi Minh dies and Colonel Muammar Gaddafi seizes power in a coup in Libya.

Man on the Moon
21st July 1969 The time has come. In the media, at work and at school, the talk is about nothing else. The Columbia command module carrying astronauts Neil Armstrong, Buzz Aldrin and Michael Collins launches on 16th July and takes four days to reach the Moon. The Eagle lunar capsule undocks and the descent to the surface begins. Two and a half hours later, Armstrong confirms: 'The Eagle has landed.' Over six hours pass before Armstrong and Aldrin release air from the Eagle's cabin and the hatch opens. At 3:56pm UK time, Neil Armstrong is the first man on the Moon and utters the famous words: 'That's one small step for a man, one giant leap for mankind.' After two hours and fifteen minutes on the Moon, the astronauts take off and link up again with Columbia. They splash down south of Hawaii on 24th August. The achievement is historic. Will the world ever be quite the same again?

The Manson family
9th August 1969 Horrific scenes greet police at film director Roman Polanski's home in Los Angeles, where they find his pregnant actress wife Sharon Tate and four others stabbed to death. A day later, Leno and Rosemary LaBianca are found dead at their home in the city, apparently by the same perpetrators. Two months later, failed musician Charles Manson is arrested on other charges and implicated in the murders by members of his sinister cult. The killings shake the music and movie worlds to their core as it emerges that other celebrities were on Manson's death list.

1969

Chappaquiddick
19th August 1969 Mary Jo Kopechne, an aide to Senator Edward Kennedy, drowns when the car he is driving leaves a bridge at Chappaquiddick Island, Massachusetts. He fails to report the accident for nine hours, for which he receives a two-month suspended jail sentence. Although the incident does not end his political career, it scuppers his chances of ever becoming President.

Internet in embryo
29th October 1969 Four computers are linked to form the US Department of Defense's Advanced Research Projects Agency Network. As the first computer network of its kind, ARPANET is the precursor of the internet.

Taylor-Burton diamond
23rd October 1969 The jewellery house Cartier buys a special diamond at auction for just over $1 million. Richard Burton misses out by underbidding but, determined to acquire it for his diamond-loving wife Elizabeth Taylor, negotiates with Cartier to buy it for $1.1 million the following day.

Jumbo journey
2nd December 1969 The Boeing 747 makes its first passenger flight from Seattle to New York. As the largest aircraft in the world and the first with a wide fuselage, allowing more than double an airliner's usual load, it changes aviation history.

 **ENTERTAINMENT**

Shelling peas
The UK's first colour TV commercial - for Birds Eye peas - airs at 10:05am on ITV in the Midlands in a break during *Thunderbirds*. Unilever, who own the Birds Eye brand, had bought the slot for just £23.

Mary, Mungo & Midge
John Ryan, creator of Captain Pugwash, is asked to create a new up-to-date animation for modern children. The result is *Mary, Mungo and Midge*, which is first broadcast on 30th December. Mary lives in on the eighth floor of a tower block with her sensible old dog, Mungo, and inquisitive mouse, Midge. The joys of modern, urban living are very much at the forefront of *Mary, Mungo and Midge*.

Lulu the elephant
Lulu the baby elephant delights viewers when she goes rogue, wreaking havoc in the *Blue Peter* studio in its 3rd July episode. She defecates on the floor and as she lumbers about the studio, barely controlled by her keeper (whose training stick had been confiscated by producer Biddy Baxter), Lulu steps on John Noakes's foot causing him to hop in agony into the pile of elephant poo. As chaos plays out around her, Valerie Singleton remains the epitome of professionalism, continuing to talk calmly about their forthcoming summer expedition to Ceylon.

1969

Waggoners Walk
The tenants in the various flats of no. 1 Waggoners Walk, Hampstead are the subject of a new Radio 2 soap opera, first broadcast on 28th April. *Waggoners Walk* replaces the long-running radio serial *The Dales*, and aims to exchange stories of cosy, rural life with a more dynamic and fast-paced world, where taboo subjects like abortion, illegitimacy, homosexuality and even murder are tackled.

Art for the masses
Art historian Kenneth Clarke presents *Civilisation,* a major 13-part documentary series about Western art, culture and progress first shown on 23rd February. Initially suggested by David Attenborough (who was BBC2 controller at the time), the series, in which great paintings are discussed, greatly benefits from being broadcast in colour.

BBC1 in colour
BBC1 is the first channel in Europe to offer full broadcast in colour from 15th November, kicking off this auspicious landmark with a Petula Clark concert from the Royal Albert Hall. Colour TV licenses become available for a higher price than those for black and white TV.

Kes
Ken Loach's second feature film, *Kes*, demonstrates the power of film to tell an unflinching truth and is intended to expose the injustices of the country's divided educational system where secondary modern schools are viewed as second-rate. When Billy adopts and trains a kestrel, it shows that every one of us has the potential to shine. The film flops in America where the thick south Yorkshire accents are unfathomable, but in the UK, word of mouth ensures this quiet, powerful, heartbreaking film will become one of the most highly regarded in British cinema.

Hats off
Children's programme *Hattytown Tales* is, quite literally, about a town where all the characters are hats, from a police officer's helmet to a Mexican sombrero. Even the buildings are hat shaped. This Filmfair production for Thames Television is one of the decade's more bizarre children's TV concepts, but it runs for four years, clocking up 52 episodes in total.

The micemen cometh
The Clangers, which makes its debut on BBC1 on 16th November, is another delight conjured up by Oliver Postgate and Peter Firmin's Smallfilms. This is the year of the Moon landings so perhaps it is no surprise that their latest creation is about a group of knitted pink, mouse-like aliens who live on (and inside) a lunar type planet. *The Clangers* characters are based on a Moonmouse who appeared in one episode of *Noggin the Nog*, they're nourished by blue string pudding and Green Soup, which is kindly provided by the Soup Dragon, and communicate through a musical, whistling language. Wonderfully strange yet charming, *The Clangers* becomes a cherished cult classic.

1969

Something completely different
Monty Python's Flying Circus crashes on to BBC1 on 5th October at 10:55pm, the kind of time where something odd and experimental could easily be buried and forgotten about. Not so with the absurd, anarchic comedy dished up by John Cleese, Graham Chapman, Terry Jones, Eric Idle, Michael Palin and Terry Gilliam (who creates animations in which pop art, Dadaism, the Victorian engraving process and slapstick all gloriously collide). The Pythons are seen as subversive and silly, anti-establishment and avant garde, the natural inheritors of Spike Milligan.

The Liver Birds
The Liver Birds, written by Carla Lane and Myra Davis, begins on BBC1 on 14th April with a theme tune by the Scaffold. Sandra and Beryl negotiate the ups and downs of their love lives, their jobs and their parents, including a magnificent Mollie Sugden as Sandra's overbearing mother, who steals every scene she's in.

Diddy, Doddy, go
Tickling stick at the ready. Ken Dodd's Diddymen have been part of the Liverpool entertainer's stage act for a while but now he and the Diddymen puppets get their own TV show, which is first shown on BBC1 on 5th January. Doddy's imagination and penchant for the absurd is encapsulated by the the Diddymen who have names like Dicky Mint, Mick the Marmaliser and the Hon. Nigel Ponsonby Smallpiece. They go to work in the Jam Butty Mines or the Broken Biscuit Repair Factory, all in the fictional Knotty Ash.

The Very Hungry Caterpillar
Will the very hungry caterpillar ever be satisfied? Kids will have to read to the end of this banquet of a book to find out. Written and illustrated by American Eric Carle, *The Very Hungry Caterpillar* is published on 3rd June and goes on to sell fifty million copies worldwide.

The delicate matter of Miss Jean Brodie
The Prime of Miss Jean Brodie, for which Maggie Smith in the title role wins an Oscar, is chosen for the Royal Film Performance on 24th February. The film has been passed by film censors with an X-certificate but organisers of the royal performance decide to cut a ten-second scene in which a drawing of a naked man appears. The *Daily Mirror* suggests the organisers should stick to organising ice cream and ticket sales, 'And leave the Queen Mother to enjoy the film. Sexy bits and all.'

Carry On topless
By the end of the decade, the laboured innuendo of Carry On films is perhaps beginning to pall. Nevertheless, *Carry on Camping*, which is released in cinemas on 29th May, includes one of the franchise's most memorable moments when bubbly blonde Babs, played by Barbara Windsor, has a surprising bikini malfunction during a campsite keep fit session.

MUSIC

1969

Rod joins the Faces
1st January 1969 Steve Marriott leaves the Small Faces to form the much more heavy rock-leaning Humble Pie with Peter Frampton. His old band team up with little known but well-regarded blues singer Rod Stewart as the Faces.

Beatles get back
29th January 1969 The Beatles finally return to performing live - on the roof of the Apple offices in London's Savile Row. *Get Back*, introduced during the session, maintains the roots-driven feel of 1968's 'white album'. Though management issues are pulling the band apart - John, George and Ringo have brought in Allen Klein, when Paul wanted father-in-law Lee Eastman - they can still create an album as elegantly contained as *Abbey Road*, on which *Here Comes the Sun* and *Something* reveal George in particularly impressive form.

King Crimson reign
9th April 1969 Performing live in London are King Crimson who, without fanfare or promotion, have become kingpins of progressive rock with  In *The Court of the Crimson King*. The LP is a jazz-rock-classical hybrid with a much imitated sleeve by artist Barry Godber.

Jethro Tull
9th May 1969 Prog rock trio Jethro Tull are rapturously received at the Royal Albert Hall. The band blend jazz, blues and folk. Complaints pour in when Tull appear on *Top of the Pops* in response to wild-man Ian Anderson's lecherous demeanour and one-legged dancing.

Tommy released
23rd May 1969 Ever since *Sgt. Pepper*, bands have been using the LP medium to develop concepts and tell stories.

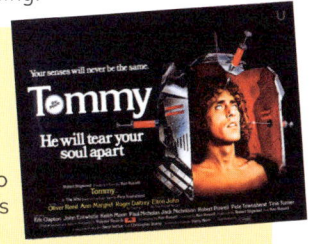

Pete Townshend of the Who creates *Tommy* - the story of a deaf, dumb and blind boy with brilliant pinball skills who becomes a religious leader. The album's success revitalises the band, while witnessing the Who perform *Tommy* live becomes one of rock music's all-time great experiences.

Sound of the Underground
12th March 1969 The Velvet Underground's self-titled third album is released to general indifference. Since forming in 1965 as part of Andy Warhol's circle, the New York band with their lowlife lyrics and bare guitar sound have offered a chilly counterpoint to expansive, laid-back west coast rock. This is their first release without John Cale who has fallen out with Lou Reed over the band's direction. Over time they will prove one of the most influential bands in rock history.

111

1969

Troubled times for the Stones
3rd July 1969 A month after leaving the Rolling Stones, Brian Jones is found dead in his swimming pool. The inquest verdict is death by misadventure. Two days later the Stones play a free concert in London's Hyde Park (photo) where Mick Jagger reads a poem by Shelley as a tribute. Brian's replacement is Mick Taylor from John Mayall's band, who stays with the Stones for five years. Although the Stones have released their most blues-based album to date, *Beggar's Banquet*, their troubled year ends with a free festival at the Altamont speedway track in San Francisco which is meant to outdo Woodstock. The decision to trust security to a local chapter of Hell's Angels backfires when they murder a spectator in full view of the band.

MY FIRST 18 YEARS — TOP 10 — 1969

1. **For Once in My Life** Stevie Wonder
2. **Blackberry Way** The Move
3. **You Got Soul** Johnny Nash
4. **Games People Play** Joe South
5. **Something** The Beatles
6. **Tracks of My Tears** Smokey Robinson
7. **Bad Moon Rising** Creedence Clearwater Rev.
8. **Born to be Wild** Steppenwolf
9. **Ruby, Don't Take Your Love** Kenny Rogers
10. **Honky Tonk Women** The Rolling Stones

Spaced out Bowie
20th September 1969 David Bowie has his first hit with *Space Oddity*, which BBC TV uses in its Moon mission coverage. Three years will pass before he charts again but *Space Oddity* has all the Bowie attributes the world will come to know - the Tony Newley-like voice, space age subject matter and his adoption of an alter ego.

Three days of peace and love
15th August 1969 'Three days of peace and music' begin at Max Yasgur's farm in upstate New York. Attended by nearly half a million, the Woodstock festival is a symbolic moment for the counter culture, made indelible by performances from rock's finest - Sly and the Family Stone, Grateful Dead, Santana, Jimi Hendrix, the Who and many more. Two weeks later 150,000 converge on the Isle of Wight for the UK's biggest festival to date, where Bob Dylan - who shunned Woodstock, even though it was close to his home - plays live with the Band.

PHOTO CREDITS Copyright 2024, TDM Rights BV.
Photos: **A** Don Morley - Hulton Archive - Getty Images / **B** INA - Getty Images / **C** Keystone-France - Gamma-Keystone - Getty Images / **D** Keystone - Hulton Royals Collection - Getty Images / **E** Bettmann - Getty Images / **F** Peter Ferraz - Hulton Archive - Getty Images / **G** Mirrorpix - Getty Images / **H** Hulton Archive - Hulton Royals Collection - Getty Images / **I** Mark and Colleen Hayward - Redferns - Getty Images / **J** NASA - Hulton Archive - Getty Images / **K** Bettmann - Getty Images / **L** Frank Edwards - Archive Photos - Getty Images / **M** Bettmann - Getty Images / **N** Mirrorpix - Getty Images / **O** Kestrel Films - Ronald Grant Archives - Mary Evans / **P** Small Films BBC - Ronald Grant Archives - Mary Evans / **Q** Michael Ochs Archives - Getty Images / **R** BBC - AF Archive - Mary Evans / **S** Landau Robert - Corbis Historical - Getty Images / **T** Michael Ochs Archives - Getty Images / **U** GAB Archive - Redferns - Getty Images / **V** Mirrorpix - Getty Images / **W** Blank Archives - Getty Images / **X** Michael Ochs Archives - Getty Images.

1970

MY FIRST 18 YEARS

SPORT

World Cup, Mexico '70
England travel to the World Cup in Mexico as defending champions, and kids around the country get busy collecting bubblegum and Panini cards and Esso medallions featuring their England heroes. England's first ever World Cup song, 'Back Home' proves prophetic and they are indeed back home sooner than anticipated after being knocked out in the quarter-finals by West Germany. In the group play-offs, they are also beaten by a magnificent Brazilian side who go on to win the tournament.

Commonwealth Games
The British Commonwealth Games are held from the 16th to 25th July in Edinburgh. England come second in the medal table, behind Australia, with a good haul of medals in track and field.

£200K move for Martin
Martin Peters becomes the first £200,000 footballer when he makes a move from West Ham to Tottenham Hotspur. The investment proves worthwhile for the North Londoners on 21st March, when he scores on his first appearance for his new team against Coventry City.

A vintage year for Jacklin
1970 is a year to remember for Tony Jacklin who receives an OBE in the New Year honours list, then goes on to win the US Open at Hazaltine, Minnesota. Away from the golf course, he even records an album of American songbook standards, *Tony Jacklin Swings Into*.

Dominance on Court
Australian Margaret Court wins all four Grand Slam tennis tournaments.

England vs. Rest of the World
The South Africa cricket team are scheduled to play England this summer but mounting pressure over apartheid leads to a cancellation of their tour. With no international fixtures for England's 1970 cricket season, a Rest of the World team is formed, captained by Gary Sobers (photo). The World XI win the test match series 4-1 but Ray Illingworth's England side put in an impressive performance against a team featuring the cream of the world's cricketers.

18 JAN 1970
The grave of Karl Marx in Highgate Cemetery is vandalised and daubed with swastikas.

11 FEB 1970
Plans are announced to decentralise the NHS by creating ninety separate regional health authorities.

6 MAR 1970
A rabies outbreak in Newmarket, Suffolk leads to a ban on imported animals to the UK.

1970

DOMESTIC NEWS

Northern Ireland
In June there are riots in Derry over the arrest of MP Bernadette Devlin, imprisoned for incitement to riot during the Battle of the Bogside in 1969, and in July three civilians and a journalist are killed by the British Army in clashes with the Irish Republican Army in Belfast. On 23rd July, Irish Nationalists throw two cans of CS or 'tear' gas into the House of Commons chamber, leading to an evacuation and one MP being hospitalised.

Thalidomide scandal
23rd March 1970 The courts award nearly £370,000 to eighteen victims of the thalidomide scandal. Thalidomide, which was marketed as an anti-nausea drug to treat morning sickness in pregnant women, caused birth defects in some 10-20,000 children worldwide.

Goodbye Minor – hello Range Rover!
18th April 1970 British Leyland announce beloved classic the Morris Minor, in production since 1948, is to be discontinued. As fans say goodbye to the Minor, a new success is on the books for Leyland with the launch of the Range Rover in June. The new vehicle proves popular as a sleeker, more urban version of the classic Land Rover.

Virgin gets going
February 1970 Richard Branson launches his first Virgin Group business. The Virgin brand begins with a mail-order business offering popular records at a discount. The business' first store will open in 1971, before other products and businesses are added under the Virgin name.

Bridge disasters
23rd May 1970 Two bridges are heavily damaged within two weeks, as a fire in the Britannia Bridge over the Menai Strait is followed by the collapse of the Cleddau Bridge in Pembrokeshire. The fire in the Britannia Bridge is caused by schoolboys playing in the structure, whilst the collapse at Cleddau occurs during construction and results in the deaths of four workers.

Reel-to-reel tape recorder

DO YOU REMEMBER THIS?

4 APR 1970
Gay Trip wins the Grand National at Aintree.

19 MAY 1970
Government agrees to bail out Rolls Royce to the tune of £20 million as it struggles with cost of developing new aero-engines.

27 JUN 1970
The Bath Festival of Blues and Progressive Festival takes place and includes a headline set by Led Zeppelin.

1970

Babes in the wood
17th June 1970 The nation is horrified as the bodies of two children, Susan Blatchford and Gary Hanlon, are found in woodland at Sewardstone, Essex, 78 days after the friends disappeared on a walk. What happened to the children remains a mystery for over twenty years, until their murderer, Ronald Jebson, finally confesses in 1998.

Dawson's Field hijacks
6th September 1970 As hijackings become part of the methodology of what are terrorists to some and freedom fighters to others, the Popular Front for the Liberation of Palestine (PFLP) hijack four passenger aircraft and force two of them to land at Dawson's Field, an airstrip in Jordan, where they are joined by a third a few days later. During intense negotiations, most of the hostages are released while the hijackers blow up the empty planes. While the Jordanian military move against Palestinian groups in the kingdom, the remaining hostages, all British, are released in exchange for captured hijackers.

Docks strike
15th July 1970 Dock workers across the United Kingdom go on strike, calling for an increase in wages of £11 a week. A state of emergency is declared as the strikes get underway, with the army standing ready to protect food imports. The strike is finally settled on the 30th, with an agreed increase in pay of 7%.

Mangrove marches
9th August 1970 Members of the black community in Notting Hill march to the local police station in protest at the frequent raids conducted on the Mangrove, a Caribbean restaurant that served as an important meeting place for black activists. Violence breaks out, and nine protesters are arrested and charged with incitement to riot. All are acquitted of incitement in a trial that sheds light on allegations of racism and brutality within the police force.

Goodbye to narrowboat freight
15th October 1970 An era draws to a close, as the last narrowboats to carry commercial freight on UK canals deliver their final load of coal from Atherstone to West London. This delivery brings to an end a way of life and transport in existence since the eighteenth century.

---

8 JUL 1970
Painter Dame Laura Knight dies at the age of 92.

24 AUG 1970
A section of Windscale power station is sealed off due to a suspected radiation leak.

12 SEP 1970
Residents complain of noise following first landing of Concorde at Heathrow.

1970

Iceland stores open
18th November 1970 Malcolm Walker opens his very first Iceland store in Oswestry, Shropshire. Iceland specialises in frozen food, initially loose items, later launching its own-label packaged food in 1977. It quickly becomes a staple of the British high street, providing cheap dinners to price-conscious shoppers.

In the Navy
Prince Charles graduates from the University of Cambridge with a 2:2 in History and joins the Royal Navy.

FOREIGN NEWS

ROYALTY & POLITICS

Surprise at the polls
A General Election takes place on 18th June, the first where people aged 18 or over can vote following the lowering of the age of majority from 21 to 18 in the Representation of the People Act the previous year. After six years of a Labour government and against expectations, Edward Heath's Conservatives win a surprise victory.

East and West meet
19th March 1970 For the first time since the division of Germany after the Second World War, West and East German leaders meet in person. West German Chancellor Willy Brandt is received warmly by East German Deputy Prime Minister Willi Stoph, heralding a normalisation of relations between the two countries. On a visit to Poland in December, Brandt is applauded when he unexpectedly kneels at the memorial to the uprising in the Warsaw ghetto in 1944.

Margaret Thatcher, milk snatcher
Free school milk in secondary schools is abolished by Ted Heath's Conservative government. The proposal is passed on to Secretary of State for Education Margaret Thatcher who argues the savings can be used to improve school buildings. Rather than abolishing all school milk, she reaches a compromise. Milk is no longer provided in secondary schools, but nursery and primary school children continue to receive a ½ pint of milk each day, dished out by whichever pupil is given the weighty responsibility of being 'milk monitor'.

Coup in Japan
25th November 1970 An attempted coup in Japan by right-wing militia leader Yukio Mishima fails. After making a public address, he commits *seppuku* – ritual suicide.

---

19 OCT 1970
BP announce they have found oil in British waters of the North Sea 110 mile east of Aberdeen.

27 NOV 1970
The Gay Liberation Front stage their first demonstration in London.

15 DEC 1970
MPs vote for an Industrial Relations Court in a bid to curb strikes.

1970

'Houston, we have a problem'

11th April 1970 Apollo 13 launches to take men to the Moon for the third time. Two days after launch, the oxygen tank explodes. Captain Jim Lovell reports the issue with the words 'Okay, Houston, we've had a problem here'. The Moon landing is aborted and all efforts are focused on improvising a way to get the three astronauts safely back to Earth. This involves sending the craft into Moon orbit, shutting down the command module's systems to conserve its resources for re-entry and transferring the crew to the lunar module, which acts as a lifeboat. They splash down on 17th April at 18:07pm UK time. The men are safe, their rescue as breathtaking and ingenious as the original Moon landing itself.

Earth Day

22nd April 1970 The first Earth Day is celebrated to show support for protecting the globe's threatened environments. More than 20 million take part in peaceful protests across the US, beginning what becomes an annual global event that is still marked a half century later.

ENTERTAINMENT

Divorced, beheaded, died

The BBC stakes its position as an expert creator of quality period dramas with *The Six Wives of Henry VIII*, which begins on 1st January with Annette Crosbie playing the first of the spouses, Catherine of Aragon. Keith Mitchell turns in an Emmy Award-winning performance as the complex Tudor king and has to age throughout the series, transforming from cultured, athletic young prince to bloated, bitter middle-aged monarch. Lavish costumes and Tudor music all enhance the authentic period atmosphere.

Nasser and de Gaulle

Two of the post-war world's most controversial politicians are no more. In September the death of General Gamal Abdel Nasser of Egypt changes the dynamic in the Middle East, as the outwardly more western-minded Anwar Sadat (photo) takes over as President. In November, the last of the Second World War leaders, former French President Charles de Gaulle, dies suddenly at the age of 80.

1970

Who changes colour
Doctor Who regenerates for the second time on 3rd January and emerges in the form of Jon Pertwee. This new version of the Doctor has the air of a flamboyant Victorian dandy, with his velvet frock coats, frilly jabots and dramatic capes, much of which is harvested from Pertwee's own wardrobe. The transformation also coincides with the sci-fi drama being shown in colour for the first time.

The Railway Children
The Railway Children, which is released on 21st December, tells the story of the three Waterbury children. When their beloved father is wrongly imprisoned, their mother (Dinah Sheridan) is obliged to leave behind a comfortable middle-class existence in suburban London and move to a modest cottage in Yorkshire. The film and its success has easily eclipsed E. Nesbit's original 1905 novel and includes a final scene guaranteed to ensure there isn't a dry eye in the cinema.

Words and Pictures
Words and Pictures, the BBC Schools programme dedicated to helping children learn to read phonetically through animations and stories, is first broadcast on 17th October.

Britain's fittest pit their wits
What will become Britain's longest-running sports quiz begins on BBC1 on 5th January. *A Question of Sport* is hosted by David Vine with boxer Henry Cooper and Welsh rugby international Cliff Morgan as team captains. The very first guests to share their sporting knowledge are footballers George Best and Tom Finney, cricketer Ray Illingworth and track and field athlete Lillian Board.

Side-splitting
The Banana Splits Adventure Hour has been on American TV for two years before it is first shown in the UK on 20th February. Coming from the Hanna-Barbera stable, *The Banana Splits* features comedy sketches and cartoons, all topped off with an ear-worm of a theme tune. It's fast-paced and action-packed so it's no surprise that one of its directors, Richard Donner, goes on to make several Hollywood blockbusters including *The Goonies* and the *Lethal Weapon* series.

1970

Scooby Dooby Doo
September sees the introduction of two new cartoon characters in the UK. On the 17th, *Scooby-Doo, Where Are You!* is shown on BBC1. Scooby is a dim but lovable Great Dane who accompanies a gang of teens who drive around in the Mystery Machine solving spooky crimes. Two days after Scooby's debut, slinky, rose-tinted sophisti-cat *The Pink Panther* prowls nonchalantly onto screens, accompanied by Henry Mancini's famous creeping saxophone theme tune.

Cat-napped
The Aristocats, the last Disney Studios film to be approved by Walt Disney himself before his death in 1966, is released in cinemas on 27th December.

Sing and bear it
Although he doesn't look a day over 10, Rupert Bear is already 50 years old when he stars in *The Adventures of Rupert Bear* on ITV this year. Now, Rupert, who lives with his mother and father in Nutwood, is brought to life as a string puppet along with his friends Bill Badger, Podge the Pig, Pong Ping the Pekingese and a host of other characters. Just thirteen episodes of *The Adventures of Rupert Bear* are initially made (the first airs on 28th October) but the series is such a success, it eventually runs for six years and 156 episodes.

The Street reaches 1,000th episode
Coronation Street celebrates its 1,000th episode on 19th August but on 30th June, actor Arthur Leslie, who plays Rovers Return landlord Jack Walker, dies suddenly of a heart attack, obliging the Street's writers to come up with a storyline to explain his absence (it is decided Jack would suffer the same fate off-screen). Key characters departing for whatever reason is a recurring issue in a long-running soap but as the novelist John Braine concludes in a piece he writes in a special 1,000th episode issue of the *TV Times*, 'the most important character in the Street is the Street itself. No matter who comes and goes, the Street remains.'

Scouting for jobs
With the advent of decimalisation, the Scout Association decide to change the name of their annual Bob-A-Job Week to the less snappy-sounding Scout Job Week.

Goodie, Goodie yum-yum
Cambridge Footlights alumni Tim Brooke-Taylor, Graeme Garden and Bill Oddie aka *The Goodies* are let loose on TV screens on 8th November. Cycling around on their 'trandem' their cartoonish humour has huge, cross-generational appeal. Viewers can't get enough of sketches like Kitten Kong (using chroma-key, green screen technology), Bill practising the ancient martial art of 'Ecky Thump' and their catalogue of silly songs including stone-cold classic, '*The Funky Gibbon*'.

1970

Page 3 provocation
Editor of the *Sun* newspaper, Larry Lamb, starts publishing a daily photograph of a topless glamour model on page 3, a controversial move that helps to double the newspaper's circulation to 2.5 million within a year. Page 3 understandably provokes protests against the sexualisation of women in what is marketed as a 'family newspaper' but it will be 45 years before the *Sun* removes Page 3 girls from its printed paper in 2015 after increasing pressure from campaigners. By 2017, topless models also disappear from its web site.

Scent of the seventies
The fragrance Aqua Manda's musky blend of mandarin, coriander, jasmine and aromatic herbs pervades every party, club and disco in the land. With its distinctive orange floral packaging and reasonable price point, Aqua Manda is the undisputed smell of the seventies.

Creedence opt out
26th March 1970 Woodstock, the film of the 1970 music festival, goes on global release. Missing from the movie is a group who performed there but vetoed their inclusion in the film - Creedence Clearwater Revival. Originally from San Francisco and one of the top groups on the planet right now, Creedence's music is barnstorming rock'n'roll that conjures up a southern landscape of swamps, riverboats and highways in piledrivers like *Proud Mary* and *Up Around the Bend*.

Butch Cassidy and the Sundance Kid
Paul Newman and Robert Redford make a pair of devastatingly handsome Wild West outlaws in *Butch Cassidy and the Sundance Kid*, which arrives in UK cinemas on 6th February. The inclusion of the Burt Bacharach song *Raindrops Keep Falling on my Head* is controversial yet the track, which is used to accompany the famous bicycle scene in the film, goes on to become a huge hit reaching No. 1 in the US Billboard chart.

The Beatles split
10th April 1970 Paul McCartney has left the Beatles. The band's dissolution is finalised in the courts at the end of the year. The *Let It Be* album is a mixed epitaph, disliked by Paul for the production sheen added by John's buddy Phil Spector. Paul is first to release a solo album with *McCartney*, while Ringo makes an LP of swing era songs as a present for his mum. John records as the Plastic Ono Band but it is a rejuvenated George who wins the most plaudits with the Spector-produced *All Things Must Pass*.

MUSIC

Jackson Five
25th April 1970 At No. 1 in the US with *ABC* are the Jackson Five, the soul-singing siblings discovered by Diana Ross. Originally from Gary, Indiana, the group are as dazzling to watch as they are to listen or dance to - much of which is down to twelve-year-old Michael's precociously emotive voice and stage presence.

1970

Simon says
28th February 1970 As news breaks that Simon and Garfunkel have parted company, their sonic masterpiece *Bridge over Troubled Water* begins its hold on the single and LP charts in the US and UK. Its soul-searching introspection has touched a real chord with America's post-Woodstock generation.

'Four dead in Ohio'
4th May 1970 Crosby, Stills, Nash and Young are America's supergroup of the moment. Formed by members of the Byrds (David Crosby), Buffalo Springfield (Steve Stills, Neil Young) and the Hollies (Graham Nash), their music is homespun but spiky - especially the impassioned *Ohio*, one of the most political songs ever to reach the US Top 40. It is Young's response to the shooting by National Guardsmen of four protesting students at Kent State University.

Everything's all Wight
26th - 31st August 1970 The second Isle of Wight Festival attracts 500,000 people. The most glowing reviews go to Emerson, Lake and Palmer, the supergroup playing live for only the second time. The most lingering memory is of Jimi Hendrix making what will be his very last live performance.

Hendrix is dead
18th September 1970 Jimi Hendrix dies in London aged 27 after taking an overdose of barbiturates and choking on his own vomit. The coroner returns an open verdict. As demonstrated indelibly by his *Are You Experienced* and *Electric Ladyland* albums, Hendrix was simply the most imaginative, most technically adept and most instinctively creative guitarist of his generation.

Just a word
3rd June 1970 Making a 6,000-mile round trip today to re-record just one word of his song *Lola* is Ray Davies of the Kinks. BBC Radio won't play the track unless its reference to Coca-Cola is changed. So Ray flies to London, enters a recording studio and sings 'cherry cola' instead, then hotfoots it back to the US. It's surprising that the BBC is prepared to play it at all, given that Lola is a transvestite.

Janis is dead
4th October 1970 Still reeling from the death of Jimi Hendrix, the rock world is shaken by the death of Janis Joplin at the same age of 27. The greatest white female blues voice of her time, her death is attributed to a heroin overdose. She had only been solo for a year, having stuck with the San Francisco band Big Brother and the Holding Company longer than she needed to.

1970

Singer-songwriters on the rise
Singer-songwriters are the flavour of the year, many of them recording for the hippest California record label, Warner Reprise. Some have been around for a while - James Taylor recorded for Apple in London, Joni Mitchell made her first LP in 1968, and Van Morrison has his roots in the UK beat boom - but the introspective nature of their songs suits the new decade's sombre mood. Taylor's *Sweet Baby James* outsells them all but August sees a young UK singer-pianist make his live US debut at the Troubadour in Los Angeles. His name is Elton John.

Eric becomes Derek
15th June 1970 Having joined Delaney and Bonnie Bramlett's touring band to expunge the excesses of his Cream and Blind Faith days, Eric Clapton forms Derek and the Dominoes with the Bramletts' rhythm section. The revitalised Clapton plays in a subtler, more concise and low-key style typified by *Layla*, a love song to George Harrison's wife Patti, who he will marry after their divorce.

MY FIRST 18 YEARS TOP 10 — 1970

1. **Layla** Derek and the Dominoes
2. **Big Yellow Taxi** Joni Mitchell
3. **Fire and Rain** James Taylor
4. **Mama Told Me Not to Come** Three Dog Night
5. **Spirit in the Sky** Norman Greenbaum
6. **Tears of a Clown** Smokey Robinson
7. **Woodstock** Matthews Southern Comfort
8. **I Hear You Knockin'** Dave Edmunds
9. **Let it Be** The Beatles
10. **Abraham, Martin and John** Marvin Gaye

Happy families
23rd September 1970 From Screen Gems, makers of *The Monkees*, comes a television music show that makes a huge star of showbiz kid David Cassidy. *The Partridge Family* is about a pop group of young siblings and their mother, played by Hollywood songstress Shirley Jones, heartthrob David's real life stepmother.

Guitar heroes
If Jimi Hendrix defined the term 'guitar hero', other axe-playing stars are ready to take on the mantle such as Rory Gallagher of Taste, Alvin Lee of Ten Years After and Led Zeppelin's Jimmy Page. For Peter Green, the adulation is too much and he leaves Fleetwood Mac before the band makes a career-changing move to the US.

PHOTO CREDITS Copyright 2024, TDM Rights BV.
Photos: **A** Peter Robinson Empics - PA Images - Getty Images / **B** PA Images - Getty Images / **C** Roger Jackson - Hulton Archive - Getty Images / **D** Bettmann - Getty Images / **E** Fox Photos - Hulton Archive - Getty Images / **F** Bettmann - Getty Images / **G** Bettmann - Getty Images / **H** Matt Stroshane - Getty Images / **I** Bettmann - Getty Images / **J** Ronald Grant Archive - Mary Evans / **K** Evening Standard - Hulton Archive - Getty Images / **L** Studiocanal Films Ltd - Mary Evans / **M** BBC - AF Archive - Mary Evans / **N** AF Archive - Mary Evans / **O** Ruby Spears Productions - Ronald Grant Archive - Mary Evans / **P** Disney - AF Archive - Mary Evans / **Q** AF Archive - Mary Evans / **R** The Scout Association - Mary Evans / **S** BBC - Ronald Grant - Mary Evans / **T** Sunset Boulevard - Corbis Historical - Getty Images / **U** Michael Ochs Archives - Getty Images / **V** Michael Ochs Archives - Getty Images / **W** Michael Ochs Archives - Getty Images / **X** Universal History Archive - Universal History Archive - Getty Images / **Y** GAB Archive - Redferns - Getty Images / **Z** GAB Archive - Redferns - Getty Images.

1971

MY FIRST 18 YEARS

SPORT

Tragedy at Ibrox
66 people are killed and 200 more are injured during the 'Old Firm' match between Glasgow Rangers and Celtic at the Ibrox Stadium in Glasgow on 2nd January, due to a crush as fans exit the game. The stadium had suffered tragedy once already when a wooden stand collapsed during an international match in 1902, killing 25. The 1971 disaster is the worst in British football history to that point and leads to a rebuilding of Rangers ground.

Arsenal win the double
Five days after becoming League champions of the 1970-1 football season Arsenal face Liverpool at Wembley on 8th May in front of a crowd of 100,000 for the FA Cup Final. They win 2-1 with goals in extra time from Eddie Kelly (helped by George Graham) and Charlie George. The win makes Arsenal only the fourth team to secure the double.

V for victory?
Show jumping rebel Harvey Smith, son of a Yorkshire builder, loses a major title and £2000 in prize money after allegedly flicking the 'V' sign at the judges at the British Show Jumping Derby with horse Mattie Brown on 15th August. Smith protests he was making a 'V for victory' gesture. Notorious for clashing with judges and officials, Smith is a great favourite with the public and after two days his disqualification is reversed.

DOMESTIC NEWS

Northern Ireland
Troubles in Northern Ireland continue with violent riots throughout the year. In August, hundreds of people are arrested by British forces and are interred in Long Kesh prison, where they are held without trial. Known as 'Operation Demetrius', this policy leads to the Ballymurphy Massacre, where eleven people are killed by British forces. The autumn sees a fourteen-year-old girl, Annette McGavigan, killed when caught in crossfire, and two women shot dead at a checkpoint in Belfast. The worst incident of the Troubles so far occurs on 4th December, when a bomb destroys McGurk's bar in Belfast killing fifteen.

The lion roars
The British Lions rugby tour of New Zealand between 12th May and 14th August sees them play in four Test series against the mighty All Blacks. The British side, captained by John Dawes and comprised of the best players from the England, Ireland, Wales and Scotland teams, win two, lose one and draw in a final, nail-biting match to secure a historic Test series win.

15 JAN 1971
George Harrison releases his first solo single *My Sweet Lord*.

6 FEB 1971
Apollo 14 astronaut Alan Shepard hits a golf ball on the moon during a two-day moonwalk.

8 MAR 1971
Brian Faulkner becomes Prime Minister of Northern Ireland.

1971

Divorce Reform
1st January 1971
The year begins with changes to divorce laws in the UK, allowing couples to divorce if they have been living separately for two years. For the first time divorce can be granted on the grounds that the relationship has irretrievably broken down, with no need for one partner to be proven at fault.

Postal workers strike
20th January 1971 Postal workers go out on strike for the first time in their history, demanding a better pay deal. The strike lasts seven weeks and sees a variety of alternatives spring up in the space left by the Post Office.

Seabed treaty
11th February 1971 Countries including the UK, USA and Soviet Union sign the Seabed Arms Control Treaty which agrees to outlaw the use of nuclear weapons on the ocean floors. The treaty covers the seabed within 12 miles of the coast and seeks to prevent the escalation of nuclear tensions.

Decimalisation day
15th February 1971 The UK and the Republic of Ireland complete the switch to a decimal currency. Pounds are now worth 100 pence, replacing the 'old money' system of 20 shillings to the pound and 12 pence to the shilling. Initially people can still pay in old money, but they receive their change in the new currency. As of September, the old penny and threepence are no longer legal tender.

Angry Brigade bombs
12th January 1971 The home of the Secretary of State for Employment, Robert Carr, is bombed along with his offices at the Department of Education. Responsibility is claimed by a left-wing group calling themselves the 'Angry Brigade'. Before the year is out, they will have struck the Biba store in Kensington, London, and the Post Office Tower.

15 APR 1971 — City of London announces plans for the building of the Barbican Centre.

11 MAY 1971 — Closure of 62-year-old paper, *The Daily Sketch*.

19 JUN 1971 — Viewing figures show talent show Opportunity Knocks is the country's most popular TV programme.

1971

Industrial Relations Act protests
1st March 1971 The proposed Industrial Relations Act prompts huge protests in London where between 120,000 and 250,000 people join 'kill the bill' strikes across the capital. The Act will ensure that only registered trade unions have negotiating power, something workers fear will lead to restrictions upon industrial action. Despite this, the bill is passed and receives royal assent in September.

Royal winner
After winning the individual medal at the world 3-day eventing championship at Burghley, aged 21, Princess Anne is voted BBC Sports Personality of the Year.

Paisley forms DUP
Protestant minister, hardline Unionist and MP for North Antrim Ian Paisley founds the Democratic Unionist Party (DUP).

Spaghetti Junction opens
10th November 1971 The infamous Gravelly Hill Interchange or 'Spaghetti Junction' opens for the first time. Initially featuring 10 routes, including the A38, A5127, and M6, it later expands to 12 in 1972.

Queen gets a big pay rise
Parliament debates an increase to the Civil List from £475,000 to £980,000. The Commons Select Committee, which makes the recommendation, justifies the increase of more than 100% stating, 'there is little further scope for economies in the Royal Household'.

ROYALTY & POLITICS

UK to join EEC
The House of Commons approves the UK's entry into Europe by a majority of 112 votes on 28th October. In his speech to the Commons, Anthony Barber, Chancellor of the Exchequer says, 'We shall join the Six as a proud and powerful country, able and ready to make its full contribution.'

6 JUL 1971
Crash helmets are to become compulsory for motorcyclists.

27-28 AUG 1971
Clashes break out between police and Hell's Angels at Weeley Festival in Essex.

3 SEP 1971
Qatar gains independence from the United Kingdom.

1971

FOREIGN NEWS

Idi the cruel
25th January 1971 General Idi Amin Dada seizes power in Uganda when President Milton Obote makes a trip abroad. The former boxing champion is welcomed at first but soon establishes a destructive dictatorship which earns him the nickname 'Slaughterer of Africa'. During his reign, Amin has 300,000 opponents eliminated.

The first email
In the US, 23 computers located at various universities are now connected to the ARPANET, the forerunner of the internet. Computer programmer Ray Tomlinson sends the first message over the network from one computer to another. He comes up with the @ sign to distinguish the domain and the recipient. The medium we know as email is born.

Starbucks starts
30th March 1971 The first branch of coffee shop giant Starbucks opens in Seattle, Washington, as a store selling varities of coffee beans.

First space station
19th April 1971 Salyut 1, the world's first space station, is launched by the Soviet Union. The first crew of cosmonauts is unable to dock while the second crew are also forced to abort after 23 days aboard in June. When their craft, Soyuz 11, returns to Earth, all three cosmonauts are found dead from an air supply leak. The decision to abandon the station is taken in October.

Pentagon Papers
30th June 1971 The US Supreme Court rules that the *New York Times* can publish the Pentagon Papers, overruling objections from the Nixon administration. The Papers are classified studies made for the Department of Defense which reveal the double-dealing and secret machinations that brought the US to war in Vietnam. The revelations strengthen opposition to the war still further in a year in which Australia and New Zealand withdraw their troops from Vietnam, the US resumes bombing of North Vietnam and the conflict spreads to Laos.

Bangladesh goes alone
31st May 1971 Four months after the devastating Cyclone Bhola, the former East Pakistan - now Bangladesh - declares its independence from Pakistan, which brutally crushes the rebellion and creates two million refugees. After Pakistan declares war on India in December, India invades Bangladesh with Bengali rebel support. Pakistan surrenders on 15th December.

1 OCT 1971
The CAT scan is first used in patient diagnosis in Wimbledon.

28 NOV 1971
51-year-old farmer, Ray Covine, uncovers an immigrant smuggling operation on his farm near Huntingdon.

30 DEC 1971
Sean Connery returns for the final time as Bond in Diamonds are Forever.

1971

Twin towers topped out
19th July 1971 The topping out of the South Tower of the new World Trade Center in New York takes place, following the topping-out ceremony for the North Tower six months earlier.

Greenpeace launches
14th October 1971 Greenpeace is founded in Vancouver, Canada, to campaign actively against US plans for nuclear tests in Alaska. As the organization grows its action-based but non-violent opposition to causes such as large-scale whaling, seal hunting and the dumping of nuclear waste at sea brings it into direct conflict with governments.

Chocolate cigarettes

ENTERTAINMENT

Top deck
The first episode of *Here Come the Double Deckers* is shown on BBC1 on 15th January. A comedy adventure series with a brilliant theme tune, it features a gang of kids - Scooper, Tiger, Brains, Sticks, Doughnut, Spring and Billie - whose HQ is an abandoned double-decker bus in a London junkyard. The Double Deckers get into various scrapes every episode, and most of us wonder where on earth their parents are.

Clackers really knacker
Possibly the worst idea for a toy ever, 'clackers', consisting of two hard acrylic balls on string, are all the rage during the summer of 1971. After several accidents, many schools ban them as a serious hazard.

1971

Kids get a *Look-In*
Look-in is launched as a junior version of the *TV Times*. Jam-packed with comic strips, interviews and pull-out posters focused on ITV's programmes, it also features pop music, cool hobbies like skateboarding and a regular column from radio DJ Ed Stewart called, 'Stewpot's Newsdesk'. Through most of the 1970s, *Look-in* covers are illustrated by Arnaldo Putzo, who also designs posters for films like *Get Carter* and the *Carry On* series.

Music for musos

On 21st September, the thinking person's music show, *The Old Grey Whistle Test* airs for the first time. This is the place to hear non-chart music and album tracks through live performances in a pared-back studio setting. *The Old Grey Whistle Test* boasts some special moments in music from Roxy Music in their glam rock pomp performing *Ladytron* to David Bowie on the eve of his 1972 Ziggy Stardust tour, rattling through a blistering performance of *Queen Bitch*.

Elizabeth R
The success of *The Six Wives of Henry VIII* in 1970 encourages the BBC to tackle the story of his daughter next; the first of six 75-minute episodes is shown on 17th February. *Elizabeth R* has Glenda Jackson in imperious form, playing the queen from a fifteen-year-old princess to the aging Gloriana.

A shocking end
Valerie Barlow (Anne Reid) and husband Ken (William Roache) are preparing to leave the Street for a new life in Jamaica in *Coronation Street*'s 27th January edition when she is electrocuted by a faulty hairdryer and killed instantly.

Playaway on Saturday
Playaway starts on 20th November and becomes a Saturday afternoon refuge for kids away from sports-dominated weekend TV schedules during the 1970s. A older sibling of the weekday programme *Playschool*, its lively variety show format includes songs, bad jokes, sketches, and general tomfoolery. Along with more familiar Playschool alumni like Brian Cant and Floella Benjamin (photo), Jeremy Irons and Tony Robinson both do time as Playaway presenters.

1971

Comedy sitcoms on-screen
Several popular British TV sitcoms capitalise on their success and get a big-screen upgrade this year with *Dad's Army*, *Up Pompeii* and *On the Buses* all made into full-length feature films.

Upstairs, Downstairs
Upstairs, Downstairs, the long-running drama about the aristocratic Bellamy family of 165 Eaton Place, SW1 and their retinue of servants below stairs, is the surprise hit drama of the decade. Originally the idea of actresses Eileen Atkins and Jean Marsh (who would play parlourmaid Rose Buck in the series), the first episode of this period drama is buried by ITV in the ignominious 10:15pm slot on Sunday 10th October, but audience figures quickly increase, eventually soaring to 18 million. Through five series, the lives of the Bellamys and their employees are interwoven with world events such as the suffragette movement and the sinking of the *Titanic*, in a dramatic formula that would be successfully revived four decades later in *Downton Abbey*.

Save us from Sesame Street
British kids have enjoyed American cartoons and comedy series since the 1950s but are introduced to a very different kind of transatlantic offering this year in a show that provokes significant controversy in advance of its broadcast on 29th March on HTV. *Sesame Street* is populated by a cast of brightly coloured puppets (many created by Jim Henson) whose daily lives form the basis of didactic teaching methods. The BBC refuses to air it since it seems specifically tailored to educating American children; ITV does so reluctantly on the understanding it 'should not be construed as endorsement of *Sesame Street* to British children'. The hand wringing of educationalists means little to parents and children, who love characters like Big Bird, Eric and Ernie and The Count (who, you've guessed it, counts!) and find novelty in exotic Americanisms such as trash, zip code and cookies - as gobbled up by Cookie Monster.

And it's goodnight from him
The Two Ronnies appear on BBC1 on 10th April in a show that will run for the next sixteen years. With many sketches based on Ronnie Barker's fondness for word play (and others playfully mocking Ronnie Corbett's short stature), their partnership produces comedy gold from a brain-teasing *Mastermind* spoof to hardware store confusion in 'Four Candles'.

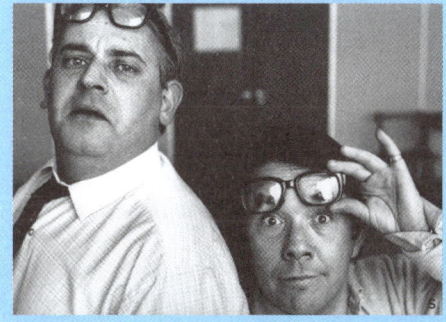

1971

A ticklish tale
The first six books in the *Mr. Men* series by advertising executive and frustrated cartoonist Roger Hargreaves are published on 10th August. The very first character is *Mr. Tickle*, whose unfeasibly long arms cause all sorts of mischief. *Mr. Men* is an instant success and becomes a cartoon series in 1974 (narrated by Arthur Lowe). Hargreaves goes on to create 46 *Mr. Men* and 33 *Little Miss* characters in total. In 2004, his widow sells the rights to *Mr. Men* to Chorion for a cool £28 million.

Beatrix Potter ballet
The Tales of Beatrix Potter, a ballet film featuring various characters created by Potter, danced by the Royal Ballet to choreography by Sir Frederick Ashton, is released in cinemas 30th June. Wayne Sleep dances the part of Squirrel Nutkin; Ashton himself plays Mrs. Tiggywinkle. The costumes by Christine Edzard form an exhibition on board the *QE2* liner this year.

Very persuasive
The pairing of Tony Curtis and Roger Moore as millionaire playboys from different sides of the tracks in *The Persuaders* is intentionally incongruous, with Curtis as the rough and ready New Yorker Danny Wilde, and Moore playing to type as the posh and polished British nobleman, Lord Brett Sinclair. Sporting equally wide sideburns and ties, *The Persuaders* embark on a series of escapades with the help of fast cars, John Barry's seventies synth soundtrack and glamorous co-stars like Susan George, Imogen Hassall and Joan Collins. Curtis, aged 46, personally performs all of his stunts.

On-screen Gangster
A grim and gloomy Newcastle-upon-Tyne is the setting for *Get Carter*, released 10th March, featuring Michael Caine as a brutal London gangster returning to his roots to seek revenge among the Geordie criminal underworld.

MUSIC

Balm for the soul
10th February 1971 After divorce from Gerry Goffin, re-marriage and a move to the Californian hills, top 60s songwriter Carole King is back with an album full of homeliness and good feeling. Including her own versions of *I Feel the Earth Move, You've Got a Friend* and *A Natural Woman*, *Tapestry* is musical balm for the soul in dark times. Over 25 million sales prove it.

Stones get sticky
12th May 1971 Negative headlines surround Mick Jagger's *très chic* wedding to Nicaraguan socialite Bianca Pérez-Mora Macías in St Tropez. The Stones are getting stick in the music press for becoming tax exiles in the south of France but they are on top form with the *Sticky Fingers* album, the first Stones release on their very own record label. Its cover has a real working zip - the work of Andy Warhol's Factory and a nightmare for record store owners the world over.

1971

Glastonbury
20th - 24th June 1971 Worthy Farm owner Michael Eavis times the first Glastonbury Festival proper - after a small event under a different name a year earlier - to coincide with the summer solstice. The line-up includes Traffic, Fairport Convention, a pre-Ziggy Stardust David Bowie and a diehard of 1970s festivals, Hawkwind.

Blue days
22nd June 1971 Joni Mitchell releases *Blue*, the outcome of a year of travelling after her relationship with Graham Nash breaks up. A searingly honest and self-revealing LP, it will dazzle and inspire scores of artists over the next 50 years.

Marvin's mission
21st May 1971 Motown superstar Marvin Gaye releases the album *What's Going On*, a huge shift from the punchy dance-driven tracks he is known for. Largely inactive since the death of his singing partner Tammi Terrell and his failing marriage to Berry Gordy's sister Anna, Marvin has set a series of socially conscious songs to a looser, expansive sound. Motown owner Gordy thinks it's commercial suicide but hands him a new deal allowing him creative freedom - at one million dollars, the most lucrative deal yet secured by a black recording artist.

Satchmo passes on
6th July 1971 Louis Armstrong, the cornet-playing father of Dixieland jazz, dies at the age of 71.

Concerts for Bangladesh
1st August 1971 George Harrison organises two Concerts for Bangladesh at Madison Square Garden, New York. Joining him on stage are Eric Clapton, Bob Dylan and sitar virtuoso Ravi Shankar. The concerts and subsequent album raise around $12 million for victims of the Bangladesh catastrophe.

Rotary dial telephone

T. Rextasy!
Singing songs about hobbits and goblins in a quavering voice, Marc Bolan of *Tyrannosaurus Rex* was an icon of late 1960s progressive rock. Now former male model Marc has truncated the band's name to T. Rex and is ditching the hippie gear for an androgynous glittery look and a much younger (and female) audience.

Gene Vincent RIP
12th October 1971 Be Bop a Lula legend Gene Vincent dies in California aged 36. Although plagued by a leg injury aggravated by the car crash that killed his friend Eddie Cochran in 1961, he epitomised the rough and greasy sound and look of classic rock'n'roll.

1971

The club of 27
3rd July 1971 Jim Morrison, charismatic leader of California band the Doors, is found dead in his bathtub at his apartment in Paris aged 27. The rest of the group try to carry on but disband at the end of 1972.

Zappa attacked
10th December 1971 Frank Zappa, musical iconoclast and satirist of the pretentious and worthy, receives life-changing injuries when he is pulled off stage by a fan at the Rainbow Theatre, Finsbury Park.

Lennon leaves UK
3rd September 1971 John Lennon leaves the UK for New York with wife Yoko. He will never return. After exploring his primal therapy treatment in *John Lennon and the Plastic Ono Band*, he makes the mellower *Imagine* but can't resist a scoff at Paul McCartney on the track *How Do You Sleep*. He and Yoko end the year by wishing everyone *Happy Xmas (War is Over)* in a Christmas single.

MY FIRST 18 YEARS — TOP 10 — 1971

1. **Maggie May** *Rod Stewart*
2. **Help Me Make it Through …** *Kris Kristofferson*
3. **Theme from Shaft** *Isaac Hayes*
4. **My Sweet Lord** *George Harrison*
5. **Sweet Caroline** *Neil Diamond*
6. **Gypsies, Tramps and Thieves** *Cher*
7. **Family Affair** *Sly and the Family Stone*
8. **Just My Imagination** *The Temptations*
9. **Coz I Luv You** *Slade*
10. **I'm Still Waiting** *Diana Ross*

Hello ELO
October 1971 As the Move call it a day with a final concert tour, Roy Wood and Jeff Lynne launch the Electric Light Orchestra (ELO) with a musical blueprint inspired by the Beatles' cello-laden *I Am the Walrus*. Within a year Wood leaves to form Wizzard and Lynne takes ELO to the next level with plans for a full string section and spectacular stage effects.

PHOTO CREDITS Copyright 2024, TDM Rights BV.
Photos: A Lynne Cameron - PA Images - Getty Images / B De bergamont - Shutterstock / C PA Images - Getty Images / D Dave Rendle - / E Mirrorpix - Getty Images / F Mirrorpix - Getty Images / G William Vanderson - ulton Archive - Getty Images / H Keystone - Hulton Archive - Getty Images / I Bettmann - Getty Images / J Bettmann - Getty Images / K Ronald Grant Archive - Mary Evans / L Mondadori Portfolio Editorial - Getty Images / M John Madden - Hulton Archive - Getty Images / N Watal Asanuma Shinko Music - ulton Archive - Getty Images / O Mirrorpix - Getty Images / P Studiocanal Films Ltd - Mary Evans / Q AF Archive - Mary Evans / R PA Images - Getty Images / S David Cairns - Hulton Archive - Getty Images / T Ronald Grant Archive - Mary Evans / U Estate of Keith Morris - Redferns - Getty Images / V Jim Britt - Michael Ochs Archives - Getty Images / W Ullstein Bild - Getty Images / X Keystone - Hulton Archive - Getty Images / Y Hulton Archive - Getty Images.

1972

MY FIRST 18 YEARS

SPORT

A league of their own
The Great Britain rugby league team arrive for the World Cup in France as the underdogs, but confound expectations and win the tournament. Great Britain is captained by Clive Sullivan, the first black player to captain a British team at any sport.

Pawns or kings?
11th July 1972 It's the Cold War in miniature: seemingly invincible world chess champion Boris Spassky of the Soviet Union versus mercurial US champion Bobby Fischer in neutral Reykjavik, Iceland. After 21 games, with Fischer leading, Spassky concedes. The final score is 12 ½ to 8 ½. Fischer becomes the first American world chess champion.

Golden girl
33-year-old Mary Peters from Belfast is Britain's Olympic champion in Munich when she triumphs over her rival, the West German Heide Rosendahl, to clinch the gold medal in the pentathlon. Peters wins by just 10 points, setting a world record in the process.

Platform shoe

Gymnastic wonder
Belarussian gymnast Olga Korbut rewrites the rule book by performing unprecedented moves at the Olympics; a back flip on the beam and what becomes known as the 'Korbut flip' on the asymmetric bars. Korbut's gobsmacking performance is hugely influential and within two years, three million British girls are members of gymnastic clubs.

Women on the ball
It is a freezing afternoon on 18th November, when England and Scotland play the first ever women's football international in the UK at Ravenscraig Stadium, Greenock. England come from 2-0 down to win 3-2.

13 JAN 1972
Royal Navy officer David Bingham is sentenced to 21 years in prison after selling defence secrets to the Soviet Union to pay family debts.

16 FEB 1972
Nine-hour blackouts imposed across the country and householders asked to heat only one room as miners' pay dispute continues.

31 MAR 1972
A revival of the anti-nuclear Aldermaston marches of the 1950s and 1960s takes place, but with just 600 participants.

1972

DOMESTIC NEWS

Bloody Sunday
30th January 1972 A dark day in British history as troops open fire on unarmed demonstrators in Derry, killing fourteen. The event becomes known as Bloody Sunday and precedes one of the worst years of the Troubles with 497 fatalities across numerous protests, clashes, and bombings. In February, the British Embassy in Dublin is burnt by rioters as days later mounted police charge protesters in London. Bombings in 1972 include explosions at Aldershot Barracks, 'Bloody Friday' bombings in Belfast, and the 'Claudy' bombing or 'Bloody Monday'. In March the British government introduces direct rule over Northern Ireland and enters secret negotiations with the Provisional IRA that prove fruitless.

Miners and dockers strike
9th January 1972 Members of the National Union of Mineworkers go out on strike for seven weeks, with the fuel shortages and a cold snap leading to the Prime Minister declaring a national state of emergency as blackouts grip the nation. The strike ends in February with a pay agreement, but on 4th August a second state of emergency is declared after dock workers go out on strike following the trial of the Pentonville Five.

Economic trouble
20th January 1972 New figures demonstrate that over 1 million people are unemployed in the UK for the first time since the 1930s. The number has almost doubled in two years, casting doubt on Prime Minister Heath's handling of the economy. In November, the government freezes pay and prices in the hope of countering inflation, which falls slightly in the following months.

27 APR 1972
Five Oxford University colleges announce plans to admit up to 100 women students in 1974.

22 MAY 1972
The Dominion of Ceylon becomes the Republic of Sri Lanka but remains within the British Commonwealth.

27 JUN 1972
The Official IRA calls a ceasefire and embarks on secret talks with the British government, but sectarian violence erupts again after two weeks.

1972

Thomas Cook & Son privatised
26th May 1972 Thomas Cook, owned by the government since 1948 as part of the British Transport Commission, is privatised. The business is purchased by a consortium including the Midland bank, which later becomes the sole controller, and continues to provide holidays to the British public well into the 21st century.

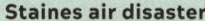

Staines air disaster
18th June 1972 British Airways Flight 548 crashes just outside Staines shortly after take-off from London Heathrow. All 118 people on their way to Brussels are killed, despite at least one person initially surviving the impact. It remains the deadliest air accident in UK history.

Battersea Fun Fair disaster
30th May 1972 The nation is horrified when the Big Dipper rollercoaster at Battersea Fun Fair comes off its rails, killing five children and injuring thirteen. An investigation finds the ride manager and engineer guilty of manslaughter, and despite attempts to reopen with a replacement ride, the park closes in 1974.

Idi Amin expels British Asians
4th August 1972 President of Uganda Idi Amin expels people of South Asian origin from the country in a wave of anti-Indian sentiment. Over the next three months, 27,200 of those who are British passport holders emigrate to the United Kingdom.

School leaving age
1st September 1972 The school leaving age in the UK is raised from 15 to 16 years old, sparking a wave of construction work across the country as schools build new classrooms to cater for the increase in student numbers.

Gay Pride
1st July 1972 The UK's very first Pride march takes place when 2,000 members of London's gay community take to the streets. The date selected is the nearest Saturday to the anniversary of the Stonewall riots in New York in 1969 and sees attendees protesting legislation targeting the gay community and demonstrating their pride in their sexuality.

28 JUL 1972
Nationwide dock strike begins and lasts until 16th August.

31 AUG 1972
American super swimmer Mark Spitz wins seven gold medals at the Munich Olympics, each in a record time.

14 SEP 1972
Death of Geoffrey Francis Fisher, former Archbishop of Canterbury who had presided over the 1953 Coronation.

1972

The Second Cod War
5th September 1972 The Second Cod War between Britain and Iceland breaks out as Iceland seeks to expand its territorial waters to 50 miles off the coast. An altercation between an Icelandic Coast Guard vessel and a British trawler, the *Peter Scott*, results in violence as the crew refuse to identify themselves and instead play *Rule Britannia!* over the radio. In November, the Foreign Secretary announces that British Navy ships will be stationed to defend trawlers in the disputed waters.

Death of Duke of Windsor
The Queen visits her uncle the Duke of Windsor on 18th May during a state visit to France. The former king is too ill to be able to attend a tea provided by the Duchess downstairs, but the Queen spends fifteen minutes with her 'Uncle David' in his first-floor sitting-room. Just ten days later he dies of complications arising from throat cancer. He is laid to rest in the Royal Burial Ground at rogmore, Windsor on 5th June after a funeral service at St. George's Chapel.

Rise of Japanese cars
1972 proves a popular year for Japanese cars, as Honda begins importing vehicles such as its Civic hatchback (photo). Nissan sells over 30,000 cars in Britain, more than three times the previous year's total, and Mazda and Toyota also enjoy success.

Tragedy for the Gloucesters
Thirty-year-old Prince William of Gloucester, elder son of the Duke and Duchess of Gloucester and cousin of the Queen, dies when his Cherokee single-engine aircraft crashes at the Goodyear International Air Trophy at Halfpenny Green near Wolverhampton on 28th August.

ROYALTY & POLITICS

Direct rule for Northern Ireland
On 30th March, the situation in Northern Ireland leads to the suspension of the Parliament of Northern Ireland which is replaced by direct rule by Westminster. William Whitelaw is appointed Secretary of State for Northern Ireland.

DO YOU REMEMBER THIS?

Rolodex

23 OCT 1972
Access credit cards - 'your flexible friend' - introduced as a rival to Barclaycard.

NOV 1972
The PEOPLE party is formed in Coventry, changing its name to the Ecology Party in 1975 and then the Green Party in 1985.

6 DEC 1972
Four members of revolutionary left-wing group The Angry Brigade are each jailed for ten years at the Old Bailey.

1972

FOREIGN NEWS

Yokoi at peace
24th January 1972 Apparently unaware of his country's surrender at the end of the Second World War, Japanese soldier Shoichi Yokoi is discovered on the Pacific island of Guam after spending 28 years hiding in the jungle.

Nixon on the world stage
21st February 1972 Richard Nixon's popularity is on a high as he becomes the first US President to visit the People's Republic of China. In May, he is the first US President to visit the Soviet Union where he agrees a drastic reduction in nuclear weaponry with Soviet leader Brezhnev.

Tricky Dicky
17th June 1972 Five men are arrested when they break into the Democratic Party headquarters in the Watergate complex in Washington DC. Dogged *Washington Post* reporters Carl Bernstein and Bob Woodward make the link between the burglars and President Nixon's re-election campaign team and uncover a much larger plan of 'dirty tricks' to thwart the Democrat challenge. Nixon defeats Senator George McGovern in a landslide in November but is already slipping towards possible impeachment.

War photo
8th June 1972 After a devastating US napalm bombardment on the Vietnamese village of Trang Bàng, Nick Ut takes the most famous war photo in history. Nine-year-old girl Phan Thi Kim Phúc is running away from her bombed village, naked and crying. The desperate moment is captured by the photographer - who then takes her to hospital. When the photo appears on the front page of the *New York Times*, it prompts a further wave of revulsion against the war.

Pocket calculator
Hewlett-Packard markets the first scientific pocket calculator, consigning the slide rule to history. The HP-35 weighs only 248 grams and measures 15 x 8.1 centimetres. It costs $395. Ultimately, 300,000 are sold.

1972

Massacre at Munich
5th - 6th September 1972 At the Olympic Games in Munich, two members of Israel's Olympic team are killed and nine kidnapped when Arab terrorist faction Black September invades the athletes' village. In an attempt by West German police to free the hostages, eleven Israelis, five terrorists and a policeman are killed. Incredibly, the Games continue.

Andean air disaster
13th October 1972 A Uruguayan plane carrying a rugby union team crashes into a glacier in the Andes on the border between Argentina and Chile. Only sixteen of the 45 passengers survive. They manage to stay alive in freezing conditions for 72 days by eating the flesh of their deceased fellow passengers.

So long Apollo
19th December 1972 With the return of Apollo 17 to Earth, the Apollo programme closes. Astronauts Gene Cernan and Harrison Schmitt are the last men to set foot on the Moon. Planning for the next crewed mission to the Moon will not begin until 2017.

The limits to growth
A new report called *The Limits to Growth* shows that humanity's future is threatened by overpopulation, environmental pollution and depletion of raw materials. Modern phosphate-based detergents are blamed for water pollution, and aerosol cans and old refrigerators spread chlorofluorocarbons (CFCs) that cause the hole in the ozone layer.

ENTERTAINMENT

Fingerbobs
Quite possibly the lowest budget children's programme ever made, *Fingerbobs*, which is first shown on 14th February, features presenter Rick Jones aka Yoffy, who sits making up stories with the help of a random selection of creatures made from gloves and sugar paper - a rodent called Fingermouse, Gulliver the seagull, Scampi the sea creature and a typically slow and steady tortoise called Flash. Simple, charming, homespun fun.

Puppy love
Andrex toilet tissue commercials featuring an adorable yellow Labrador puppy are shown for the first time this year. With guaranteed 'aah' factor, the puppy becomes the brand's enduring mascot, and helps Andrex build their market share to 30% by the end of the decade.

And...action
On the April, *Clapperboard* begins on ITV. Presented by Chris Kelly, *Clapperboard* offers a fascinating insight into the world of film and television, past and present. It's a fount of knowledge for any budding movie buff.

1972

Here is the news
John Craven's Newsround, explaining serious news in simple terms for kids, is broadcast on 4th April on BBC1. Craven fronts over 3,000 bulletins for *Newsround* until he leaves the programme in 1989. He also becomes resident news specialist on *Multicoloured Swap Shop* and *Saturday Superstore*.

Cosmo girls
The first UK issue of the notoriously racy *Cosmopolitan* magazine is published in March. Alongside articles on fabulous fashion, beauty and careers, *Cosmo* delivers frank advice on sex and relationships. Over in the US, the April issue causes a sensation when it features a naked Burt Reynolds as the first male centrefold. No subject is taboo to the magazine's international editor-in-chief, Helen Gurley-Brown, whose 1962 international bestseller, *Sex and the Single Girl*, sets the tone. Cosmo readers are single career girls; ambitious, glamorous, and sexually adventurous. Can women have it all? Cosmo says 'yes'!

Evel Knievel doll released
Ideal Toys release a six-inch action figure of American stunt motorcyclist Evel Knievel in the same year the real Evel attempts a high-publicised jump across the Snake River Canyon in Idaho (his parachute releases prematurely, ruining the stunt, but he gets away with only minor injuries).

Watership Down
Richard Adams' epic novel about a band of rabbits risking everything to establish a new warren goes on to sell 50 million copies worldwide. The 1978 animation film is an instant classic, fuelled by the Art Garfunkel's song *Bright Eyes*.

Pebble Mill at One
In January, the government lifts the restrictions on the numbers of hours of broadcasting and schedulers begin to look at expanding daytime programming. *Pebble Mill at One*, the magazine programme filmed in the foyer of the BBC's Pebble Mill studios in Birmingham, is first broadcast at 1pm on 2nd October and remains a fixture of daytime television until 1986.

Give us a wave
As the 1970s becomes renowned as the decade of the disaster movie, *The Poseidon Adventure*, about an ailing ocean liner capsized by a tidal wave, vies to be the one filled with the most hysterical screaming. An ensemble cast play a small group of survivors led by Gene Hackman's maverick preacher, taking their chances and dicing with death as they navigate their way out of the topsy-turvy vessel.

I've started so I'll finish
Hopeful quizzers take to the black chair to face questions asked by Magnus Magnusson in *Mastermind*, which is first broadcast on BBC1 late at night on 11th September (it's moved to a primetime slot the following year).

1972

A British *Jesus Christ Superstar*
Andrew Lloyd-Webber and Tim Rice's biblical rock opera *Jesus Christ Superstar* opens at the Palace Theatre on 9th August with Paul Nicholas moving from *Hair* to take on the role of Jesus, Stephen Tate as Judas and Dana Gillespie playing Mary Magdalene. *Jesus Christ Superstar* began as an album before stage musical adaptations on Broadway and in Australia and by the time it opens in London, the timing, the anticipation and the buzz ensure it's a smash hit. *Jesus Christ Superstar* runs for 3,358 performances until 1980, then tours the UK from 1983.

Retail therapy
There's rarely a dull moment at Grace Brothers Department Store, what with Mr Humphries camping it up in his latest outrageous sales promotion costume, or Mrs Slocombe, head of the ladies' department, changing her hair colour and worrying about her pussy. The pilot episode of the retail comedy *Are You Being Served?* is broadcast on 8th September. Famed for its double entendres, a series follows in 1973, with nine more, and a 1977 feature film, produced over the next twelve years.

The Adventures of Black Beauty
The Adventures of Black Beauty begins on ITV on 27th September and although inspired by Anna Sewell's 1877 novel, the action is instead shifted forward to the turn of the twentieth century and places Beauty in the care of widower Dr. James Gordon and his two children Vicky and the very un-Edwardian-sounding Kevin. Featured in ITV's family-friendly Sunday teatime slot, the uplifting *Black Beauty* theme tune, Denis King's *Galloping Home*, becomes more famous than the series itself, ingrained in the memory of every 1970s kid.

The Godfather
'A bloody good story, or a good bloody story' is how Derek Malcolm describes *The Godfather* in his *Guardian* review. Francis Ford Coppola's monumental gangster film based on Mario Puzo's novel about the Corleone family is released in the UK on 24th August. Conflict over casting decisions had dogged the early stages of production, with Coppola digging in his heels to cast Marlon Brando as Vito Corleone and Al Pacino as his son and heir, Michael; Brando wins an Oscar and *The Godfather* becomes the highest-grossing film of 1972.

Birth of Pong
The video game revolution begins in America with the release of the Pong arcade game on 29th November. Three years later, the simple table-tennis game is adapted for play on a console connected to a television allowing early gamers to pong and ping to their heart's content from the comfort of their armchair.

1972

MUSIC

Paul spreads his Wings
8th February 1972 Paul and Linda McCartney hit the road with their new band Wings. They make their live debut at Nottingham University when they turn up unannounced and offer to do a lunchtime gig. Tickets are just 40 pence.

American Pie
15th January 1972 Don McLean was inspired to write his seven minute-epic *American Pie*, now at No. 1 in the US, by the death of his idol Buddy Holly in 1959. It tells the story of rock music with biblical imagery and cloaked allusions to Dylan, the Beatles, the Rolling Stones, Janis Joplin and others.

Far from plain
21st January 1972 A session on John Peel's Radio 1 evening show introduces Roxy Music, who don't even have a record deal yet. The band is an art-cum-music project fronted by Bryan Ferry, whose strangled diction makes for a sneering vocal style. Musically and visually they mix Hollywood cool with futuristic sonic wizardry and costumes to match. A dazzlingly inventive debut album is followed by the single *Virginia Plain*, its rococo lyrics referencing everything from Fred Astaire movies to casinos and chic American cars.

Heartbreak tale
11th March 1972 At No. 1 in the UK is one of the most affecting heartbreak ballads ever, *Without You* by Harry Nilsson, who is best known for singing *Everybody's Talkin'* over the *Midnight Cowboy* credits. Written by Pete Ham and Tom Evans of Badfinger, its sales are so huge that the two young songwriters should be set up for life. Instead, disputes over royalties lead to the suicides of both men, in 1975 and 1983 respectively.

Bowie breakthrough
16th June 1972 After years as one of UK rock's fringe figures, David Bowie makes a huge breakthrough with *The Rise and Fall of Ziggy Stardust and the Spiders from Mars*. On the album he assumes the role of an androgynous rock star who soars to fame as the Earth awaits an apocalypse. The Bowie look and style defines glam rock at its most serious and sexually questioning, underpinned by Mick Ronson's searing guitar.

Bagpipe blast
15th April 1972 Over the years the record chart has featured singing nuns, chickens, dogs and even ventriloquists, but never bagpipe bands. Standing proudly at No. 1 are the Pipes and Drums and Military Band of the Royal Scots Dragoon Guards with the eighteenth-century hymn *Amazing Grace*. Its million-selling success is generally credited to (or blamed on) Radio 1 DJ Tony Blackburn. A vocal-only version by folk singer Judy Collins is also one of the year's top sellers.

1972

School's Out!
29th July 1972 As schools break for summer, never has a record release been better timed than *School's Out* by Alice Cooper. Alice and his horror movie-derived stage show, his pet snake, garage band sound and all-American sweetheart name are calculated to appal parents and delight adolescents.

MY FIRST 18 YEARS TOP 10 1972

1. Let's Stay Together *Al Green*
2. All the Young Dudes *Mott the Hoople*
3. Sylvia's Mother *Dr Hook and the Medicine Show*
4. Me and Mrs Jones *Billy Paul*
5. Starman *David Bowie*
6. Mama Weer All Crazee Now *Slade*
7. Rocket Man *Elton John*
8. Ain't No Sunshine *Michael Jackson*
9. I Can See Clearly Now *Johnny Nash*
10. Guitar Man *Bread*

Osmonds everywhere
Osmondmania grips the country. Twelve year-old Donny revives *Puppy Love* and *Too Young* and joins his Mormon brothers on a string of Top Tenners before his younger brother Jimmy - just nine years old - bags the Christmas No. 1 with *Long Haired Lover from Liverpool*. Waiting in the wings is sister Marie, soon to top the chart with *Paper Roses*.

The Philly sound
Challenging Motown's grip on making precision-tuned radio-friendly soul music are producers Kenny Gamble and Leon Huff at the Philadelphia International label. The 'Philly sound' they have perfected matches great rhythm tracks to sweet orchestral backings on hits for Harold Melvin, Billy Paul and the O'Jays. Another Philly producer, Thom Bell, is behind the hits of the Stylistics while Barry White gives the template a twist with his vocal group Love Unlimited.

All crazee now
While glam rock avatars T. Rex are beginning to stutter, Wolverhampton band Slade's raucous and cheeky brand of updated rock'n'roll reaches out to the guys as well as the girls. Their trademarks are hits with deliberately misspelt song titles like *Take Me Bak 'Ome* and *Mama Weer All Crazee Now*, while guitarist Dave Hill's platform boots and singer Noddy Holder's mutton-chop sideburns make the Clockwork Orange-influenced look the height of teen fashion.

PHOTO CREDITS Copyright 2024, TDM Rights BV.
Photos: **A** Picture Alliance - Getty Images / **B** David Attie - Archive Photos - Getty Images / **C** R. Viner - Hulton Archive - Getty Images / **D** Independent News and Media - Hulton Archive - Getty Images / **E** Evening Standard - Hulton Archive - Getty Images / **F** Evening Standard - Hulton Archive - Getty Images / **G** Keystone - Hulton Royals Collection - Getty Images / **H** Bettmann - Getty Images / **I** Alessandra Benedetti - Corbis News - Getty Images / **J** Express - Archive Photos - Getty Images / **K** Photo12 - Universal Images Group Editorial - Getty Images / **L** Tim Roney - Hulton Archive - Getty Images / **M** Tony Evans Timelapse Library Ltd - Hulton Archive - Getty Images / **N** D Morrison - Hulton Archive - Getty Images / **O** Studiocanal Films Ltd - Mary Evans / **P** Silver Screen Collection - Moviepix - Getty Images / **Q** Brian Cooke - Redferns - Getty Images / **R** Michael Ochs Archives - Redferns - Getty Images / **S** Hulton Archive - Getty Images / **T** George Wilkes Archive - Hulton Archive - Getty Images.

1973

MY FIRST 18 YEARS

SPORT

Football's FA Cup Fairytale
When Second Division side Sunderland arrive at Wembley on 5th May for their FA Cup final match against Leeds, few people fancy their chances against a tough team who are the 1972 Cup winners and have dominated First Division football over the past couple of seasons. But in one of the most spectacular examples of giant-killing football, the Black Cats win 1-0, with Ian Porterfield's goal coming in the thirty-second minute, and several outstanding saves from the Wearsiders' goalie Jimmy Montgomery to keep them ahead. When the final whistle goes and Sunderland's manager Bob Stokoe runs onto the pitch, it's a fairytale ending for a team whose fanbase is as loyal as it is large.

Flying Scot quits at the top
Following the death of his Tyrrell-Ford team-mate Francois Cevert in a practice race at Watkins Glen on 6th October, three-times world F1 champion, Jackie Stewart announces his retirement.

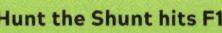

Hunt the Shunt hits F1
James Hunt makes his debut in Formula One racing as a driver for Hesketh; his highest position is second in the US Grand Prix. The RAC award him with the Campbell trophy at the end of the season for best British driver.

Battle of the Sexes
In the year the US Open pays equal prize money to male and female players, a tennis match between 55-year-old Bobby Riggs and 29-year-old Billie Jean King takes place on 20th September. Billed as the 'Battle of the Sexes' the contest had arisen due to Riggs's public declarations about the inferiority of the women's game. After a $100,000 prize is offered, King agrees to take up the challenge. Watched by a global television audience of 90 million, King wins 6-4, 6-4, 6-3, a significant point scored in King's long-running battle for equality in the sport.

7 JAN 1973
British Darts Organisation is founded.

5 FEB 1973
The Wombles begins on BBC1, narrated by Bernard Cribbins and with music by Mike Batt.

27 MAR 1973
The first women traders are admitted onto the floor of the London Stock Exchange.

1973

The Sunshine Showdown
Number-one-ranked heavyweight boxer George Foreman and heavyweight champion Joe Frazier slug it out on 22nd January in Kingston, Jamaica in a bid to become WBA, WBC and The Ring champion. Foreman overpowers Frazier who hits the canvas six times in just two rounds before the match is stopped and Foreman declared the winner.

DOMESTIC NEWS

IRA bombs England
1973 sees the trouble in Northern Ireland spread to London and Manchester, with a series of bombings taking place across the country. Thirteen bombs are planted in the capital, ten of which detonate. These include bombs at Whitehall and the Old Bailey, and in stations such as Victoria, King's Cross and Euston, injuring over 60 people. In March, a referendum on sovereignty in Northern Ireland sees 98.9% of voters choose to remain within the UK, although turn-out for Catholics is less than 1%.

European Economic Community
1st January 1973 Britain enters the EEC alongside fellow new members Ireland and Denmark.

Everton shelled by Iceland
26 May 1973 British Trawler *Everton* refuses to follow instructions from the Icelandic Coast Guard and is shelled as it flees to the protection of British Navy ship HMS *Jupiter*. This latest incident in the Second Cod War precedes a number of escalations and collisions throughout the year before an agreement is signed in November bringing the conflict to an end.

London Bridge opens
17th March 1973 The newly completed London Bridge, at least the fourth to stand on the site, is opened by Her Majesty the Queen. Traffic flows over the newly widened bridge, reducing the congestion that has been prevalent in the city since the old bridge was dismantled in 1968.

Secondary banking crisis
The country's economic problems continue in 1973, as the end of the year witnesses the start of the secondary banking crisis, which would last into 1974. The sharp drop in property prices and an increase in interest rates threatens many secondary lending banks with bankruptcy.

---

8 APR 1973
Jackie Stewart wins the BRDC International Trophy at Silverstone.

18 MAY 1973
Soviet party leader Leonid Brezhnev visits West Germany.

24 JUN 1973
90-year-old Eamon de Valera, the world's oldest head of state, resigns as President of Ireland.

1973

New radio stations
8th October 1973 The London Broadcasting Company (photo David Jessel) begins broadcasting and becomes the first commercial independent radio station to operate legally within the UK. LBC's talk radio content is followed eight days later by the launch of Capital Radio, which focuses on music programming.

Value added tax
1st April 1973 Value added tax replaces purchase tax in the UK. Unlike its predecessor, VAT is applied at the point of sale, not at the point of manufacture, and is fixed at 10%. Purchase tax had varied based on the perceived luxuriousness of the goods in question, from 13% for small items, up to 55% for purchases such as motor vehicles.

Oil crisis
4th November 1973 Angered by western support for Israel in the Yom Kippur War, the Organization of the Petroleum Exporting Countries (OPEC) hits back by raising prices and reducing supplies, triggering an oil crisis with huge consequences for all western economies, forcing the introduction of petrol rationing by some and pushing up material and transport costs.

Pizza Hut opens
American restaurant chain Pizza Hut opens its first UK branch in Islington, London. Pizza Hut expands to offer a variety of branches, from diner-style restaurants to take-away premises, and quickly becomes a firm high street favourite.

ROYALTY & POLITICS

Princess Anne marries at the Abbey
On 14th November, the same day as her brother Prince Charles turns twenty-five, Princess Anne marries Captain Mark Phillips at Westminster Abbey wearing a medieval-style gown and Queen Mary's fringe tiara.

Queen opens Opera House of Oz
During a tour of Australia, on 20th October, the Queen opens the Sydney Opera House.

Tory sex scandals
Government ministers Lord Lambton and Earl Jellicoe both resign this year after the secret service discover their associations with prostitutes. The story breaks when photographs of Lambton are sold to the papers.

1 JUL 1973
A merger of the British Museum Library and the National Lending Library for Science & Technology at Boston Spa, creates the British Library.

15 AUG 1973
Sitcom *Man About the House* starring Richard O'Sullivan begins on ITV.

3 SEP 1973
Death of J. R. R. Tolkien, scholarly creator of *'Lord of the Rings'*.

1973

FOREIGN NEWS

LBJ dies
22nd January 1973 Lyndon Baines Johnson, 36th President of the US, dies at his Texas home aged 64.

'Peace with honour'
27th January 1973 US President Richard Nixon signs the Paris Peace Accords. The historic agreement with the governments of North and South Vietnam ensures a temporary ceasefire, after which US troops will withdraw.

Skylab
14th May 1973 Skylab, the US space station, is launched. Three extended manned missions are completed aboard the station by the end of November.

Watergate rumbles on
16th July 1973 The revelation that President Nixon has been secretly recording conversations in the Oval Office opens a whole new avenue of investigation into the Watergate burglary and whether he knew of it or approved it. The newly convened US Senate Watergate Committee demands access to the tapes and Nixon refuses.

Mobile calling
3rd April 1973 Inventor Martin Cooper makes the very first cell phone call with a prototype of the Motorola DynaTAC, a 2.5lb cordless phone connected to an antenna on the roof of the hotel across the street. Cheekily, Cooper calls a major competitor to report that Motorola has succeeded in making mobile phone calls.

Yom Kippur War
6th October 1973 On Israel's holiest day, Yom Kippur, Egypt and Syria launch a surprise attack to recapture the territories lost in the Six-Day War in 1967. Egyptian troops cross the Suez Canal and enter the Sinai Desert as Syria retakes the Golan Heights. Israel launches a counter-offensive and pushes the Egyptians back across the Suez Canal. On 24th October, when Israeli troops are within one hundred kilometres of Cairo, the US presses Israel to sign an armistice.

Picasso
8th April 1973 Pablo Picasso dies at the age of 91. He was the founder of cubism and creator of masterpieces such as *Guernica*, depicting the German-Italian bombardment of the city during the Spanish Civil War.

17 OCT 1973
The price of oil increases by 70% leading to rocketing petrol prices and pressure on the UK economy.

1 NOV 1973
Final issue of the underground, counterculture magazine *Oz* is published.

5 DEC 1973
50mph speed limits put in place on UK roads in a bid to save fuel.

1973

Dictator Pinochet
11th September 1973 With CIA support, General Augusto Pinochet stages a military coup against Chile's socialist President Salvador Allende. The object is to ensure that the country will not be the next domino to fall to communism. During the coup, the presidential palace is bombed and Allende is killed. Pinochet's tenure as President is vicious and uncompromising.

High, wide and handsome
It's a giddy year for architecture as dazzling new structures are unveiled in different parts of the world. The Sears Tower in Chicago becomes the world's tallest building at 442 metres. The iconic Sydney Opera House is opened by Queen Elizabeth II. In Istanbul, the Bosphorus Bridge connects Europe and Asia for the first time across the Bosphorus Strait. But the new buildings of most long-term significance are the twin towers of the new World Trade Center: construction has taken ten years and final costs are estimated at $900 million.

ETA attacks
20th December 1973 Luis Carrero Blanco, General Franco's (photo) Prime Minister and right-hand man, is killed in a bomb attack by the Basque separatist movement ETA.

Kissinger controversy
10th December 1973 The most surprising and controversial award in the history of the Nobel Prize is made as US Secretary of State Henry Kissinger and North Vietnamese negotiator Le Duc Tho are jointly awarded the Nobel Prize for Peace. Kissinger is widely seen as a power broker who has acted with a consistent disregard for democracy and human rights. Tho declines the prize but Kissinger accepts.

Fisher Price Tree-house

147

1973

ENTERTAINMENT

Delia's Debut
After appearing in the cookery slot on East Anglia Television's *Look East* programme, Delia Smith fronts her own BBC1 programme, *Family Fare*, which is first broadcast on 15th May. She writes several successful cookbooks this decade including 1978's best-selling *Complete Cookery Course* and is rapidly on track to become the doyenne of British food writers and television cooks.

Teddy Edward
Based on the books by Mollie and Patrick Edward, *Teddy Edward* is a gentle tale of a toy bear and his friends, told through still photographs and narrated by Richard Baker. It begins on BBC1 on 5th January.

Game of the Year
The game Mastermind, which pits code-maker against code-breaker, with the help of a series of coloured, plastic pegs, is announced as Game of the Year. First launched in 1970, Mastermind has huge international success selling 30 million during the decade.

Big biba
Biba moves into the old seven-storey Derry and Tom's store in Kensington High Street. 'Big' Biba is a phenomenon, offering the complete Biba lifestyle and becoming London's second-biggest tourist attraction after the Tower of London.

Let's do the time warp
Richard O'Brien's musical fantasy, *The Rocky Horror Show*, opens at the 63-seat performance space, Royal Court Theatre Upstairs on 19th June. Made on a shoestring budget, with costumes begged, borrowed and adapted, *The Rocky Horror Show* takes inspiration from old Hollywood sci-fi B-movies, goth horror and burlesque and blends it with a witty and knowingly camp celebration of seventies sexual fluidity. The production later moves to the King's Road Theatre where it continues until 1979. With the release of a 1975 film, *The Rocky Horror Picture Show*, this wickedly wacky musical gains a loyal, global following cementing Rocky Horror's status as a cult classic.

Charley says…
Kids in 1973 are kept safe from daily hazards with the help of Tony and his pet cat Charley, whose feline wisdom warns against going off with strangers or playing with matches. Charley's meowed advice is in fact the voice of radio DJ Kenny Everett.

1973

The Wicker Man
A folk horror about paganism and sacrifice, The Wicker Man, released 6th December, is British film-making at its most weird and inventive. The sacrificial target in question is Edward Woodward, playing a devoutly Christian police officer who travels to a remote Scottish island in search of a missing girl, only to discover the inhabitants are fully-fledged pagans under the patriarchal leadership of Christopher Lee's fiendish Lord Summerisle. The film's horrifying climax goes on to have a wide-ranging cultural impact.

Wheely, wheely funny
Half man, half walking disaster, Frank Spencer, of Some Mothers Do 'Ave 'Em, goes to a roller disco and finds himself accidentally flying through the exit doors and dodging the traffic of Edmonton in the episode 'Fathers' Clinic' which airs on 20th December. Michael Crawford, who plays the luckless, neurotic but ultimately adorable Spencer (ably supported by Michele Dotrice as wife Betty), performs all his own stunts in the series.

Lizzie Dripping
In East Midlands dialect, 'Lizzie Dripping' is a term for a girl with an overly active imagination and a tendency to tell fibs. Prolific children's author Helen Cresswell uses this as the premise for a children's drama serial, which begins on BBC1 on 13th March. Cresswell's main character, Penelope Arbuckle, is a typical 'Lizzie Dripping' who discovers a mischievous witch in her village. Of course, only Lizzie can see her. Tina Heath who plays Lizzie goes on to become Blue Peter's tenth presenter in 1979.

Away you go!
We Are the Champions, presented by Ron Pickering, begins on BBC1 on 13th June - an inter-school competition which is 70% school sports day and 30% It's a Knockout. The highlight of every episode comes after the swimming races when Pickering shouts, 'Away you go!' and the kids forget their savage rivalry and dive bomb into the pool en masse. Joyful chaos.

Enter the Dragon, exit Bruce Lee
On 20th July, Bruce Lee, legendary martial arts expert and actor, is found dead in his Hong Kong hotel room of cerebral edema. He is just 32. Lee's last film, Enter the Dragon, acquires almost mythological status when it is released a month after his death, becoming the highest-grossing martial arts film of all time.

1973

Petrifying puppets
The hallowed halls of children's TV puppetry welcome a number of strange new arrivals this year. *Pipkins* (photo) introduces attention-seeking Hartley Hare along with a motley selection of animal friends all of whom have a different regional accent. Pig is a Brummie, Mrs Penguin a Geordie and the blank-eyed, frankly petrifying Topov the Monkey is a Cockney. If the *Pipkins* posse wasn't odd enough, then over at *Hickory House*, which first broadcasts on 12th March, there is sleepy, banana-guzzling Humphrey the Cushion, and a red-nosed, obsessively houseproud kitchen mop called Dusty Mop!

Wholegrain nostalgia
Ridley Scott directs a TV commercial for Hovis bread that strikes a chord with nostalgic Brits. Showing a boy pushing a bike up a cobbled hill (the famously picturesque Gold Hill in Shaftesbury) to the strains of Dvorak's *New World Symphony* played with mournful tones by the Ashington Colliery Brass Band, the tune will forever more be known as 'the Hovis tune' and the advert is later voted the UK's favourite of all time in a 2006 poll.

Pucker up
The lip balm revolution begins when skincare company Bonne Bell develop a special balm to help protect skiers' lips. Before long the balm is sold in a range of sickly flavours for the teen market under the name Lip Smackers.

Why Don't You?
Why don't you just switch off television set and go out and do something less boring instead? That is the rather ironic question posed by the opening credits of *Why Don't You*, which becomes a fixture of morning telly through the school summer holidays as of 20th August 1973.

 **MUSIC**

Guess the subject
January 1973 Peaking at No. 3 in the UK, Carly Simon's *You're So Vain* has everybody guessing who she has in mind. The betting is on infamous womaniser Warren Beatty but could it be Mick Jagger, who can be heard on backing vocals?

On the dark side
1st March 1973 Pink Floyd release *The Dark Side of the Moon*, an album exploring the theme of madness that has taken over a year to record and fine-tune. Their most emotional work, it propels them into the big league of British bands in the US, where it spends over 730 weeks in the LP chart.

1973

Tubular Bells
25th May 1973 The first release from Richard Branson's new Virgin record label is Mike Oldfield's *Tubular Bells*. It's a mesmeric, slow-building 50-minute work featuring scores of overdubs by Oldfield playing different instruments and narration by Viv Stanshall of the Bonzo Dog Doo Dah Band. The album is not only a surprise hit, its main theme is heard in *The Exorcist*.

Second time unlucky
7th April 1973 Ever hopeful, Cliff Richard has another go at winning Eurovision with *Power to All Our Friends*. He comes third. Anne Marie David wins it for Luxembourg with *Wonderful Dream*.

Join the love train!
24th March 1973 Philadelphia soulsters the O'Jays invite the people of every nation to join hands and form a *Love Train*. The song's mentions of Egypt, Israel, Russia and China catalogue the enmities that characterise global politics in 1973. Hopelessly idealistic, *Love Train* makes the world seem just a little more jolly

Yellow ribbons
21st April 1973 At No. 1 in the UK is the year's biggest-selling global hit. Dawn's *Tie A Yellow Ribbon Round The Old Oak Tree* is a story song that resonates with returning servicemen from prison camps in Vietnam who really are welcomed home by yellow ribbons.

Rhymin' Simon
6th May 1973 Paul Simon starts his first solo tour since splitting with Art Garfunkel to promote *There Goes Rhymin' Simon*, an album embracing gospel, reggae and doo-wop styles and including his comment on Watergate malaise, *American Tune*.

Bowie and Reed
3rd July 1973 David Bowie announces his retirement from live performing but his real aim is to abandon his alter ego stage creations, Ziggy Stardust and Aladdin Sane. His skills as a producer benefit Velvet Underground founder Lou Reed, whose *Transformer* takes him from cult figure to major star. Amazingly, iconic track *Walk on the Wild Side* is added to the Radio 1 playlist, despite clear references to cross-dressing, drugs and oral sex.

Suzi Q
Under the Chinnichap banner, songwriting team Nicky Chinn and Mike Chapman and veteran producer Mickie Most deliver hit after hit for Sweet, Mud, Suzi Quatro and more. Suzi is a leather-clad, bass-playing rock'n'roller from Detroit whose sound is pared-down and punky. It's no wonder that she'll be chosen to play streetwise Leather Truscadero in the 1950s-set US TV comedy *Happy Days*.

1973

Stevie feels the sunshine
6th August 1973 Stevie Wonder lies in a coma for four days after a car accident in North Carolina but returns to live performing within weeks. Having won full creative freedom from Motown, his albums retain the soulful accessibility of earlier records but are now explorative, innovatory and deeply philosophical. When asked by an interviewer how he can write *You Are the Sunshine of My Life* when he has never seen the Sun, he explains 'but I can feel it, man'.

Slade stalled
4th July 1973 With a US tour beckoning, Slade drummer Don Powell is seriously injured in a car crash that kills his girlfriend. The band opt to stay in the UK and help him learn to play the drums again. They return to form in December with the song that Noddy Holder will call his pension because it is released year after year - *Merry Xmas Everybody*. Recorded during a New York heatwave, it brings much-needed hope and fun to a nation about to knuckle down to a three-day week.

MY FIRST 18 YEARS TOP 10 — 1973
1. **Superstition** Stevie Wonder
2. **Stuck in the Middle with You** Stealers Wheel
3. **Nutbush City Limits** Ike and Tina Turner
4. **Loving and Free** Kiki Dee
5. **Like Sister and Brother** The Drifters
6. **Goodbye Yellow Brick Road** Elton John
7. **Live and Let Die** Paul McCartney and Wings
8. **Roll Away the Stone** Mott the Hoople
9. **See My Baby Jive** Wizzard
10. **Reelin' in the Years** Steely Dan

Golden oldies
7th July 1973 As the Carpenters proclaim it's *Yesterday Once More*, the hits of 1973 prove their point. There are revivals and comebacks galore, by Neil Sedaka, the Drifters, Perry Como, Ike and Tina Turner and many more, while TV-advertised compilations of past hits clog the album charts and 'golden oldie' radio explodes in the US. Roy Wood's new band Wizzard bring back the Phil Spector wall of sound, 10cc recall the Beach Boys on *The Dean and I*, while David Essex stars as a would-be early 1960s rock star in the film *That'll Be The Day* and storms the chart with *Rock On*, which name-checks James Dean and blue suede shoes.

Walrus of Love
After working for years as an arranger and producer, the rotund Barry White has become an unlikely superstar and sex icon. His every record is soaked in lush orchestrations and bass rhythms as belly-deep as his voice.

1974

MY FIRST 18 YEARS

SPORT

Sunday league
In 1974, Sundays are still viewed as a day of rest. But an energy crisis caused by spiralling oil costs and a strike by the National Union of Mineworkers is the catalyst for the introduction of Sunday football league matches this year. With Edward Heath's three-day week affecting the UK in the first two months of the year, energy saving measures are crucial, including daytime matches that require no floodlights. The first Sunday match is played between Millwall and Fulham at The Den at 11:30am on 20th January. Millwall wins 1-0.

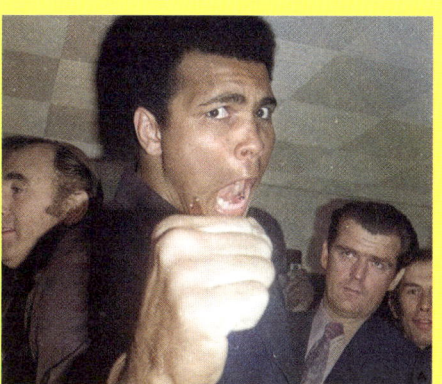

Rumble in the Jungle
The long-awaited and much-hyped fight between champion heavyweight George Foreman and Muhammad Ali takes place in Kinshasa, Zaire on 30th October. Foreman's heft and power is more than matched by Ali's clever tactics, including his dope-and-rope technique, and after eight rounds, Foreman is floored by a straight punch to the face from Ali. The fight attracts an estimated global audience of one billion and is considered one of the greatest sporting moments of all time.

DO YOU REMEMBER THIS?

Monchichi monkey

Nude interruption
A streaker makes the front pages after he runs onto the pitch stark naked at Twickenham on 20th April during a friendly rugby international between England and France. The man had made the streak for a £10 bet after drinking several pints of lager. The police officers who catch up with him cover his genitals with a helmet before carting him off to Twickenham magistrates' court (where his £10 bet is immediately handed over as a fine for 'insulting behaviour'). He returns to the ground as one of the founding fathers of a streaking craze which continues throughout the 70s and beyond.

1 JAN 1974
News Year's Day becomes a public holiday for the first time.

1 FEB 1974
Ronnie Biggs, one of the perpetrators of the Great Train Robbery is arrested in Brazil.

6 MAR 1974
Miners' strike ends after a 35% wage increase is agreed and two days later, the UK returns to a five-day working week.

1974

Love match
There is romance in the air at Wimbledon this year when American golden couple Jimmy Connors and Chris Evert arrive at the tournament engaged to be married. When they each win the singles title, it seems like the perfect outcome. At the Wimbledon Champions' Dinner the pair dance to 'The Girl That I Marry' but in October, they break off their engagement, deciding that tennis must come before love.

Conteh the champion
Liverpudlian John Conteh becomes WBC World Light Heavyweight Champion after defeating Jorge Ahumada at the Empire Pool, London on 1st October. It's an excellent year for Conteh, who not only has an episode of *This Is Your Life* dedicated to him, but also wins the second series of masters of sport TV competition *Superstars*.

Flixborough Disaster
1st June 1974 The chemical industry reels as news breaks of an explosion at a chemical plant near the village of Flixborough, North Lincolnshire. Faulty, modified equipment leads to a large cloud of hydrogen leaking and igniting, killing 28 people and injuring 36 more. There is a national outcry over the event, which occurs as a new Health and Safety at Work Act is passed through Parliament.

DOMESTIC NEWS

Three-day week
1st January 1974 Coal shortages caused by industrial action lead to a reduction in the generation of electricity, with Prime Minister Edward Heath introducing the three-day working week. Businesses are limited to three consecutive days of electricity consumption in a seven-day period. It lasts until 7th March.

First McDonald's
13th November 1974 Britain gets its first McDonald's restaurant, in Woolwich, southeast London. Soon the restaurant chain begins to compete with established brands like Wimpy, and the so-called 'Golden Arches' become a familiar site on British high streets.

Oil embargo ends
18th March 1974 The Organisation of Arab Petroleum Exporting Countries finally lift their embargo on oil exports to the United Kingdom, relieving the pressure on the fuel shortages felt across the country.

2 APR 1974
Tatum O'Neil, aged 10, becomes youngest recipient of an Academy Award for Best Supporting Actress.

6 MAY 1974
Chancellor Willy Brandt resigns amidst controversy over his aide's ties with the Stasi.

13 JUN 1974
Prince Charles makes his maiden speech in the House of Lords.

1974

Red Lion Square
15th June 1974 Members of the National Front marching through London clash with counter-protesters in Red Lion Square. Individuals representing the International Marxist Group charge a police cordon separating them from the marchers, and riots break out. In the melee twenty-year-old student Kevin Gately is killed.

Ceefax launched
23rd September 1974 The BBC launches Ceefax, a pun on the words 'see facts', as the first teletext service in the world. Starting with 30 pages, viewers can use their television remotes to type in a page number before viewing useful information on a variety of topics

Economic trouble
Economic trouble for the UK continues throughout 1974. Aside from the strikes and the three-day week implemented in January, figures launched at the beginning of the year show the country had entered its first post-war recession at the end of 1973. Inflation reaches a 34 year high of 17.2%.

Lord Lucan disappears!
7th November 1974 London is rocked by the disappearance of Lord Lucan, following the murder of the children's nanny. Lucan's wife is found injured, claiming that her husband has attacked her and murdered the nanny. Lucan's car is found abandoned and stained with blood, and the peer disappears, never to be heard from again.

The Birmingham Six
21st November 1974 The bombing of two pubs in Birmingham kills 21 people and is the single most deadly attack on the country since the end of the Second World War. Six Irish men are arrested almost immediately amid concerns the IRA is to blame and undergo brutal treatment at the hands of the police. Their conviction, on flawed evidence, becomes one of the country's most famous miscarriages of justice.

The Troubles
Trouble in Northern Ireland continues as the collapse of the Sunnydale agreement leads to the re-establishment of direct rule. 1974 sees many bombings across the country, including the M62 massacre which kills 12 people. Bombs in the summer detonate in Dublin and Monaghan planted by the Ulster Volunteer Force, and in London at the Houses of Parliament and the Tower of London by the IRA. October brings the Guildford pub bombings, killing five, and an attack on Brook's club in London. Sports Minister Denis Howell's family survive a car bomb, and the home of Edward Heath is targeted.

3 JUL 1974
Long-standing Leeds United coach Don Revie accepts £200,000 to become the new England manager.

29 AUG 1974
Hippies and police clash when the latter try to close down the illegal, Windsor Free Festival.

14 SEP 1974
Giant pandas Chia-Chia and Ching-Ching arrive at London Zoo, the result of a diplomatic deal with China brokered by Edward Heath.

1974

ROYALTY & POLITICS

The balance of power
Juggling several crises and locked in a battle with trade unions, a beleaguered Edward Heath calls a General Election for 28th February to secure a new mandate for his policies. His gamble backfires and he resigns, and Harold Wilson returns as Labour Prime Minister. Labour wins a second election on 11th October with a tiny majority of just three seats. It is the first time since 1910 that two general elections have been held in one year.

Attempted kidnapping
20th March 1974 Princess Anne narrowly escapes a kidnapping as she and husband Captain Mark Philips wrestle with attacker Ian Bail. Bail stops the Princess's car and shoots her driver and protection officer, before attempting to drag her from the vehicle. He is foiled by intervening citizens and the timely arrival of the police, despite shooting a police officer and a member of the public. No one is killed, and Bail is detained under the Mental Health Act.

Death of the Duke of Gloucester
Henry, Duke of Gloucester, uncle to the Queen and the last surviving son of George V, dies on 10th June at his home, Barnwell Manor, following a period of ill health.

Hover bother
During his General Election campaign, Liberal leader Jeremy Thorpe tours the coastal towns of south-west Britain via hovercraft, the transport mode of the moment.

FOREIGN NEWS

Worst air disaster
3rd March 1974 The highest fatalities to date in an air disaster occur when the rear cargo hatch of a DC-10 of Turkish Airlines Flight 981 flies open over Meaux, France. The sudden pressure difference causes the hull to burst and all 340 passengers and crew are killed instantly.

Terracotta Army
29th March 1974 A magnificently preserved Terracotta Army of life-size figures is discovered at Xi'an in China. The sculptures date from 210-209 BC and were buried with the body of Emperor Qin Shi Huang to protect him in the afterlife. The three pits in which they are found contain more than 8,000 soldiers, 130 chariots with 520 horses, and 150 cavalry horses.

---

16 OCT 1974
Riots break out at the Maze prison in Belfast.

27 NOV 1974
The Prevention of Terrorism Act is passed giving police special powers when they suspect terrorism.

22 DEC 1974
The London home of Conservative party leader and ex-PM Edward Heath is bombed by the Provisional IRA.

1974

Golf launch
30th March 1974 A worthy successor to the immensely popular but outdated Beetle rolls off the Volkswagen production line at Wolfsburg. An affordable small family hatchback, the first Golf model sells around thirty million.

Four billion
1st April 1974 The US Census Bureau calculates that for the first time there are more than four billion people on the planet - a doubling of the world's population since 1930.

Pompidou est mort, Brandt tritt zurück
April - May 1974 Within a month, Europe loses two of its most effective political leaders. French President Georges Pompidou dies aged 62 having initiated the large-scale industrialisation of France. On 6th May, West German Chancellor Willy Brandt resigns with his secretary revealed as an East German spy and the oil crisis threatening his social reforms.

Rubik's cube
19th May 1974 Hungarian mathematician Ernő Rubik has a question: 'How can I make part of an object move without the whole object falling apart?' He builds a cube to answer that question and shows it to his students. Put into mass production, it becomes one of the biggest fads of the 1970s and 1980s.

Nixon resigns
9th August 1974 Facing impeachment over his role in the Watergate burglary and subsequent cover-up, President Richard Nixon announces his resignation. The final straw was the US Supreme Court decision the day before to order the release of tapes of Oval Office conversations. He is succeeded by his Vice President Gerald Ford, who pardons Nixon for any federal offences he might have committed. Nixon is the first US President to resign from office.

Haile Selassie deposed
12th September 1974 After more than 700 years, the Ethiopian Empire comes to an end. Plagued by famine and economic malaise, citizens strike in protest against Emperor Haile Selassie. The army and police seize their opportunity, place Haile Selassie under house arrest and take power.

Perón dead
1st July 1974 General Perón, stripped of power by a coup in 1955, returns to Argentina from exile with his wife Isabel and is elected President for the third time. Two days later, he suffers a fatal heart attack and Isabel assumes the presidency.

1974

PLO recognized
1st October 1974 The Palestine Liberation Organisation is recognised by the UN and the Arab League as the representative of the Palestinian people. PLO leader Yasser Arafat addresses the UN: 'Today I came with an olive branch and the weapon of the freedom fighter. Don't let the olive branch fall from my hands.'

Lucy in the ground
24th November 1974 Bones of a 3.2 million year old hominid are found in Ethiopia. The fossil is named Lucy, after the Beatles song *Lucy in the Sky with Diamonds*. Lucy, probably 1.10 metres tall and weighing 29 kilos when alive, is the oldest two-legged animal ever recovered and one of the most important excavations in history.

The Flake girl
Since the 1960s, the TV commercials for Cadbury's Flake have focused on the sensual, languorous pleasure of solo chocolate consumption, with a succession of Flake girls showing us how it's done.

'Just an old, saggy cloth cat'
Bagpuss, is first shown on BBC1 on 12th February. Full of gentle, old-world charm, the inhabitants of a Victorian shop run by a little girl called Emily, come to life whenever she brings a new thing to be repaired. It's Bagpuss, a plump, quizzical-looking pink and white striped cat who is the catalyst for the others to wake; a woodpecker bookend called Professor Yaffle, Madeleine the doll, Gabriel the toad and his banjo, and an army of industrious little mice. A 1999 poll votes *Bagpuss* the UK's favourite children's programme.

ENTERTAINMENT

Paint the whole world with a rainbow
Geoffrey Hughes, who has been a jobbing actor in dramas like *Z Cars* and *Dixon of Dock Green*, joins the Thames Television children's programme *Rainbow* this year and now spends his days with a large, absent-minded bear called Bungle, a sheepish pink hippo called George, and Zippy, a talkative orange creature of indistinct species. Over the next eighteen years, Geff-wee (as George pronounces it) takes on the role of teacher, parent, and peacekeeper to his furry, fuzzy colleagues.

Tiswas - Saturday morning mayhem
Saturday mornings are never the same again after *Tiswas* begins on 5th January on ITV. *Tiswas*, which comes from ATV's Birmingham studios, is chaotic, subversive and a bit rebellious with a gaggle of hyperactive presenters including Chris Tarrant and Sally James, who embrace the custard pies and slapstick, the buckets of water, mischief and mayhem. Bad jokes and impressions are provided by Bob Carolgees and Spit the dog and local comedian Lenny Henry, while Spike Milligan and Jasper Carrot are two more names who often pop up to join in the anarchic fun.

1974

Goodnight, John Boy

Already a huge hit in America, *The Waltons* comes to the UK this year, airing on BBC2 on 18th February. The Waltons - seven siblings, Ma and Pa, Grandma and Grandpa - live in Depression-era Virginia, run a sawmill, wear mainly denim dungarees and every night insist on calling goodnight to each other as they turn out their lights. It's an unapologetic slice of very sweet American apple pie and Britain adores it.

Kubrick withdraws *Clockwork Orange*

When Stanley Kubrick's *A Clockwork Orange* was released in cinemas in 1971, the film's controversial themes and 'ultraviolence' divided opinion. But following a spate of real-life crimes which some argue are strongly influenced by the rapes and murders depicted in the film, Kubrick and his family begin to receive death threats. In an unprecedented example of self-censorship, he insists Warner Brothers withdraw the film from circulation in the UK. *A Clockwork Orange* remains an underground cult movie until it is once again permitted general release in 2000, a year after Kubrick's death.

Roobarb (and Custard)

Roobarb bounces onto television screens for the first time on 21st October on BBC1 in a cartoon perfectly capturing the universally recognised differences between cats and dogs. Roobarb is an exuberant green dog, and his rival, the laid-back Custard, is a puce-coloured cat who spends most his days calculating how to get the better of Roobarb.

Opportunity Knocks for Lena

Diminutive Italian-Scottish singing sensation Lena Zavaroni, aged ten, appears on Hughie Green's talent show, *Opportunity Knocks* and becomes the only contestant to win five weeks in a row. Her version of 'Ma - He's Making Eyes at Me' becomes a chart hit for her at the age of thirteen.

Baker Who?

Doctor Who number four is introduced to audiences for the first time on 28th December in an episode called 'Robot'. Tom Baker's Doctor wears a floppy hat, an unfeasibly long stripey scarf, has a penetrating gaze and seems quite excitable. It doesn't take long to win viewers round and for many, Baker remains the definitive Doctor Who, delighting many middle-aged fans when he appears in the show's 50th anniversary special, 'Day of the Doctor' in 2014.

Miss Pears turns 21

Pears Soap celebrates the 21st birthday of its famous Miss Pears competition by inviting all the past winners to a special party. Since 1958, hopeful parents around the country submit photographs of their offspring each year for this highly-publicised contest in which one little girl is chosen to be the face and brand ambassador for the classic glycerine soap.

1974

Hysteria and tragedy at Cassidy concert
26th May 1974 Fourteen-year old Bernadette Whelan dies in a hysterical stampede at a David Cassidy concert at White City Stadium in London. The incident has a profound effect on the singer, who quits live performing and his *Partridge Family* TV show.

Smash hit
Instant mash brand Smash score a smash hit with a TV advertising campaign created by ad agency BMP DDB, featuring metallic aliens chortling over the primitive and labour-intensive way in which earthlings peel and boil their potatoes. 'Get Mash, Get Smash' is the advertising jingle on everyone's lips and the Smash Aliens go on to be voted among the top UK advertisements of all time by the public and advertising industry alike.

Good clean fun?
Robin Askwith puts on his best cheeky chappie persona as he takes on the role of disaster-prone window cleaner, Timothy Lea, who spends more time in bed with his customers than he does actually cleaning their windows. *Confessions of a Window Cleaner*, releaed 16th August, treads a fine line between sauce and soft porn but the promise of lewd slapstick, full frontal female nudity, and constant views of Askwith's derrière somehow compels people to see it.

Head-swivelling horror
When William Friedkin's film *The Exorcist* is released in UK cinemas on 14th March, its reputation precedes it, with reports of American audiences suffering shock, fainting and vomiting after witnessing the terrifying demonic possession of twelve-year-old Regan MacNeil, played by Linda Blair. There has never been a horror like *The Exorcist*; seeing it becomes a test of bravery and endurance.

Bedsits and Beckinsale
September treats TV viewers to the launch of not one but two winning sitcoms. ITV's *Rising Damp* starts on 2nd September, with Leonard Rossiter playing Rigsby, the miserly landlord of a creaking Victorian townhouse, whose bedsits are occupied by Richard Beckinsale's medical student, a suave Don Warrington and Frances de la Tour as the romantic spinster Miss Jones, with whom Rigsby is besotted. On BBC1 on 5th September, Beckinsale appears a second time this week as Lennie Godber, the cell mate of Ronnie Barker's Norman Stanley Fletcher ('Fletch') in prison comedy *Porridge*.

 **MUSIC**

Streets of London
30th January 1974 Singer-songwriter Ralph McTell packs London's Royal Albert Hall on his first headlining appearance. Croydon-born Ralph is best known for the contemporary folk standard *Streets of London*, which he wrote in 1968. He has a surprise hit with the song over Christmas 1974 when its no-room-at-the-inn sentiments strike a chord with a broader audience.

1974

Queen on tour
1st March 1974 Queen headline their first UK tour. Initially regarded as yet another glam-rock outfit, they are starting to make a big impact as an album band thanks to Freddie Mercury's charismatic vocals and the uniquely sonorous, melody-driven guitar style of former astronomy student Brian May.

Dolly's debut year
21st April 1974 Country singer-songwriter Dolly Parton says goodbye to her long-time singing partner Porter Wagoner with the heartfelt *I Will Always Love You*. In her first solo year, Dolly tops the US country chart with this, *Jolene* and *Love is Like a Butterfly*.

Abba win Eurovision
6th April 1974 A landmark day in pop music as the Eurovision Song Contest - hosted by the UK at the Brighton Dome - introduces the world to Abba. Comprising two wonderfully costumed Swedish couples who sing in English, they win with *Waterloo*, written by members Bjorn Ulvaeus and Benny Andersson with producer Stig Anderson. It's the start of an incredible six years for the group who will be the world's leading singles act by 1980.

Northern soul
In industrial Lancashire, 'northern soul' rules. Fans and disc jockeys hunt out the best 1960s soul records from the US - the more obscure the better - and dance to them at 'all nighters' at venues such as Wigan Casino. It's now common for the tracks to be turned into national hits by radio play, as happens with R. Dean Taylor's *There's a Ghost in My House* and Robert Knight's *Love on a Mountaintop*.

Lennon's lost weekend
March 1974 Having parted from Yoko Ono and with the threat of deportation from the US hanging over him, a drunken John Lennon is thrown out of the Troubadour in Los Angeles. He is in the middle of what he will later call his 'lost weekend'; reconciliation with Yoko follows a Thanksgiving Night concert in New York in at which Lennon joins Elton John on stage.

Cass Elliot dies
29th July 1974 Aged just 32, the ebullient, wise-cracking Cass Elliot of the Mamas and the Papas dies in her sleep at Harry Nilsson's London flat, where she has been staying during an exhausting two-week spot at the London Palladium.

Reggae for it now
26th October 1974 Thanks to names like Desmond Dekker and Jimmy Cliff, Jamaican reggae is no stranger to the UK charts. A No. 1 is a rarity, however. *Everything I Own* by Kingston's Ken Boothe is a reggae version of a song by David Gates of Bread who wrote it as a tribute to his late father.

1974

A song for Annie
12th October 1974 Best known for writing *Take Me Home Country Roads* and *Leavin' on a Jet Plane*, country-folk singer John Denver has his only UK chart hit - a No. 1 - with *Annie's Song*, dedicated to his wife of seven years.

MY FIRST 18 YEARS
TOP 10 — 1974

1. **Tiger Feet** Mud
2. **Jolene** Dolly Parton
3. **Rock Your Baby** George McCrae
4. **The Air That I Breathe** The Hollies
5. **Band on the Run** Wings
6. **Raised on Robbery** Joni Mitchell
7. **I Know What I Like (In Your Wardrobe)** Genesis
8. **Midnight at the Oasis** Maria Muldaur
9. **When Will I See You Again?** The Three Degrees
10. **Spiders and Snakes** Jim Stafford

Open | Search | Scan

Wailers 'too good'
Having been famously fired from supporting Sly and the Family Stone on tour for being too good, Bob Marley and the Wailers continue to nurture the US and UK markets with their reggae-rock fusion. Eric Clapton's chart-topping US cover of Marley's *I Shot the Sheriff* raises the band's profile despite the departures of key men Peter Tosh and Bunny Wailer.

King of clubs
21st September 1974 Reaching the UK Top Ten is the runaway dance hit of the year, *Queen Of Clubs* by Miami-based showband KC and the Sunshine Band. KC (Howie Casey) is the man behind the airy production sound of the TK label, which has just sold a million with the slinky, sensuous *Rock Your Baby* by George McCrae (photo).

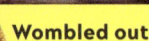

Wombled out
Bizarrely, the UK's leading chart act of 1974 is not a real group at all but the Wombles, who are songwriter Mike Batt and chums dressed in furry clothing. They follow up *The Wombling Song* with further variations on the wombling theme like *Remember You're A Womble*, *Wombling White Tie And Tails* and *Wombling Merry Christmas*.

PHOTO CREDITS Copyright 2024, TDM Rights BV.
Photos: **A** Harry Dempster - Hulton Archive - Getty Images / **B** David Cannon - Getty Images / **C** Bettmann - Getty Images / **D** Mirrorpix - Getty Images / **E** Independent News and Media - Hulton Archive - Getty Images / **F** Hulton Archive - Hulton Royals Collection - Getty Images / **G** Ulstein Bild - Getty Images / **H** Wally McNamee - Getty Images / **I** Bettmann - Getty Images / **J** Thames Television - Ronald Grant Archive - Mary Evans / **K** Gareth Cattermole - Getty Images / **L** TV Times - Getty Images / **M** Silver Screen Collection - Moviepix - Getty Images / **N** Anwar Hussein - Getty Images / **O** Ronald Grant Archive - Mary Evans / **P** Sunset Boulevard - Corbis Historical - Getty Images / **Q** Michael Putland - Hulton Archive - Getty Images / **R** Hulton Deutsch - Corbis Historical - Getty Images / **S** Steve Morley - Redferns - Getty Images / **T** Robert Riger - Getty Images / **U** David Redfern - Redferns - Getty Images / **V** David Warner Ellis - Redferns - Getty Images.

1975 MY FIRST 18 YEARS

SPORT

Fitness guru gets royal recognition
Fitness pioneer Eileen Fowler, who has inspired the nation to keep fit since the 1950s with her exercise programmes on radio, records, and TV, is awarded an MBE. Fowler continues to evangelise about the benefits of exercise and even after moving into a retirement home in her nineties, encourages other residents to join her in a daily fitness routine.

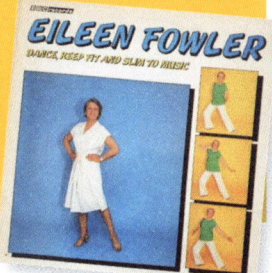

The Thrilla in Manila
In a decade defined by epic boxing confrontations, the Thrilla in Manila, between Muhammad Ali and Joe Frazier on 1st October, is perhaps the biggest and the most brutal. It's a gruelling, forty-two-minute marathon with temperatures reaching a muggy 49 degrees, as the two heavyweights slug it out in what is their third meeting. Ali prevails when Frazier's team stop the fight in the fourteenth round, the victory cementing his status as 'The Greatest'.

Terror on the terraces
Football hooliganism is rampant by the mid-1970s and has serious consequences for Leeds United who are defeated by Bayern Munich in the European Cup Final. Riots by Leeds fans break out during the match, triggered by a disallowed Peter Lorimer goal. The club is handed a four-year ban from European football which is reduced to two years after an appeal. Two years later, Liverpool is also banned from Europe after riots at a Cup Winners' Cup game against St. Etienne. The so-called 'English disease' will overshadow football for the next decade.

Arthur Ashe conquers Wimbledon
It's an all-American affair for the men's singles final at Wimbledon on 5th July as defending champion and favourite Jimmy Connors meets Arthur Ashe in the final. Ashe plays a perfect, tactical match, and when he beats Connors in four sets, he becomes (and remains) the only black man to win the Wimbledon as well as the US and Australian Open titles.

World Cup cricket
The cricket World Cup takes place in England from 7th to 21st June, the first major tournament in the history of one-day international cricket. The West Indies under Clive Lloyd emerge the victors.

2 JAN 1975
It is announced Charlie Chaplin will receive a knighthood in the New Year Honours.

26 FEB 1975
Off-duty Metropolitan Police officer Stephen Tibble, aged 22, is shot and killed at point blank range while pursuing a member of the Provisional IRA.

15 MAR 1975
The Army is drafted in to clear 70,000 tonnes of rubbish accumulated during a nine-week binmen's strike in Glasgow.

1975

New start for Martina in the States
Czech player and rising tennis star Martina Navratilova announces her defection from Czechoslovakia to the US.

Sobers becomes Sir
On 19th February, during her Commonwealth tour of the West Indies, the Queen knights cricket hero Gary Sobers at Bridgetown racecourse, in front of a crowd of 10,000 cheering Barbadians.

Moorgate tube crash
28th February 1975 London is left reeling when a train entering its final stop at Moorgate underground station fails to slow down and collides with the end of the tunnel. 43 people are killed and 74 injured, prompting the introduction of an automatic system to slow speeding trains on the network, known as the 'Moorgate' protection.

Local government in Scotland
16th May 1975 Following major changes to the administrative map in England the previous year, Scotland's local government areas are redrawn leading to the creation of nine new regions and a two-tier system of regions and districts.

DOMESTIC NEWS

Black Panther
14th January 1975 Headlines are dominated by the kidnapping of 17-year-old Leslie Whittle, an heiress taken from her home in Bridgnorth, Shropshire. The kidnapper demands a £50,000 ransom, but confusion regarding the kidnapper's instructions means it is never delivered. On 7th March her body is discovered, and the killer identified as the 'Black Panther', a serial burglar and murderer. Newspapers cover the investigation until Donald Nielson is arrested in December. He spends the rest of his life in prison.

Cassette carousel

Dibbles Bridge coach crash
27th May 1975 Tragedy strikes as the brakes fail on a coach carrying 45 female pensioners on a day trip to Grassington. The bus plunges off a bridge near Hebden, North Yorkshire, killing 33 and injuring everyone else on board.

International Women's Year
15th January 1975 The United Nations declares 1975 'International Women's Year' in the hope of prompting nations to examine inequality. In November, the UK introduces the Employment Protection Act, which establishes the provision of paid maternity leave, and in December the Sex Discrimination Act 1975 and Equal Pay Act 1970 come into force.

23 APR 1975
As South Vietnam falls to the Communists, the British Embassy in Saigon is closed and staff evacuated.

22 MAY 1975
One of Britain's leading sculptors, Barbara Hepworth, is killed in a fire at her St. Ives studio.

19 JUN 1975
Striking stable-boys march around the course at Royal Ascot on Gold Cup Day. They accept a 19% pay rise in July.

1975

European Space Agency
31st May 1975 The UK becomes one of the ten founding members of the European Space Agency, which launches its first mission later in the year. The Cos-B space probe is launched to study sources of gamma radiation in the cosmos.

Snow in June
2nd June 1975 England is stunned when June brings unexpected snow showers. The brief flurries fall as far south as London, the first time the capital has seen snow in June in almost 200 years.

EEC referendum
5th June 1975 The country goes to the polls for a referendum on membership of the European Economic Community, which would later become the European Union. The 'Yes' vote is successful with 67% choosing to remain within the community.

The Spaghetti House siege
28th September 1975 The Spaghetti House restaurant in Knightsbridge, London, is robbed by three gunmen who take the staff hostage when the police are called. On the advice of psychologists, police allow the siege to continue for six days in the hope that the gunmen will feel sympathy for their hostages. Eventually, the gunmen release the staff and surrender.

Balcombe Street siege
6th December 1975 A year of continuing violence regarding Northern Ireland culminates with the Balcombe Street siege. After months of bombings in London, police give chase to four Provisional IRA operatives who had fired shots into a Mayfair restaurant. The chase ends with the operatives breaking into a flat and taking the two occupants hostage for six days, before eventually surrendering. Events are broadcast live on television across the country. Two of the operatives, Harry Duggan and Hugh Doherty, had been responsible for the assassination of Guinness Book of Records founder Ross McWhirter in November, after he had offered a reward for information about their activities.

First Ripper victim
30th October 1975 The murder of 28-year-old Wilma McCann in Leeds is the first in a string of killings committed by the so-called 'Yorkshire Ripper' Peter Sutcliffe. The search for the Yorkshire Ripper becomes one of the decades' biggest news stories.

18 JUL 1975
British racing driver Graham Hill announces his retirement from the sport. He is killed in an air crash on 29th November.

7 AUG 1975
Temperatures soar to 32 degrees centigrade in London, the highest recorded in 35 years.

19 SEP 1975
British Forces Broadcasting Services broadcasts television programmes for the first time from the Trenchard Barracks, Celle, near Hanover.

1975

ROYALTY & POLITICS

Thatcher becomes Tory leader
On 11th February, Margaret Thatcher, becomes the first woman leader of a British political party when she defeats four other (male) candidates with 146 out of 215 votes. 'I beat four chaps. Now let's get down to work,' says the 49-year-old mother of twins.

Politics on the radio
The idea of broadcasting Parliamentary proceedings has been resisted for some time but on 24th February, a Commons vote approves the presence of microphones in the chamber and in June, during a month-long experiment, Radio 4 listeners can hear for the first time what is debated in Westminster; Labour minister Tony Benn is the first MP to be heard. Permanent radio coverage of Parliament is introduced in 1978, but television must wait until November 1989.

Queen visits Japan
Thirty years after the end of the Second World War, the Queen makes the first state visit to Japan as the guest of Emperor Hirohito. She and the Duke of Edinburgh attend a welcome banquet on 7th May and they experience plenty of Japanese culture and tradition during the visit.

Order of the Bath anniversary
Prince Charles, sporting a moustache, is installed as Great Master of the Most Honourable Order of the Bath at Westminster Abbey on 25th May, in a service marking the 250th anniversary of the founding of the order by George I.

FOREIGN NEWS

Digital watches
Too expensive and out of reach for the average consumer, digital LED watches start to take off when Texas Instruments starts mass production in a plastic housing. These watches sell for $20 and cost half the price a year later.

Microsoft launch
4th April 1975 After developing an operating system called an interpreter for the Altair 8800, which makes the microcomputer interesting for hobby programmers, childhood friends Bill Gates and Paul Allen launch their own company. Allen coins the name 'Micro-Soft', short for 'microcomputer software'.

---

30 OCT 1975
A report is published stating that 6.5 million elm trees have been destroyed due to Dutch elm disease.

27 NOV 1975
Ross McWhirter, co-founder of the Guinness Book of World Records with his twin Norris, is shot and killed by the Provisional IRA.

25 DEC 1975
Heavy metal band Iron Maiden are formed in east London by bassist Steve Harris.

1975

Fall of Saigon
30th April 1975 After nearly twenty years of fighting, North Vietnamese forces penetrate Saigon and 'liberate' the capital of South Vietnam. Without the support of the US, South Vietnam is lost. News cameras capture the mass panic of the final moments in the fall of Saigon, as desperate civilians mass around US helicopters sent to rescue the remaining American Embassy staff.

Khmer Rouge
17th April 1975 Despite three years of bombing by the US, the Khmer Rouge emerge victorious in the Cambodian civil war. On 17th April, their forces enter the capital Phnom Penh, where they expel the rulers and install dictator Pol Pot as leader. The stage set is set for one of the most brutal regimes in human history.

Carlos the Jackal
21st December 1975 With five accomplices, Venezuelan terrorist Ilich Ramírez Sánchez, nicknamed Carlos and called 'the Jackal' by the press, kidnaps delegates to the ministerial conference of the Organization of the Petroleum Exporting Countries (OPEC) in Vienna. They capture 60 and kill three. A day later, the hostage takers are given a free exit by plane to Algiers and Tripoli, where the hostages are freed in return for a ransom of more than $20 million.

Franco is dead
20th November 1975 After a three-week-long coma, Spain's fascist dictator General Francisco Franco dies. Two days after his death, the monarchy returns, as he had wished. But against expectations, King Juan Carlos pushes for reconciliation with the socialists, a return to democracy and more freedom for regions such as Catalonia and the Basque Country.

ENTERTAINMENT

High-rise horrors
'A night of blazing suspense' is perhaps an understatement for *The Towering Inferno*, a collaboration between Warner Bros. and Twentieth Century Fox based on two separate books about a skyscraper uncontrollably ablaze. This is the disaster movie to end all disaster movies and when it's released in the UK on 29th January, audiences flock to see not only the scorching special effects but an A-list cast who must find a way to escape as the flames lick at their heels. Who will survive, and who will get roasted? *The Towering Inferno* is 165 minutes of catastrophic, nail-biting conflagration and becomes the year's biggest box-office hit.

1975

Six Million Dollar toys

The Six Million Dollar Man action figure is launched in the UK, based on the hit US TV series starring Lee Majors as NASA astronaut Steve Austin who is rebuilt with bionic body parts following a deadly crash. Now kids can have their own thirteen-inch-high Steve Austin, who comes wearing a natty red NASA tracksuit and sneakers. Steve can show off his power by lifting a car engine, you can look through his bionic eye via a hole in his head, and his rubber skin peels back to reveal those $6,000,000 bionics.

Little House on the Prairie

Following on from the success of *The Waltons*, the next historical family drama from America to hit these shores (on 25th February) is *Little House on the Prairie*. Loosely based on the books by Laura Ingalls Wilder about growing up in the nineteenth-century Mid-West as a child of pioneer settlers, *Little House on the Prairie* isn't afraid to tackle some thorny subjects from racism to disability and has no qualms about tugging at viewers' heartstrings - many were moved to tears when Mary Ingalls wakes up to discover she has gone blind. It also fuels a growing taste for prairie style as frilled floral maxi dresses, patchwork bed covers and characters such as Hollie Hobbie gain in popularity.

Shark attack

Jaws may be one of Stephen Spielberg's earliest films but his ability to keep the tension taut, and to play on audiences' fear of the unseen, turns it into a major movie event in the US this summer before it has its UK film premiere on Christmas Day. Roy Scheider, Richard Dreyfus and Robert Shaw do battle with an underwater menace terrorising the East Coast resort of Amity Island before it picks off any more of its swimmers for a mid-morning snack. The suspense is intensified by John Williams's menacing music, and brilliant lines like, 'We're gonna need a bigger boat.' *Jaws* becomes an instant classic.

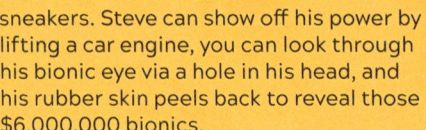

Tune in to Doonican

Irish crooner Val Doonican, known for his easy manner, cosy cardigans, and relaxing rocking chair performances, returns to BBC1 on 24th May with *The Val Doonican Show* after several years at ATV (ITV). A regular on British TV screens since 1963, Doonican is comfortable with his uncool status, having sold millions of records including the completely unthreatening *Val Doonican Rocks, But Gently* in 1967.

Toffee transformation

Chewy sweets Toff-o-Lux are rebranded as Toffos this year, and if that wasn't enough to rattle toffee fans, they are also launched in a fruit-flavoured version featuring strawberry and banana toffees.

1975

Music hall for the masses
The Good Old Days, a recreation for television of the late Victorian and Edwardian music hall, presented with great flourish by Leonard Sachs, and with songs and sketches performed in the style of greats like Marie Lloyd or Harry Lauder, began way back in 1953 and continues to enjoy a loyal following throughout its long, thirty-year run. The live audience is encouraged to dress up in costume and sing along at the end to 'The Old Bull and Bush'. During the 1970s, the waiting list to be part of that audience is 24,000.

The Good Life
The Good Life appears on our screens for the first time on 4th April, with Richard Briers and Felicity Kendal as Surbiton's ever-optimistic pioneers of suburban self-sufficiency, Tom and Barbara Good. *The Good Life* taps into - and encourages - a resurgence in growing your own vegetables, jam making and experimenting with homemade wine, but we tune in just as much to laugh at the barely suppressed snobbery and bemusement of socially mobile, kaftan-wearing neighbour Margo Leadbetter (a magnificent Penelope Keith) and her long-suffering husband Jerry (Paul Eddington).

Chop Phooey
'Who IS the superhero? Sarge? No. Rosemary? The telephone operator? No. Penry? The mild-mannered janitor? Could be!' *Hong Kong Phooey* karate chops his way onto British TV screens on 17th March, a canine crime-fighter full of enthusiasm but with ambitions far beyond his capabilities. He regularly has to stop to consult the 'Hong Kong Book of Kung Fu', and even his transformation into superhero is marred by getting stuck in a filing cabinet drawer. Thank goodness for Spot the cat (who is actually striped) who covers for his friend's incompetence with casual efficiency.

TV cops get tough
The Sweeney airs on ITV on 2nd January and introduces a whole new side of policing to the British public. This is no cosy drama along the lines of *Dixon of Dock Green*. Taking its title from Sweeney Todd, the Cockney rhyming slang for the Flying Squad, Detective Inspector Jack Regan (John Thaw) and Detective Sergeant George Carter (Dennis Waterman) tackle violent crime head on, frequently throwing out the rule book to bring hardened criminals to heel. Police slang terms are revealed (a 'snout' is an informer, a 'stoppo' is a getaway car), and with so much filming done on location around London, this is drama with a heavy dose of reality.

Trainspotting
Trainspotters and rail enthusiasts assemble as the National Railway Museum is opened in York this year. The first national museum outside of the capital, the National Railway Museum welcomes 2 million visitors in the first twelve months.

1975

Faultlessly Fawlty
In 1967, the Monty Python team stay at the Gleneagles Hotel in Torquay and are amused and fascinated by the hotel owner who John Cleese describes as 'the rudest man I have ever come across in my life'. That hotelier becomes the inspiration for Basil Fawlty, the misanthropic owner of *Fawlty Towers*, which begins on BBC2. Written by Cleese and his then-wife Connie Booth (who plays maid Polly), the pair spend weeks writing and fine tuning the script for each episode, and then more weeks editing, during which time Cleese appears in several TV commercials to earn income. The show first airs on 19th September, with Cleese as Basil, Prunella Scales as his domineering wife Sybil and Andrew Sachs as Manuel, the hapless Spanish waiter whose mix-ups and accidents are always because, 'He's from Barcelona'. Just twelve episodes of Fawlty Towers are made, divided into two series. But it's quality not quantity and Cleese and Booth's pursuit of perfection pays off. In 2000, *Fawlty Towers* is voted first out of the 100 best British television programmes of all time by the British Film Institute.

How we used to live
Queen Elizabeth, the Queen Mother, visits Beamish Museum near Stanley, Co. Durham on 17th July. Beamish is an open-air museum and pioneer of living history, preserving north-east heritage by authentically recreating typical communities and industries of the area in the late nineteenth and early twentieth centuries.

Runaround
Cockney geezer Mike Reid is the MC of ITV's kids' quiz show *Runaround*, which airs for the first time on 2nd September. It's high energy fun with teams zooming around the studio when Reid asks a question and shouts, 'G-g-g-g-g-GO!' jumping in front of what they think is the correct answer. The elusive yellow ball – and two extra points – goes to any brainbox who selects the right answer when nobody else does.

Bod
Bod first appears on the BBC in 1974 in a story read on *Playschool*. The BBC decide to bring Bod to life on screen and the resulting animation airs on 23rd December, narrated by John Le Mesurier with a jazzy theme tune by *Playschool* and *Playaway* regular Derek Griffiths. *Bod* is quite odd; a bald little figure of indeterminate gender in a yellow smock and with a circle of acquaintances limited to a policeman, a farmer, a postman and his aunt Flo.

Comedy's Holy Grail
'Sets the film industry back 900 years!' and 'Makes Ben Hur look like an epic' are just some of tongue-in-cheek slogans across the film poster for *Monty Python and the Holy Grail*, which opens in the UK on 3rd April. A farcical retelling of the Arthurian legend with non-stop jokes and silliness, it's a film crammed with memorable (and quotable) moments from the ridiculous Knights of 'Ni' to the gory duel where the Dark Knight insists 'Tis only a scratch' as Graham Chapman's King Arthur systematically dismembers him.

1975

Big potato
Mr Potato Head, first launched in 1952, expands in size this year making him safe for small children to play with too.

A right royal drama
ITV's historical royal drama *Edward the Seventh* begins on 1st April, and traces the life and eventual reign of Edward VII, whose older self is played by Timothy West, with Annette Crosbie as his mother, Queen Victoria. Through the years we witness the appearance of figures both central and peripheral to European history, played by an eclectic cast.

One Flew Over the Cuckoo's Nest
When Randle P. McMurphy (Jack Nicholson) claims insanity so he can get himself transferred to a state psychiatric hospital in order to avoid hard labour, he doesn't factor in a formidable foe in the form of sadistic Nurse Ratched (Louise Fletcher). Produced by Michael Douglas, whose father Kirk owned the film rights to Ken Kesey's best-selling novel about his experiences working in a Californian Veterans Hospital, *One Flew Over the Cuckoo's Nest* wins five Oscars including Best Actor for Nicholson and Best Actress for Fletcher.

Galileo, Galileo
31st October 1975
Queen close out the year with one of the records of the decade. *Bohemian Rhapsody* is a six minute-long multi-layered five-part mini-opera that takes three weeks to record. The band also make their own film for television stations to play when they can't appear live - effectively the first promotional video of the kind that will become commonplace in the 1980s. *Bohemian Rhapsody* stays at No. 1 in the UK for nine weeks.

Ch-Changes
March 1975 David Bowie changes style again. As he prepares for filming *The Man Who Fell to Earth*, his *Young Americans* album reveals a new soul-based direction. *Fame*, a collaboration with John Lennon and Carlos Alomar, gives him his first US No. 1.

Rollermania!
22nd March 1975 'Rollermania' explodes as the Bay City Rollers spend five weeks at No. 1 with an old Four Seasons tune, *Bye Bye Baby*. From the Glasgow area, they appeal most to teenage and pre-teenage girls with a tinny and clanky sound that's deliberately under-produced to underline their ingenuousness. In the charts and on teen magazine covers, it is difficult to escape the tartan-covered quintet during 1975. The Rollers offer a final blast of pop hysteria before punk rock and disco take hold.

MUSIC

Mac additions
1st January 1975 US rock duo Lindsey Buckingham and Stevie Nicks join Fleetwood Mac, setting the once all-British blues band on a whole new course.

1975

Voulez-vous coucher?
23rd March 1975 One of the cheekiest lines in songwriting history - *'Voulez vous couchez avec moi, ce soir?'* - is heard in *Lady Marmalade* by Labelle, now No. 1 in the US. Fronted by Patti LaBelle, Labelle is an all-female trio whose space-age stage suits and in-your-face attitude put them light years ahead of previous all-female outfits like the Supremes.

Gabriel leaves
28th May 1975 Peter Gabriel leaves Genesis (photo), the art rock band he formed with fellow Charterhouse public schoolboys Mike Rutherford and Tony Banks in 1967. Stepping up as vocalist is Phil Collins, drummer with the band since 1970, who once played the Artful Dodger in *Oliver!* in the West End. Far from jeopardising the band's future, as some suggest, the switch gives the band a more mainstream direction and a new lease of life.

Rod goes west
As Rod Stewart admits he is considering US citizenship, his debut album for Warner Brothers has the appropriate title of *Atlantic Crossing*. Meanwhile Rod's private life goes public as he begins an affair with actress Britt Ekland.

MY FIRST 18 YEARS TOP 10 — 1975

1. **I'm Not in Love** *10cc*
2. **Lovin' You** *Minnie Riperton*
3. **This Old Heart of Mine** *Rod Stewart*
4. **Jive Talkin'** *The Bee Gees*
5. **At Seventeen** *Janis Ian*
6. **Cat's in the Cradle** - *Harry Chapin*
7. **You Ain't Seen Nothing Yet** *Bachman-Turner...*
8. **December '63** *The Four Seasons*
9. **No Woman No Cry** *Bob Marley*
10. **Mamma Mia** *Abba*

Zeppelin in exile
May - June 1975 Now the biggest band in the world in terms of earnings, Led Zeppelin enter tax exile in Switzerland after playing a series of four hour shows at Earl's Court. Their first release on their own SwanSong label, *Physical Graffiti*, is an instant chart-topping album in the US and UK.

Lennon can stay
7th October 1975 With John Lennon and Yoko Ono now reconciled, son Sean is born two days after Lennon's deportation order is rescinded. He receives his Green Card allowing him permanent residence in the US nine months later.

PHOTO CREDITS Copyright 2024, TDM Rights BV.
Photos: A Bettmann - Getty Images / B Bettmann - Getty Images / C PA Images - Getty Images / D Philippe Achache - Gamma Rapho - Getty Images / E Keystone - Hulton Royals Collection - Getty Images / F Doug Wilson - Corbis Historical - Getty Images / G Roland Neveu - LightRocket - Getty Images / H Keystone France - Gamma-Keystone - Getty Images / I Keystone - Hulton Archives - Getty Images / J Fotos International - Archive Photos - Getty Images / K Tony Russell - Redferns - Getty Images / L Ian Tyas - Hulton Archive - Getty Images / M Yorkshire Television - AF Archive - Mary Evans / N Ronald Grant Archive - Mary Evans / O Ronald Grant Archive - Mary Evans / P Ronald Grant Archive - Mary Evans / Q LMPC - Getty Images / R Michael Putland - Hulton Archive - Getty Images / S The Land of Lost Content Collection - Mary Evans Picture Library / T Michael Ochs Archives - Getty Images / U RB - Redferns - Getty Images / V Jorgen Angel - Redferns - Getty Images.

1976

MY FIRST 18 YEARS

SPORT

Ice gold perfection
On 11th February, at the Winter Olympics in Stockholm, Birmingham's John Curry wins the gold medal in the men's figure skating. Curry's early ambitions to be a ballet dancer were quashed by his father but there is a balletic quality to his performance, which combines grace with athleticism.

Borg begins
On 3rd July, cool, calm and collected Swede Bjorn Borg defeats Ile Nastase in the men's singles final at Wimbledon in three sets and secures the first of five consecutive titles at the All England club.

Life in the fast lane
Marlboro Maclaren's chances of victory in this year's Formula One Championship rest on the final race at the Fuji Speedway track in Japan, and the ability of their British driver, James Hunt, to secure a place in the top four. Hunt has been chasing his Austrian rival, Niki Lauda, all season and when they line up on the grid on 24th October, he needs just three points to take the championship. In treacherous, monsoon conditions James Hunt has the drive of his life, continuing through the spray despite a puncture, and a delayed pit stop, while Lauda is forced to withdraw from the race. Hunt comes third, enough to win the championship by a single point. Charismatic with dashing good looks and a playboy reputation, the win seals Hunt's position as one of the country's modern-day heroes.

Seven times Derby winner
Lester Piggott becomes the most successful jockey ever in the Derby when he wins the race for the seventh time on Empery on 2nd June. Piggott's seven titles put him ahead of the six wins of both Jim Robinson in the 1830s, and the legendary Steve Donoghue. He will go on to consolidate his achievement, winning the race twice more, in 1977 and 1983.

13 JAN 1976
Queen of crime writing Agatha Christie dies at the age of 85.

2 FEB 1976
The Queen opens the huge National Exhibition Centre (NEC) in Birmingham.

20 MAR 1976
The speedy Oxford crew win the Boat Race in 16 minutes, 58 seconds; a record for the event.

1976

Montreal Olympics
One of Britain's three gold medals is thanks to swimmer David Wilkie who sets a new world record of 2:15:11 in the men's 200 metre breaststroke. It is the first Olympic gold swimming medal for Great Britain in 68 years. Elsewhere, sporting history is made by Romanian gymnast Nadia Comaneci who is awarded the first ever 10.0 score on the asymmetric bars in the team competition, followed by six more perfect scores in individual events on her way to winning three gold medals

Montréal 1976

Concorde arrives!
21st January 1976 Supersonic jet Concorde makes its first commercial flight between London and Bahrain, launching the era of supersonic passenger flights. Concorde becomes an icon of luxury and modernity but suffers with sales thanks to its high cost and the difficulties flying it over land thanks to its sonic boom.

DOMESTIC NEWS

Northern Ireland
5th January 1976 A year of continuing violence in Northern Ireland begins with the Kingsmill Massacre in South Armagh, in which ten protestant men are killed by members of the Provisional IRA. Twelve bombs strike the West End of London later in the month, and in July Christopher Ewart-Biggs, the UK's ambassador to Ireland, is assassinated by landmine. The year also brings large peace demonstrations, with 10,000 Protestant and Catholic women marching in August, and a Derry Peace March attracting 25,000 people in September. The same year the Guildford Four and the Maguire Seven are wrongly convicted for the Guildford pub bombings, their convictions overturned in 1989 and 1991.

Britain's Buddhist temple
Britain gets its very first purpose-built Buddhist temple. Following the Thai style of Buddhism, the Wat Buddhapadipa opens in Wimbledon following a move from its original location on a residential street in East Sheen.

DO YOU REMEMBER THIS?

Marbles

Third Cod War
1st June 1976 Iceland and the UK finally agree an end to the Third Cod War, with the UK accepting Iceland's definition of its territorial waters. The eleven-month conflict has resulted in 55 separate incidents, mostly involving the aggressive ramming of ships on both sides.

26 APR 1976
Comedy actor and *Carry On* star Sid James dies after suffering a heart attack on stage at the Sunderland Empire.

10 MAY 1976
Embroiled in scandal, Jeremy Thorpe resigns as leader of the Liberal Party.

22 JUN 1976
The sizzling 'summer of '76' begins with a heatwave that will be remembered for decades to come.

1976

Ford Fiesta launches
14th July 1976 Nation's favourite the Fiesta is launched by Ford, due to be manufactured at the company's Dagenham plant in Essex. The three-door hatchback is the smallest car Ford has produced so far and becomes popular as a 'run-around' vehicle and especially with learner drivers, making it one of the best-selling cars of the next 40 years.

Art fraud exposed
16th July 1976 A series of articles published in *The Times* begin to unravel the story of prolific forger Tom Keating. Convinced dealers are interested only in big names and not the artistic value of a work, Keating has been saturating the market with hundreds of fakes since the 1950s. He is convicted in 1979 and goes on to lead a successful Channel 4 documentary about painting in the 1980s.

Riots at Notting Hill
30th August 1976 The Notting Hill Carnival descends into chaos as mounted police officers attempt to break up the 150,000-strong crowd. Whilst arresting pickpockets at the event, tension had risen between the police and young black attendees who felt unfairly targeted. Violence breaks out and 100 police officers and 60 carnival attendees are injured.

Hull Prison riot
1st September 1976 A three-day long riot breaks out at HM Prison Hull. Protesting against alleged prison guard brutality, 100 prisoners take over the prison, destroying two-thirds of the compound. The riot ends peacefully, but the prison closes for a year to allow for the £3 million worth of repairs.

Big Ben clock stops
5th August 1976 After more than 100 years of use, the chiming mechanism in the Great Clock of Westminster breaks. The mechanism is badly damaged and is shut down for 26 days while repair is made, the longest break in service since its construction. Westminster feels eerily quiet without its familiar tolls.

Renee MacRae disappearance
12th November 1976 36-year-old mother Renee MacRae disappears with her three-year-old son Andrew in what becomes the country's longest-running missing persons case. In 2022, MacRae's lover, and Andrew's father, William MacDowell is found guilty of their murders, although their bodies are never found.

14 JUL 1976
Drought Bill introduced to tackle the country's worst drought in 250 years.

1 AUG 1976
Grand Prix champion Niki Lauda suffers severe burns in an accident during the German Grand Prix.

29 SEP 1976
With the pound falling to $1.64, Britain applies to borrow £2.3 billion from the IMF.

1976

Bank of America robbery
16th November 1976 The perpetrators of what is believed to be the world's largest bank heist are sentenced to a total of 100 years in prison. The seven men are responsible for a robbery at the Mayfair branch of the Bank of America last year, in which safety deposit boxes worth £8 million were stolen, and only £500,000 of the loot is ever recovered.

International Monetary Fund loan
15th December 1976 Chancellor of the Exchequer, Denis Healey, announces an agreed £2,300,000,000 loan from the International Monetary Fund to ease the country's financial woes. The loan comes on the condition that public spending be cut and is received against a backdrop of pay freezes and inflation at 16.5%, one of the highest levels since records began.

Extreme weather
1976 brings extreme weather to the United Kingdom. In January, the Gale of 1976 sees hurricane-force winds of 105 miles per hour. In June and July, an extreme heat wave sees fifteen consecutive days of temperatures over 26.7°C. The temperature reaches a peak of 35.9°C before August and September bring drought.

Callaghan takes over at No. 10

On 16th March, Prime Minister Harold Wilson announces his resignation and recommends Foreign Secretary and former Home Secretary James Callaghan (photo) as his successor. Callaghan, aged 64, becomes Prime Minister on 5th April. Wilson's departure triggers controversy when he includes some questionable individuals in his resignation honours list.

Divorce in the Firm
A statement from Kensington Palace on 19th March announces that Princess Margaret and Lord Snowdon have mutually agreed to live apart. Although the statement goes on to say 'There are no plans for divorce proceedings' the couple do indeed divorce two years later.

FOREIGN NEWS

Dirty War

24th March 1976 In Argentina, President Isabel Perón is kidnapped and deposed by the military, and replaced by Lieutenant General Jorge Videla. Under the name 'Dirty War', the Videla junta is responsible for the disappearance of tens of thousands of trade union workers, students and other left-wing activists.

ROYALTY & POLITICS

Hot property
The Queen buys the 730-acre Gatcombe Park estate in Gloucestershire for Princess Anne and Captain Phillips at a reported cost of £300,000, leading to criticism by several Labour MPs.

4 OCT 1976
British Rail launch the new Intercity 125 train which initially runs out of Paddington to Bristol and South Wales.

27 NOV 1976
The Mini continues to be a popular choice of motor. The four millionth rolls off the assembly line this month.

10 DEC 1976
Mairead Corrigan and Betty Williams, founders of the Ulster Peace Movement, are awarded the Nobel Peace Prize.

1976

First Apple
1st April 1976 Having built a prototype of an assembled personal computer with Steve Jobs in 1975, Steve Wozniak offers the design to his employer HP and to game console manufacturer Atari, but neither party is interested. Wozniak and Jobs then decide to market their computer themselves. Jobs, who follows a fruit diet, comes up with the name: Apple Computer Company. From 11th April, the Apple I is on sale for $666.66.

Judgement of Paris
1st May 1976 In a blind wine tasting soon to be known as 'the judgement of Paris', an eleven-member jury of nine connoisseurs from France, the UK and US chooses both the white chardonnay and the red cabernet sauvignon from California over the French chardonnay and Bordeaux - a serious blow to the French ego. The so-called 'new wines' are conquering the world.

CN Tower opened
26th June 1976 The Canadian National (CN) Tower is opened in Toronto, Canada, at this point the highest free-standing structure on the planet at 553 metres.

Operation Entebbe
27th June 1976 Palestinian militants hijack an Air France plane in Greece and fly it to Entebbe in Uganda, where they are welcomed by dictator Idi Amin. They demand the release of militants imprisoned in Israel and other countries in return for the hostages. 148 non-Jewish hostages are released over the next two days but an Israeli force of 100 commandos mounts a rescue of the remaining hostages on 4th July. Three hostages are killed but 102 are brought to safety, while all the hijackers and 45 Ugandan soldiers are killed. The rescuers' sole fatality is Yonatan Netanyahu, brother of future Israeli Prime Minister Benjamim Netanyahu.

Soweto uprising
16th June 1976 In South Africa, the apartheid regime comes under further pressure when police in Soweto open fire on students demonstrating against the introduction of Afrikaans as the dominant language of education. Several hundred demonstrators are killed. A photo of the shot twelve-year-old student Hector Pieterson being carried away shocks the world.

Red planet
20th July 1976 In the search for life on other planets, NASA sent an unmanned space mission to Mars on 20th August 1975. Now Viking 1 becomes the first spacecraft in history to successfully soft land on the red planet. The probe soon transmits the first images of Mars to Mother Earth.

1976

Robbery of the century
16th – 17th July 1976 Six robbers spend four months drilling their way through the sewer system to the vaults of the Société Générale bank in Nice. During the weekend after the 14th July national holiday, the robbers strike: 337 safes are emptied containing almost 50 million French francs. Before they leave, the thieves leave a message: 'Without weapons, without hatred and without violence.' Not a single franc from the loot is ever recovered.

Mao is dead
9th September 1976 The architect of Chinese communism and one of the dominant political figures of the 20th century, Chairman Mao Zedong of the People's Republic of China dies in Beijing aged 82.

Carter is President
2nd November 1976 Jimmy Carter (photo right) wins the US presidential election, defeating incumbent Gerald Ford in a close race. He is the first candidate from the southern states to become President since the American Civil War.

ENTERTAINMENT

Emu attacks Parky
On 27th November, Rod Hull and Emu are invited onto chat show *Parkinson* but Emu takes a marked dislike to host Michael Parkinson, rips up his notes and eventually attacks and unseats him. Rod, meanwhile, is powerless to stop him.

Roy of the Rovers scores
Roy Race of Melchester Rovers, aka Roy of the Rovers, first made an appearance in *Tiger* comic back in 1954, but 22 years later, his continuing popularity means he's promoted to the first division and gets to headline his own comic with the first issue on 25th September. With guest appearances by real-life players and even the former England manager Alf Ramsey popping up, plus dramatic storylines including a worrying number of kidnappings, at its peak *Roy of the Rovers* sells an extremely respectable 450,000 copies.

Carry On Budgie
Budgerigars have been popular pets since the Victorian era but in the 1970s, it seems as if every home has a cage hanging in the corner with a gaudy plastic cover. Riding on the crest of the budgerigar wave is *World of Budgerigars*, a short film on how to care for your feathered friends, starring, unexpectedly, Sid James, who listens attentively to the advice delivered with deadpan solemnity by budgie expert Philip Marsden.

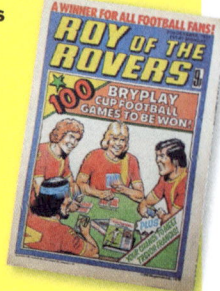

1976

Green Cross Code for roads

Since the 1950s, children have been schooled in crossing the road safely by Tufty the Squirrel. Tufty appears as a puppet in public information films and is the face of the Tufty Club which by the early 1970s has two million members. But there is a new road safety kid on the block by this year, with special superpowers. The Green Cross man extols the importance of the Green Cross Code's essential rules of Stop, Look, Listen, Think and, if he spots anyone ignoring this advice, can teleport in an instant to intervene and save kids getting squashed by an Austin Allegro. The Central Office of Information engages 6 ft 6 in bodybuilder, weightlifter and actor David Prowse, who dons the special green and white suit in his quest to rid the world of road accidents.

Open All Hours

Ronnie Barker creates another sitcom anti-hero in the form of Albert Arkwright, the penny-pinching, stuttering shopkeeper of a Doncaster corner shop, assisted by his luckless nephew Granville (David Jason) as he tries to charm Lynda Baron's Nurse Gladys and avoid injury by a temperamental cash register. Barker's comic timing and knack for verbal acrobatics, not to mention the on-screen chemistry with Jason, guarantees *Open All Hours* - which opens on BBC1 on 20th February - is a comedy classic.

High spirits

They've got spooks and ghouls and freaks and fools at *Rentaghost*, an agency run by ghosts for all your haunting needs. Unfortunately, the three ghosts available - Mr Timothy Claypole, a Tudor jester, a fey Victorian gent called Hubert Davenport, and the more recently deceased Fred Mumford - were all failures in life and are equally hopeless in death. The first series of *Rentaghost* begins on BBC1 on 6th January.

Starsky and Hutch

Some of TV's most successful crime-busting duos are based on a personality balance of yin and yang. That's the case with Starsky & Hutch, who first appear on British TV screens on 23rd April. Starsky is a streetwise, ex-US Army veteran from Brooklyn, prone to moodiness and fond of shawl-collars. His partner Hutch is a more reserved, cerebral type with Nordic good looks. Together they tear around the streets of Bay City, California in a red and white striped Ford Gran Torina, on the hunt for drug dealers, pimps and other lowlifes, often tipped off by their friend, fly guy and bar owner Huggy Bear.

1976

Saturday Swap Shop
Swapping things is the basic premise for the BBC's new Saturday morning show, the *Multi-Coloured Swap Shop* which opens for business on BBC1 at 9:30am on 2nd October, hosted by Noel Edmonds. Kids can phone in to swap their action man for a Stylograph; their stamp albums for a Viewmaster, while out in the field, perpetually excited Keith Chegwin supervises outdoor 'swaporamas' at various venues around the country. Interspersed with the swapping are interviews with celebrity guests, news segments courtesy of John Craven, interactions with Posh Paws (Edmonds' prehistoric, purple sidekick), music performances and videos.

Muppetry
The Muppet Show is Jim Henson's move away from *Sesame Street* to a puppet show with a broader appeal. *The Muppet Show* is made at Elstree Studios and airs on ITV on 5th September with a vivid cast of hundreds including a skinny green frog called Kermit who acts as MC; temperamental diva, Miss Piggy; a struggling stand-up called Fozzie Bear, a groovy house band - Dr. Teeth and the Electric Mayhem (with a lunatic, Keith Moon-style drummer called Animal); Gonzo, Rowlf, and many more.

I, Claudius
Showered with BAFTA awards and still considered a taboo-breaking landmark in historical television drama, *I, Claudius* begins on BBC1 on 20th September. Based on the novels of Robert Graves, the adaptation by Jack Pulman does a fine job at leading the viewer through the complicated web of corruption, debauchery, power struggles, treachery and murder marking the early days of Imperial Rome, with Derek Jacobi, as the Emperor Claudius, unravelling the story as narrator. The huge cast includes Sian Phillips as the scheming Livia (never far from a vial of poison), John Hurt as Caligula and Brian Blessed, in booming form, as Augustus.

Happy Days
16th October 1976 The show's central character, Arthur 'Fonzie' Fonzarelli, played by Henry Winkler, is a global phenomenon. Kids everywhere try to channel The Fonz's cool, impersonating the click of his fingers, the thumbs up and the drawled, 'He-ey'. Fonzie appears on magazine covers, annuals, posters, bubblegum packets and there is, of course, a play figure. Goofy teen Richie Cunningham is played by Ron Howard, who goes on to become a successful Hollywood film director.

MUSIC

Patti's in town
16th March 1976 Punk rock may come to be seen as a very British phenomenon but its roots are on the US east coast with Iggy and the Stooges, the New York Dolls and Television. Another big influence is the Ramones, whose buzzsaw sound is what every punk band wants to emulate. Now rock journalist and poet Patti Smith adds another dimension with the stunningly unadorned and daring debut album *Horses*, produced by Velvet Underground's John Cale.

Eurovision win
3rd April 1976 This year's Eurovision Song Contest, held in the Hague, sees Brotherhood of Man represent the UK with *Save Your Kisses For Me*. And what do you know, the UK has a winner for only the third time in Eurovision history. A cutesy love song from a father to his three-year-old, it gives the group a whole now lease of life after a couple of hits in the early 70s.

On a dark desert highway
As ego clashes and general excess start to pull the Eagles apart, they peak with an album that articulates all that's enervating and vacuous about the cocaine-fuelled Californian rock lifestyle. *Hotel California* has elements of the country rock they once championed on *Desperado* and *Take It Easy* but it's a self-loathing set that nevertheless becomes the sixth best selling album of the whole decade.

Frampton live
8th April 1976 Peter Frampton achieves platinum status for sales of his double album *Frampton Comes Alive!*, which includes the hit *Show Me The Way*. Recorded at San Francisco's Winterland Ballroom, it's a stunning comeback for a guitarist whose career stalled after leaving Humble Pie.

Forever Demis
17th July 1976 Sitting atop the singles chart is the long-haired, kaftan-clad Demis Roussos, whose distinctive high trill once adorned the progressive rock band Aphrodite's Child. He has a huge fanbase among British holidaymakers who first heard his music in the tavernas and discotheques of the Greek islands. The single is made up of four tracks and titled *Roussos Phenomenon*, with most radio airplay going to the dreamy *Forever And Ever*.

Elton and Kiki
24th July 1976 The big hit of the long, hot drought-ridden summer of 1976 is Elton John's duet with Kiki Dee, *Don't Go Breaking My Heart*. Oddly, they don't actually record the track together: Elton makes his vocal in Canada and ex-Motown artist Kiki adds hers in London. It is Elton's first UK No. 1.

1976

Here comes Summer

Clubs and discotheques playing black-originated dance music have been part of the New York scene since the late 60s. Now disco music becomes a truly global phenomenon as producers Giorgio Moroder and Pete Bellotte and former *Hair* performer Donna Summer begin collaborating at the Musicland studios in Munich. On *Love to Love You Baby*, over a looping part-synthesised backing track, Summer adds moans of ecstasy as if approaching climax. Released as a seventeen-minute twelve-inch single, it causes a sensation in the discos and clubs of Europe. By the time Summer makes the even more orgasmic *I Feel Love* in 1977, they have established the blueprint for what becomes known as 'Eurodisco'.

MY FIRST 18 YEARS TOP 10 — 1976

1. The Boys are Back in Town — Thin Lizzy
2. This Masquerade — George Benson
3. If You Leave Me Now — Chicago
4. You to Me are Everything — The Real Thing
5. Let's Stick Together — Bryan Ferry
6. Beautiful Noise — Neil Diamond
7. All By Myself — Eric Carmen
8. Blitzkrieg Bop — The Ramones
9. Free — Deniece Williams
10. Golden Years — David Bowie

Abba go regal

4th September 1976 A triumphant year for Abba brings no fewer than three No. 1s including their majestic contribution to the growing disco boom, *Dancing Queen*. It is quintessential Abba: soaring, heart touching and an instant dancefloor filler.

Punk grabs the headlines

1st December 1976 Punk rock has been making waves in the press all year. Now comes the moment when its notoriety goes national. On the TV programme *Today*, the Sex Pistols scoff and swear their way through a live interview with unamused host Bill Grundy. Even though they haven't played a note, suddenly they are every stroppy and disaffected kid's dream. With their *Anarchy in the UK* tour about to start, sixteen of the nineteen planned gigs are cancelled on local authority orders.

10cc split

27th November 1976 Founder members Lol Creme and Kevin Godley leave 10cc to pursue other projects, including a new guitar-attachable gadget called a 'Gizmo'. Graham Gouldman and Eric Stewart - the creators of No. 1s *I'm Not in Love* and *Dreadlock Holiday* - will carry on as a duo under the 10cc banner.

PHOTO CREDITS Copyright 2024, TDM Rights BV.

Photos: A Bettmann - Getty Images / B Tony Evans Timelapse Library Ltd - Hulton Archive - Getty Images / C PA Images Archive - PA Images - Getty Images / D BWP Media - Getty Images / E Classicsworld - New retro-ads - Getty Images / F PA Images - Getty Images / G European Communities - Christian Lambiotte - / H SSPL - Getty Images / I Keystone - Hulton Archive - Getty Images / J Wally McNamee - Corbis Historical - Getty Images / K Central Press - Hulton Archive - Getty Images / L Denis Tabler - Shutterstock / M BBC TV - AF Archive - Mary Evans / O Evening Standard - Hulton Archive - Getty Images / P ABC - AF Archive - Mary Evans / Q PA Images - Getty Images / R BBC - Ronald Grant Archive - Mary Evans / S The Jim Henson Company - AF Archive - Mary Evans / T Ronald Grant Archive - Mary Evans / U Andrew Putler - Redferns - Getty Images / V David Redfern - Redferns - Getty Images / W GAB Archive - Redferns - Getty Images / X Michael Ochs Archives - Getty Images / Y Mirrorpix - Getty Images.

 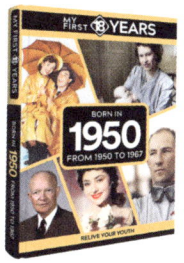 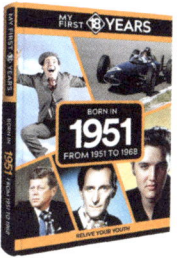 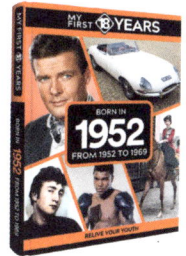

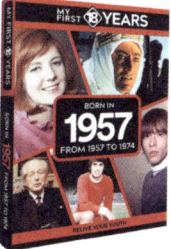 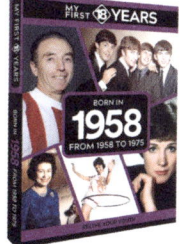 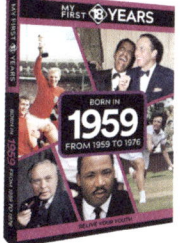 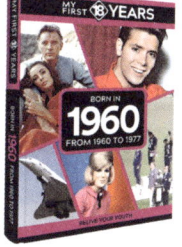

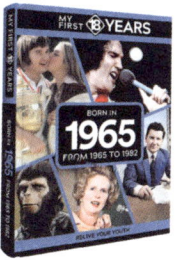  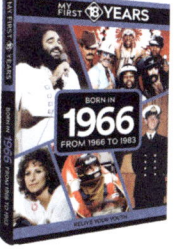

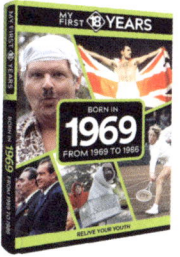   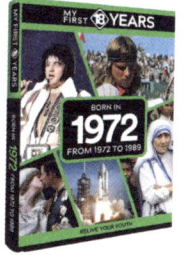

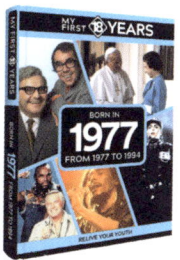 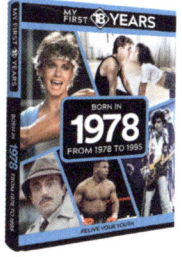 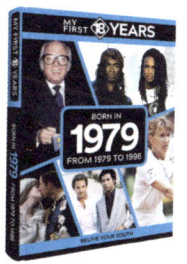